HUNTING MARCO POLO

CO-AUTHORED BY PAUL EDDY

Destination Disaster
The Hughes Papers
The Plumbat Affair
Siege!
War in the Falklands
The DeLorean Tapes
The Cocaine Wars

CO-AUTHORED BY SARA WALDEN

The DeLorean Tapes
The Cocaine Wars

Hunting
MARCO
POLO

The Pursuit of the Drug Smuggler
Who Couldn't Be Caught, by the Agent
Who Wouldn't Quit

PAUL EDDY AND SARA WALDEN

Little, Brown and Company

BOSTON TORONTO LONDON

First American Edition

ISBN 0-316-21056-0

Library of Congress Cataloging-in-Publication information is available.

10 9 8 7 6 5 4 3 2 1

RRD-VA

Published simultaneously in Canada by Little, Brown & Company
(Canada) Limited

Printed in the United States of America

To the memory of our fathers

Research
Patricia Barry

Reporting in London
Peter Gillman

With special thanks to
James McFadden and Nigel Bowden

CONTENTS

Polo, Marco (b. *c.* 1245, Venice or Curzola, Venetian Dalmatia—d. Jan 8, 1324, Venice), Venetian merchant, adventurer, and outstanding traveller. . . The actual personality of Marco is somewhat elusive. . . For some he was a genius, a man of prodigious memory, a most conscientious observer. . . For others he was a braggart, who made too much of himself. . .

—Encyclopedia Britannica

I have not told half of what I saw.

—Marco Polo on his deathbed

THE PLAYERS

The Hunters
Drug Enforcement Administration (DEA)
Craig Lovato: Madrid and Miami, Case Agent
Wendy Lovato: Miami
Ed Wezain: Miami, Lovato's partner
Harlan Bowe: Las Vegas and Karachi
George Pasenelli: Houston, intelligence analyst
Julie Desm: Los Angeles
Art Scalzo: Manila
Neil Van Horn: Los Angeles
Peter Shigeta: Los Angeles
Steve Austin: San Diego, Technical Agent
Gil Charette: Miami, undercover agent
Dodge Galanos: Miami, Special Agent in Charge
Mike Campbell: London, Country Attaché

Tom Cash: Miami, Special Agent in Charge
Dave Herrera: Madrid, Country Attaché

United States Attorney's Office
Bob O'Neill: Miami

United States Customs Service
Mark Bastan: San Francisco
Lawrence Ladage: New Orleans, Special Agent in Charge

Naval Investigative Service (NIS)
John Dill: Alameda
Randall Waddell: South-East Asia and New Orleans

Internal Revenue Service (IRS)
Brad Whites: Washington DC, Case Agent

Spanish National Police
José 'Pepe' Villar: Madrid
Adolfo Rodriguez: Palma

Her Majesty's Customs and Excise (HMCE)
Michael Stephenson: Karachi
Peter Nelson: London

London Metropolitan Police (Scotland Yard)
Tony Lundy: London
Phil Corbett: London
Terry Burke: London and Miami, Case Officer

Australian Federal Police (AFP)
Trevor Young: Sydney
John Robinson: Manila

Royal Canadian Mounted Police (RCMP)
Ken Ross: Vancouver
Murry Dauk: Vancouver, Case Agent
Stan Brooks: Vancouver and Miami

The Hunted
Palma, Majorca, Spain
Dennis Howard Marks: 'Marco Polo'
Judith Marks: Marks's wife
Geoffrey Kenion: 'the Sewage Engineer'
Roger Reaves: 'Roger the Agronomist'

Karachi, Pakistan
George Lane: Marks's brother-in-law
Saleem Malik: hashish supplier
Aftab Malik: Saleem's nephew

Amsterdam, The Netherlands
Frederick James Hobbs: messenger and courier

Manila, The Philippines
Antony Moynihan: exiled British peer
William Robb: messenger

Bangkok, Thailand
Phillip Sparrowhawk: marijuana supplier

London, England
John Denbigh: 'the Vicar'
James Newton: supplier of fake passports
Balendo Lo: manager, Hong Kong International Travel

United States
California
Ernest 'Peter' Combs: main West Coast distributor
Patti Hayes: Combs's common-law wife
Gerald Wills: transporter, owner of the *Axel D*
Wyvonna Meyer: Wills's ex-wife
Ronald Allen: Wills's partner
Bradley Weller: courier

Miami
Patrick Lane: Marks's brother-in-law

New York
John Francis: money launderer

The Men in the Middle
Reiner Jacobi: alias Rex Johnson
Thomas Sunde: alias Major Ross Woods

HUNTING MARCO POLO

P R O L O G U E

Taiwan, Republic of China, Tuesday, 19 July 1988

An hour and a half's drive from Taipei, beyond the small fishing port of Tanshui, there stands a temple not listed in any of the guides to Taiwan's tourist attractions.

It's really more a shrine than a temple. It stands near a beach overlooking the Formosa Straits, an eight-foot-high statue of a dog of uncertain breed, protected from the elements by a rude wooden shack that also accommodates the faithful.

The dog keeps vigil over a portion of coastline where, in February 1956, thirty-three souls lost their lives in the wreck of a sampan. They were laid to rest in a common grave near the beach and, according to local legend, a dog jumped into the pit and refused all entreaties to leave.

So the Taiwanese, being a pragmatic people, buried the dog – alive – together with the thirty-three victims. The temple stands as a tribute to the dog's unquestioning loyalty, and for reasons that are not entirely clear it has become a mecca for some of the other lost souls of Taiwan: prostitutes, pickpockets, common thieves, and even those whose crimes are more carefully organized.

'What a marvellous story,' said Howard Marks. 'I should go there immediately.'

He was, when he said that, somewhat the worse for wear, having enjoyed a liberal feast at a Mongolian barbecue restaurant and any amount of after-dinner drinks at Nesty's Bar in Taipei. But roaring drunk or stone cold sober, Howard Marks could not possibly resist

1

a temple that caters to reprobates. He demanded a cab to take him to Tanshui at once.

It was well after midnight when Marks arrived at the temple, yet the parking lot was filled with motor bikes and scooters, ubiquitous Yue-Loong automobiles made in Taiwan, much more expensive imports, and even buses. On the other side of the coast road where the temple stands there were, by Marks's estimates, at least 1,000 people: among them men in expensive suits who, despite the hour, wore dark glasses; beggers and urchins; fearsome-looking bikers; and exquisitely beautiful hookers.

Marks threaded his way through the crowd to the shack where the dog sits on its haunches gazing out to sea.

It is carved out of black rock, but over the years the statue has taken on a ghostly golden sheen as countless worshippers have sought a little luck by making offerings of gold: actually tiny strips of gold-leaf with adhesive backing, sold by ever-present hawkers, which the faithful stick to the statue while offering silent prayer.

'Please let me see my wife and children soon,' was Marks's prayer. In the circumstances, it was, he thought, a lot to ask.

On Wednesday morning, after a few hours of deep sleep induced by a generous joint of Thai marijuana, Marks rode an air-conditioned limousine to Chiang Kai-shek international airport where he checked in at the Singapore Airlines counter, first class as always. Then he lined up to complete the formalities required to leave Taiwan and, as always on these occasions, he felt the flutterings begin.

For all of his adult life, Howard Marks had never checked in for an international flight, never crossed an international border, without feeling the flutterings. No matter which passport he used, his own or any one of the fakes he had acquired, he could not look at an immigration official without wondering, 'This time?' It was an occupational hazard and something he'd got used to, but there were times when the particular circumstances or his own paranoia made the flutterings almost unbearable.

As Marks stood in line at the airport, waiting to change his Taiwan dollars into some more negotiable currency, he convinced himself that the man in front of him was an agent of the US Drug Enforcement Administration, his nemesis. Marks's suspicion was based on nothing more than his belief that the man was American, but it was indicative of his state of mind.

Marks had known for months that the DEA was about to indict him, that his phone had been tapped, and that for the last three years he had been under surveillance in more countries than most people get to visit in a lifetime. He also knew that the DEA had a confidential informant – a 'CI' in the lexicon of the trade – who had betrayed him. Marks, too, had a CI who regularly betrayed the DEA and who promised Marks that the indictment could be delayed almost indefinitely, so long as he kept paying.

He had paid over and over, and he'd offered gold and silent prayer at the temple of the dog. Yet, as he waited in the line at passport control, Marks could not kick the feeling that his luck had finally run out. When it came to his turn to present his documents he fully expected to hear that polite but ominous demand: 'Just a moment, sir. Will you please come with me?'

But nothing happened. Or rather, the immigration official merely satisfied himself that Marks had not overstayed the expiry of his tourist's visa, and waved him through. Marks sought the sanctuary of Singapore Airlines' first-class lounge and drowned the flutterings in complimentary alcohol.

By the time he boarded the plane he was in much better spirits, not least because he found that for only the second time, out of the literally hundreds of flights he had taken in his career, he was seated next to a truly beautiful woman. The first time it had been Elizabeth Taylor, who'd given Marks her autograph. This time it was a Korean woman who, though she resolutely ignored Marks, was still sufficiently lovely to cheer him up enormously.

In the early afternoon, as the Boeing 747 lifted off the runway, Marks took two Rohypmol tablets. Rohypmol is a sedative which, when mixed with large amounts of complimentary alcohol, will guarantee just about anybody the sleep of the innocent.

Miami, Florida, Wednesday, 20 July 1988

Some 9,000 miles away, in the home of Craig and Wendy Lovato, the telephone rang. It was two o'clock in the morning in Miami but the Lovatos were thoroughly accustomed to phone calls at all hours, particularly when Howard Marks was on the move. On the nights when the phone calls became too disruptive, they took it in turns to sleep.

'He's checking out of the hotel,' said the man on the other end of the phone, one of a small army of often anonymous watchers around the world who reported to the DEA on Marks's movements. 'He's got reservations on Singapore Airlines flight 79.'

'Where's it going?' asked Lovato.

'Singapore, Dubai, Zürich,' said the watcher.

'Does it stop in Manila or Bangkok?'

'No.'

'Damn.'

He might have expected it. Since the chase had begun, Marks had travelled to south-east Asia so many times – twenty-two – that the DEA had taken to calling him Marco Polo, and Manila or Bangkok were almost always on his itinerary. Now, when the Philippines or Thailand were the two countries in the world where Lovato wanted him to go, he was avoiding them.

Did Marks know? Had he spotted the surveillance? Had he been warned that the US government had sent provisional warrants for his arrest to both countries? (And, in the case of the Philippines, had reached a tacit understanding with the authorities that if Marks set one foot in Manila, he would be delivered, quietly and without fuss, to the US naval base at Subic Bay, where what awaited him was an involuntary one-way flight to Miami.)

Lovato did not know, but he had learned the hard way that where Marks was concerned it was always wise to assume the worst.

So, for the next twenty-three hours, the progress of Singapore Airlines' Boeing 747, and Marks's presence on it, was monitored as carefully as the space shuttle. From the DEA office or their bedside telephone, Craig – or, more often, Wendy – directed the army of watchers.

It was four o'clock in the morning Miami time when the 747 made its first stop in Singapore. Agents of the Singapore Central Narcotics Bureau, hastily recruited by telephone, watched as Marks stepped off the plane. There was no arrest warrant for Marks in Singapore, and if he had chosen to walk through Immigration there was nothing they could have done to stop him. But, totally unaware of the suspense he was creating, he strolled only as far as Singapore Airlines' business centre in the transit lounge. Three hours later he re-boarded the flight.

'He's on his way to Dubai,' one of the Singapore agents reported to Lovato, who had, by then, abandoned any hope of further sleep and driven to the office.

It was good news, and bad. It seemed to indicate that Marks suspected nothing and was simply following an itinerary that would take him to Zürich. But there was nothing to stop him getting off the plane in Dubai. And Dubai, one of seven Trucial States that make up the United Arab Emirates, was where the DEA believed Marks had stashed much of his fortune.

What was Dubai's attitude towards the extradition of foreign nationals, particularly very rich foreign nationals? Lovato did not know, but he was not optimistic. All he could do was wait.

Meanwhile, there was no shortage of things for him to do. If and when Marks landed in a country where the US government had prepared the ground to have him arrested, the ripples would immediately spread to six other countries in five different time zones. In what Lovato hoped was great secrecy, the DEA had obtained grand jury indictments against twenty-one other members of what it called 'the Marks organization'. Arrest warrants had been sent to Canada, England, the Netherlands, Pakistan, Thailand and Spain. Arrest teams were also standing by in Miami, New York and Los Angeles. But all of the arrest teams had been given the same sanction: 'Wait until Howard is in the bag.'

It made strategic sense. Marks had already demonstrated his ability to survive for years as a fugitive. If any of the arrest teams moved too soon, and Marks got word of it, he would flee, Lovato was sure. On the other hand, the longer they waited, the more chance there was that other members of the organization would slip away.

And the weekend was approaching, and any idea of making co-ordinated international swoops on a weekend is a pipe dream.

For much of Wednesday Lovato stalled, making and fielding calls from around the world, trying to keep nine different balls in the air. In Canada, England, the Netherlands, Pakistan, Thailand and Spain, and in Los Angeles, Miami, and New York, they all wanted to know the same thing. When could they move? When and where would Marks be arrested? The truth was Lovato didn't know, and couldn't begin to know, until the news came in from Dubai.

The one certainty was, wherever and whenever it happened, Craig Lovato would be there.

By July of 1988, Lovato and Marks had played a game of cat and mouse for two-and-a-half years. Lovato had listened to hundreds of Marks's telephone calls. He had followed him for days at a time, sat at the next table to him in restaurants, watched him play tennis. It would be nonsense to say he liked Marks (or Howard, as he always referred to him), but he felt he knew him, felt they had developed a certain rapport.

So in Lovato's mind, once Howard was in custody they would sit down together and do business. Craig would explain that it was useless to resist extradition, that this time there really was no escape. And Howard, being highly intelligent, would realize that the game finally was over.

There was a more personal reason, too. Lovato wanted to be there to see them put the handcuffs on – for George's sake.

George Pasenelli was a DEA intelligence analyst whom they called 'the Computer'. Actually, he was much too set in his ways to have any time for computers, but his mind worked like one. He had somehow absorbed and retained thousands of pieces of information about Marks, his methods, his associates and his rivals. Feed Pasenelli the most obscure name that nobody else could remember, and out would come a date, or a list of associations, or the details of a long-forgotten incident.

Lovato always insisted that the investigation and pursuit of Marks had been a team effort. He also insisted that there was no more dedicated member of the team than Pasenelli. Call him at his office in San Diego at six in the morning, and he'd be there. Call him again at ten o'clock at night and he'd still be there, pouring over the intelligence reports that he kept in bulging manila folders.

He had never balked at any task, never asked for overtime, and he'd never asked Lovato for a favour – until now.

Two days before he'd called.

'Craig, did you receive a package from me?'

'No. What's in it?'

'You'll understand when you get it.'

The next day Federal Express had delivered a pair of silver handcuffs with Pasenelli's name inscribed on them.

Lovato called him up and said, 'I got your package.'

'Well, you know what I want done with them, don't you?' said Pasenelli.

Howard Marks did leave the plane in Dubai, though only to spend a little of his fortune buying gifts in the airport's duty-free shops. Shortly after five o'clock on Wednesday afternoon, Miami time, the watchers reported: 'He's on his way to Zürich.'

The flying time from Dubai to Zürich is almost eight hours. That meant it would be the early hours of Thursday morning in Miami before Marks arrived in Zürich and made his next move. Lovato went home, to share another all-night vigil by the telephone with Wendy.

6

Their best guess was that Marks would fly from Zürich to his Spanish home near Palma on the Mediterranean island of Majorca. But he also had a home in London, and at least one numbered Swiss bank account in Zürich, and from Zürich he could fly to just about anywhere. The Lovatos spent much of the night on the telephone, talking to the arrest teams, renewing the appeal: 'Wait.'

It was almost four o'clock in the morning when Zürich finally called. Dennis Howard Marks was at the airport and had booked himself on Swissair flight number 670, to Palma, Majorca.

Howard was going home.

It took Lovato forty-eight hours to get there. The US government insists that its employees travelling on business do so on American carriers if at all possible. No American airline flew direct from Miami to Spain, so Lovato had to go to New York.

In Madrid, protocol required that before going to Palma, Lovato report to the DEA country attaché at the American embassy. Protocol also required that for such a momentous event as the arrest of Dennis Howard Marks, the country attaché be present, too.

The country attaché decided that since there was no time left to make all the arrests before the weekend, there was no urgency. Instead of flying to Palma, he would drive the 350 miles to Barcelona and take the ferry. It would give him a chance to see the Spanish countryside.

Lovato flew to Palma on Saturday morning. The Palma police assured him that Marks had safely arrived on the island.

Good, said Lovato. Where was he now?

They couldn't say. They'd lost him.

ACT ONE
The Opening

It is axiomatic in chess that it is easier to achieve a winning game than to win it. One bad move nullifies forty good ones, and precision technique is of the essence even when the game is well in hand.

I.A. Horowitz, *All About Chess*

O N E

This is a story with any number of possible beginnings, a spectrum of moments when you would say that Howard Marks and Craig Lovato were set on their inexorable collision course.

It could begin in the 1960s when Howard Marks, already thoroughly steeped in the drug culture, accepted that he would never make it as a rock 'n' roll singer and that becoming a dope dealer or an Oxford academic were his only career alternatives, and when Craig Lovato joined the Las Vegas sheriff's department.

It could begin in 1973, when 700lb of Howard Marks's hashish was found ingeniously concealed in twenty-eight sound speakers in Craig Lovato's Las Vegas, causing Marks to become a celebrated, if reckless, international fugitive from both British and American justice.

It could begin in 1981, when Howard Marks, finally brought to book, went on trial at London's Old Bailey on drug trafficking charges and produced a successful defence so riddled with dissimulation and outright perjury that it left his adversaries, in their words, 'astonished, disbelieving and incredulous'.

But 1984 is, perhaps, the most compelling starting point because that is when the contest between Marks and Lovato became almost inevitable – when, unaware of each other's existence, they both moved to Spain.

For Howard the move from England to Majorca, 200 miles from the Spanish mainland, was a prudent decision.

11

In London the Inland Revenue, not impressed by Howard's acquittal at the Old Bailey, was demanding some £1.8 million in back taxes, as its share of what it assessed to be Howard's ill-gotten gains from drug trafficking.

Then there was the matter of the imminent publication in Britain of *High Time – the Shocking Life and Times of Howard Marks*, a book about Howard's life on which he had collaborated in return for a half share in the anticipated profits. The book would boast about Howard's perjury at the Old Bailey. Adding insult to injury, it would also say, in effect, that plodding policemen were no match for Howard Marks. He was simply too smart to get caught.

Finally, for anyone intending to renew a career in the international dope business, Spain – with its relatively moderate penalties for drug trafficking, and an institutional reluctance to grant foreign extradition requests – was not a bad place to be.

In April 1984 Howard and his wife, Judy, bought an old, secluded house in La Vileta, a small village on the outskirts of Palma, Majorca's capital. They put their two daughters into the island's English school, and began work on renovating the house.

Meanwhile, in Las Vegas, Craig Lovato reluctantly agreed to leave his wife. He had by then been a DEA agent for six years. His second wife, Wendy, had been a DEA agent for just two days when news came through of Craig's transfer to Madrid. He saw only two alternatives: he could refuse the two-year posting, or she could give up her own career with the DEA and join him in Spain.

Wendy said nothing. She pulled the Yellow Pages out of her desk drawer and called a travel agent to establish the cost of a round-trip ticket to Spain. 'It's not that bad,' she said. 'So, we'll commute.' Three months later, she was stationed in Miami, and he was on his way to Spain.

There was a time when DEA agents posted overseas were essentially diplomats; men in suits, tied to a desk at the American embassy and primarily concerned with administration, nor enforcement. But times (or perhaps it is the agents) have changed.

Lovato's journey from Las Vegas to Spain, via Miami and New York, took five days. He finally arrived in Madrid at seven in the morning, checked into his hotel and, by midday, was on the streets, working a surveillance operation with Madrid's small but enthusiastic undercover drugs squad.

The first day set the pattern. The half dozen 'narcs' who made up Group 3 of the Servicio Central de Estupefacientes might have been chosen by Central Casting for their undercover roles as pimps and pushers. They could move through the clubs and bars and brothels of Madrid's underworld without causing a ripple. But sometimes they needed help, and in providing it Craig Lovato was in his element.

He had at least two identities, one of them as Johnny Luna, a documented cat burglar with a genuine police record in Las Vegas (lest anyone should check) and a pilot's licence. Johnny Luna had moved into drugs, and he could convince almost anybody that he could fly, buy, or sell just about any illegal substance they wanted. Working with the undercover narcs of Group 3, Lovato became 'the American connection' in Madrid, and many people went to jail because of him.

Then events conspired to make Craig Lovato aware of the existence and activities of Howard Marks and, though he would deny it, he became obsessed with him. So began, in Hollywood's terms, an epic contest – a marathon chess game played out on a universal board – between a target who was too smart to be caught, and a hunter who would not quit.

In the course of it, Marks and Lovato gained a grudging respect for each other. That is despite the fact that in attitude, background, character, temperament and belief, they had nothing in common – save for the fact that in Spain they each had a dog called Rocky.

Howard's Rocky was a golden labrador, delightful, reckless, and incorrigible. Craig's Rocky was a pit bull terrier, indomitable, persistent, and utterly loyal. When Howard's Rocky became too difficult to manage, Howard gave him to somebody else to care for. When Craig's Rocky became too senile to manage, Craig took him out into the garden and shot him in the head.

The first moves were made long before Craig Lovato even knew he was to be a player in the game. He was still packing his bags for Spain, still unaware of the existence of Howard Marks, when the hashish was pressed, the deposit paid, and clever plans were laid to deceive the government of the United States into furthering the conspiracy. This was one consignment of drugs the government was unlikely to seize, because the government itself was going to import it.

Karachi, Pakistan, 14 June 1984

'Mr Dennis', as he called himself, was about six feet tall and slim, with modestly long brown wavy hair; a handsome man, thought

13

Asad, the clerk. Judging by his accent he was obviously British, which seemed strange to Asad, for Mr Dennis insisted that it was the Americans he worked for, at the US embassy in Hong Kong. What did he do? asked Asad. Just a job, said Mr Dennis, lighting yet another cigarette.

Asad took the hint. He was a new and very junior employee at Forbes, Forbes, Campbell & Company, one of Karachi's leading shipping agents, and it was not his place to interrogate the customers. He switched the conversation to the future of Hong Kong, in light of China's impending takeover of the British colony, but Mr Dennis wasn't much interested. In awkward silence, and the steamy heat of a Karachi summer, the two men waited for the arrival of someone more senior who could deal with Mr Dennis's consignment.

It sat outside the shipping office, loaded on a shining new, blue Mazda truck; four substantial wooden crates of unusual dimensions. Each crate was twelve feet long and four feet square. Together they weighed more than two tons.

'Aircraft propeller parts', said the scrap of paper that Mr Dennis produced when the traffic supervisor for Forbes, Forbes, Campbell & Company, the man with the authority to accept or refuse any consignment, returned to his office. The supervisor was not impressed with Mr Dennis in his well-worn jeans and white T-shirt, for such clothes are widely regarded in Karachi as the uniform of hippies, who are not welcome in Pakistan, and certainly not suitable attire for someone who claimed to be from the US Military Sealift Command, Special Missions branch.

The supervisor was even less impressed with Mr Dennis's documentation. Waybills, and commercial invoices, and export licences are the currency of the shipping business, and a scrap of paper requesting that the crates be sent to the US naval air base in Alameda, near Oakland, California, could not possibly meet the company's standards. Where was the proper documentation?

Coming, from the American consulate in Karachi, said Mr Dennis. Or, perhaps direct from the naval attaché at the US embassy in Islamabad.

Well, said the supervisor, he certainly could not accept the consignment without proper documentation. Mr Dennis would have to return with the crates at a later date.

Impossible, said Mr Dennis. He was required to return to Hong Kong immediately, to undertake another urgent mission. Couldn't they just store the crates until the documentation arrived?

No, said the supervisor, with the assurance of a bureaucrat used to getting his own way. He had no men available to unload the crates from the truck.

Fine, said Mr Dennis, he would leave the truck. And he handed over the keys.

Against his better judgement, the supervisor accepted them. Mr Dennis didn't even ask for a receipt.

What was Mr Dennis's address? Sorry, said Mr Dennis, he was not allowed to reveal that. 'I'll be in touch,' he promised as he left.

Nobody at Forbes, Forbes, Campbell & Company ever saw or heard from Mr Dennis again.

For the rest of June, all of July, and on into August, the crates and the truck remained where they were, to the growing irritation of Syed Bashir, general manager of Forbes, Forbes, Campbell & Company, who made no secret of his view that the consignment should never have been accepted in the first place.

All appeals for documentation addressed to the US consulate in Karachi produced nothing more than the vaguest of responses. On the other hand, the naval attaché at the embassy in Islamabad was precise but unhelpful. He insisted he knew nothing about the consignment, and he had never heard of Mr Dennis.

It was not until late August that Bashir saw any hope of resolving the situation, when he made what was for him an annual pilgrimage to California, to visit the Oakland headquarters of American President Lines.

Forbes, Forbes, Campbell & Company are sole agents in Karachi for President Lines, which has a virtual monopoly of the marine cargo trade between Pakistan and the United States. And, since the naval air station in Alameda has frequent need to ship military equipment to and from Pakistan, it is a good customer of President Lines, and its officials warranted a courtesy visit from the Karachi agent.

So in August 1984, Syed Bashir met Frederick Hilliard, a large, gregarious man with grey hair and an explosive temper that he usually concealed behind a brash exterior. Fred Hilliard knew all about Bashir's bothersome consignment. He assured Bashir that the delays were due to red tape and nothing more. The proper documentation, he promised, would soon be forthcoming.

A grateful Bashir gave Hilliard his business card. Hilliard gave Bashir a tie-pin depicting an airplane. Very much in character,

Hilliard said it was a miniature copy of America's latest and still secret spy plane.

Crystal City, Virginia, 23 September 1984

Fred Hilliard was being treated by his doctor for high blood pressure, diabetes and 'poor dietary control'. Nevertheless, for his last meal he ate red meat, french fries and stuffed potato skins, according to the analysis of the indigested remains found in his stomach. He died of acute coronary failure. Death probably occurred on the previous Friday evening but it was not until Sunday lunchtime that the house detective at the Marriott Hotel, where Hilliard was staying, forced open the door of room 1626. Hilliard was found wearing shorts, sitting in an armchair, his feet propped up on a coffee table. His reading glasses were perched on his forehead and a copy of Friday's *Washington Post* lay on his lap.

There was nothing suspicious about the circumstances, but by law every 'unattended death' in Virginia requires at least a nominal police investigation. The detectives who went to the Marriott found a fairly orderly room, a bed that had not been slept in, and curtains that had not been drawn.

They also found binoculars; a miniature Minox camera suitable for copying documents; a parking permit for the White House; an envelope addressed to the director of the Central Intelligence Agency; a handwritten note with the words 'CIA CITY 661-2752'; and a brown leather briefcase containing $36,371 in cash.

There were also documents showing that Hilliard was a US government employee, engaged as an aerospace engineer by Naval Air Systems Command. On the totem pole of government service Hilliard did not rank high. He was a journeyman, with an official grade of 12, on a scale of 7 to 17. He did, however, enjoy considerable security clearance.

Three days after Hilliard's body was found, the Naval Investigative Service (NIS) began a full-scale investigation into what it called – with the blunt irreverence of policemen everywhere – 'The Dead Fred Case'.

NIS works for the US Navy, though all its agents are civilians. Their remit is all and any crimes committed by or against US Navy personnel or property anywhere in the world. Though they rarely get media credit in major cases, their brief includes the detection of espionage.

Everything about the Dead Fred affair screamed espionage. Until the previous December, Hilliard had struggled to get by on his monthly salary of $1,400. Then, in six months, he had deposited a total of more than $78,000 in cash into his bank account. He had paid more than $20,000, again in cash, for a new sporty Saab. He had acquired a girlfriend almost half his age and sent her on expensive trips, including one to Mexico. And, just before his death, Hilliard had put down a $10,000 deposit, in 100-dollar bills, on a condominium in Crystal City. At his insistence, the contract stipulated that the balance of the purchase price, a little less than a quarter of a million dollars, would also be paid in cash.

Where had the money come from, if not from the sale of secrets? Hilliard had told friends and colleagues any number of stories to explain his sudden wealth, none of them true. But then, as NIS investigators quickly discovered, everything about Frederick Edgar Robert Duncan Hilliard's life was a mosaic of lies.

Hilliard's version of his life was contained in the resumé he had submitted to Naval Air Systems Command in Virginia when applying for his recent transfer from the naval air station at Alameda. The resumé chronicled years of achievement from 1943 when, just seventeen years old, he had joined the Marines: how he had been awarded the Navy Cross; held a Guggenheim research fellowship in aeronautical engineering at Princeton University; worked for the Navy on 'top secret' military projects; implemented the Air America Operations for the CIA in Laos during the Vietnam War; worked for the Pacific Institute in San Francisco on 'various designs for operations of the intelligence community'.

A very different story was told by Hilliard's full personnel record at Alameda, where he had worked as an aerospace engineer from 1978 until July 1984. That file revealed that Hilliard had already been investigated frequently from 1961 onwards for a host of petty, and not so petty, violations, including failing to return a rental car so that it was listed as stolen; giving the name of Congressman John Brademas as a personal reference on a job qualifications statement, though Brademas said he didn't know him; and passing dud cheques for which he was arrested three times.

Then there were Hilliard's impersonations or, more accurately, misrepresentations. At various times he had passed himself off as a consultant to the National Security Council, a member of the Committee on Science and Astronautics, and a lieutenant-colonel

17

in the US Marine Corps, attached to the White House staff at San Clemente. (In fact, Hilliard's military career in the Marines came to an end in 1955 when he was wounded in the right leg in Korea. He was then a mere second lieutenant.)

The picture that emerged from the NIS investigation of Fred Hilliard was of a man who loved an audience, a man who was generous to his friends but who could shock them with outbursts of uncontrollable temper, a gambler who was often in debt, a chronic braggart who was actually incompetent in his work – and, above all, a man who continually hinted of 'hush-hush operations' within the intelligence community, of having connections with the CIA.

Some of his co-workers at Alameda told NIS they had dismissed Hilliard's CIA stories as fantasies. Others believed them. They were the only explanation as to how Hilliard could possibly have held down his job.

Karachi, 4 November 1984

Finally, nineteen weeks after Mr Dennis vanished, Syed Bashir, general manager of Forbes, Forbes, Campbell & Company, was able to rid himself of the four abandoned crates.

The proper documentation arrived from Alameda. The US Embassy in Islamabad formally applied to the Pakistan authorities for an export licence, making the necessary declaration that the crates contained no antiquities. The Pakistan Ministry of Foreign affairs granted it.

Cranes lifted the crates on to the S.S. *Ulanga* and she sailed for Dubai, where the S.S. *President Lincoln* was waiting to take them on to California.

A much relieved Syed Bashir submitted his bill – for $2,328.90 – to the United States government.

Alameda, California, 6 November 1984

In his office at the Alameda naval station, NIS agent John Dill pondered the progress of the investigation into the Dead Fred affair. Six weeks into the case, it amounted to somewhere between slender and zero. Every lead had turned into a dead end.

Pursuing the espionage theory, Dill had persuaded the Navy top brass at Alameda to review all the classified material Fred Hilliard had ever had access to. Nothing was missing, and none of the documents contained secrets worth hundreds of thousands of dollars.

For a while the CIA connection had seemed promising. Hilliard's young girlfriend was convinced he had been involved in intelligence work, if only because in the midst of an argument he had told her: 'Don't you move out of this room because I can kill you. I do it for a living.'

The CIA, however, was adamant: Hilliard had *never* worked for the agency. Everything said that Hilliard was simply a liar and a braggart. But he hadn't lied about coming into sudden money.

So where had it come from? Dill's best and last hope for finding the answer was the person who knew Hilliard best, a college professor in Washington DC named Dr Robert Hemmes. He had first met Hilliard in 1954, in a naval hospital in New York, where they were both recuperating from wounds received in Korea. Over the years, Hemmes had loaned Hilliard money, got him a job, and was endlessly tolerant of Hilliard's 'stories', which, he said, nobody took very seriously. Hemmes lived in McLean, Virginia, only a few miles from the hotel where Hilliard died. He had identified the body and organized the funeral.

Hemmes had already been interviewed twice by NIS, but although he was helpful on Hilliard's background and personality, he knew nothing about the money – or so he said.

Then, on 6 November, as John Dill sat in his office at Alameda wondering where on earth to look next, Dr Hemmes telephoned.

There was, he said, something else he knew that he has previously withheld but now wanted to say.

Because he was Hilliard's closest friend, the police had given him some of the papers found in the hotel room. They included documents that described defective aircraft propeller parts which had been shipped from Pakistan to the naval base at Alameda.

Hemmes said he had discussed these papers with Hilliard's girlfriend. She knew about the crates: she told Hemmes that Hilliard had somehow intercepted them at Alameda, and taken something out of them.

Whatever it was, she said, someone had paid him $1 million for his trouble.

Ernest Franz Combs – or 'Peter', as he preferred to be called – had always been rich, or so it seemed. His father had sold 2,800 acres of California land to Walt Disney, who turned it into Disneyland, and he owned his own oil business, so the family was more than comfortably off.

Not that Peter was spoiled. His father kept him on a tight rein

19

and there weren't any handouts. He drifted into dope dealing almost naturally, just to make living expenses. When he was a student at the University of Southern California, he'd drive down the coast to San Diego, just shy of the Mexican border, and buy marijuana that could be sold for a nice little profit back in San Francisco. It was no big deal; everybody he knew was doing it.

Then Combs began importing hashish from Europe, a more challenging business which tripled the profit. He began modestly, with 200lb of hash smuggled from England, hidden inside a metal sculpture. Soon he was employing relays of people to import cars and camper-vans into the US, stuffed in every concealed space with hash from the Lebanon or marijuana from Afghanistan. He used a boat to bring in marijuana from Thailand, but some of it got wet. (He dried it with his mother's heat lamp.) A better idea was importing almost a ton of hash, hidden in the boom of a huge yellow construction crane.

He always insisted it was the challenge and excitement, rather than the profit, that appealed to him. He was exceptionally casual about money. It was his habit to pick out the 10-dollar bills from the bagfuls of cash that came in, and put them in a box. The box, which might contain $100,000 or more, was for Patti Hayes, his common-law wife. 'I keep the tens for Patti so she can shop,' he would say. Another story about his laid-back attitude became legendary in the dope business. A brand-new employee, who had never met Combs, phoned him from Oregon to say that the latest load had been sold locally, and what should he do with the several hundred thousand dollars of Combs's profits?

'Look, I'm real busy right now,' said Combs. 'Just hang on to it. Don't worry about it.'

In 1981, Combs decided to retire, at the age of thirty-five. In just the last six years of his career he had made, by his own estimate, $20 million.

He'd banked a lot of it, laundering it through his high-priced Los Angeles attorney. The attorney would give suitcases crammed with cash to his wife – or, sometimes, his mistress – to take across the border into Mexico. The cash was deposited in a Tijuana bank, then wire-transferred to Combs's account at the Bank of Bermuda. There was so much money that Combs didn't mind too much when the attorney borrowed half a million dollars to buy a classy house in Los Angeles, and neglected to pay it back. Or when the attorney developed a heavy cocaine habit, and Combs had to 'lend' him $25,000 a month to keep his practice going.

The attorney was his friend. In 1979, when Combs was diagnosed as having thyroid cancer, it was the attorney who found one of the best cancer specialists in America, and who got him into the Cedars Sinai hospital in Beverly Hills for surgery. In Combs's view, his attorney had saved his life. So, what was a few hundred thousand dollars?

After he had announced his retirement to his friends and associates, Combs asked his attorney for an accounting of the funds amassed in the Bank of Bermuda. The attorney stalled. Eventually he admitted the account was nearly out of money.

'Out of money? Are you crazy?' said Combs. 'There should be at least 12 million in there.'

But there wasn't. It had all been lost on bad investments, the attorney said.

Combs fumed for a while, then fretted, then shrugged. Thirty-five was too young to retire, anyway.

Lake Tahoe, California, November 1984

Peter Combs sat in his house, set amid the spectacular mountain scenery of the sierras on the California–Nevada border, and considered the dilemma caused by the sudden death of Fred Hilliard.

Alameda – some 150 miles to the south-west – wasn't exactly Fort Knox, but it was a military base. How could he spirit four crates, weighing more than 2 tons, out of there?

'Easy,' said Tom Sunde. 'We'll go in there and get them for you.'

It was exactly the kind of thing Sunde (pronounced like Sunday) would say. He was nothing if not anxious to please. At times he reminded Combs of his favourite breed of dog, Dobermans; always faithful to their masters, always seeking approval. He was particularly adept at perceiving the kind of jobs that Combs hated – like washing the car or taking out the garbage – and doing them himself, unasked.

For years he had treated Combs and Patti as surrogate parents, hanging around them so closely that, when they were living in San Francisco, they finally insisted he get his own apartment, eight floors above theirs. It didn't work. He'd turn up at breakfast and stay till bedtime and beyond, or until Combs yelled, 'Tom, *go home.*' Sometimes they would send him away for weeks, just to get a break.

Combs would say, 'Tom, go to London,' and he'd be on the next plane, up and gone in an hour. Then after a while they'd miss him and say, 'Hey, Tom, come on back.'

He always did exactly what Combs told him to do. Combs would send him to Pakistan or Thailand, to deliver money or oversee the dispatch of loads, and Sunde would follow his instructions to the letter. He wouldn't deviate, he wouldn't get smart. He was reliable, loyal and appreciative – qualities which, in Combs's experience, were rare indeed in the dope business.

Even when Combs fired him, upon his own retirement, Sunde accepted the dismissal as though it were a favour. That's OK, he said, he had a new job anyway. He told Combs he was going to work for the CIA, at a salary of $65,000 a year.

It was nonsense, of course. As Combs said dismissively: 'Tom always wanted to be a spy.'

But then came dramatic changes in Sunde's lifestyle. He stopped using drugs, smartened up his appearance considerably, and began talking knowledgeably about politics, weapons and unarmed combat. He also introduced Combs to his 'CIA partner', a charming if slightly menacing West German named Reiner Jacobi, who, as Combs soon discovered, could sell religion to the Pope.

There were times Combs was convinced that Sunde and Jacobi were a couple of confidence tricksters whose elaborate 'CIA covert actions' were scams devised to enrich themselves, often at Combs's expense. There were other times he wasn't so sure.

It wasn't just the outward appearances: the blue bomber jackets Sunde liked to wear, decorated with a discreet seal of the United States; the briefcase handcuffed to Jacobi's wrist; their walkie-talkie radios with mysteriously blocked frequencies; the official-looking cars that would arrive to collect them, minutes after they sent the signal.

More convincing were the classified documents, on highly sensitive subjects, that Jacobi would sometimes produce from his briefcase. Or the telephone calls he would make to obtain, presumably from official files, full and accurate details on anyone Combs wanted information about. Or the time when Patti's nephew was accused of rape in Santa Rosa, California, and Jacobi said he'd fix it, and within days the state prosecutor was complaining of 'pressure from the CIA' to drop the case.

Sunde and Jacobi were always rushing off to Europe, or South Africa, or Israel or the Far East, yet Combs could reach them night or day. Jacobi gave him an unlisted number in Washington

DC, where he could leave a message. Within hours they would call him back from some exotic foreign location.

Combs noticed that their foreign travels often coincided with those of Ronald Reagan. He didn't know what to make of that. He also didn't know what to make of a photograph, clipped from a newspaper, that Sunde carried in his wallet. It showed two men walking along an apparently deserted beach. One of them was Sunde. The other was the president of the United States.

Perhaps they did work for the CIA? Perhaps they could somehow penetrate the Alameda base and spirit away four wooden crates of unusual dimensions?

'What the heck,' said Combs to Sunde. 'Go do it.'

Oakland, California, 8 November 1984

In America's much-vaunted war on drugs, the special forces – the troops who fight behind enemy lines – are mainly mercenaries. They are called Confidential Informants, or in the lexicon, 'CIs'. Some of them do it to save themselves from jail. Some do it for money. 'Rex' said he did it out of patriotism, which was remarkable since he wasn't even an American citizen.

Mark Bastan had never met anybody like him. Bastan had gone to their agreed rendezvous at the Marriott Airport Hotel in Oakland, unsure as to how they would recognize each other. He had barely entered the lobby when a man in his early forties came up to him and said: 'Are you Mark? I'm Rex. Let's go and sit down over there.'

Sitting on a sofa in the lobby of the Marriott, Rex told Bastan his astonishing story.

His primary concern, he explained in his precise German accent, was disrupting the activities of international terrorists. Terrorism and drug trafficking sometimes walked hand in hand. At that very moment, he said, a large load of Pakistani hashish was sitting in the Alameda naval base, just down the road from the Marriott, and when it was sold, at least some of the proceeds would flow into the coffers of the IRA.

The hashish had been shipped to Alameda in four crates, and had arrived some time in October, Rex said. The load had been imported by a US Navy employee named Fred Hilliard. It was going to be distributed by two California dopers – and here Rex carefully spelled out their names, and dictated their telephone numbers.

And, by the way, he added, the police and the navy thought Hilliard was dead. He wasn't. The corpse they'd found was that of somebody else. The hands had been cut off, to prevent identification.

Mark Bastan had been a special agent for the US Customs service for less than a year, and this was the first time anybody had dropped the prospect of a multi-ton drug seizure into his lap. He was much too excited to call ahead. He drove straight to the Alameda base and presented his badge at the gate. Within minutes of leaving Rex, Bastan was sitting in the offices of the Naval Investigative Service, repeating the story to an incredulous John Dill.

So that was it! Ever since the telephone call from Dr Hemmes two days before, Dill had prowled the base, trying to find anybody who remembered a shipment of aircraft parts from Pakistan that Hilliard had arranged – and that might have also contained something worth $1 million.

He'd discovered there had been such a shipment. People remembered it because on the paperwork Hilliard had used an irregular control number, one that had already been assigned to a previous consignment. When challenged about this gross breach of naval regulations, Hilliard had told co-workers the shipment was 'covert', something 'hush-hush', something they shouldn't concern themselves with.

But, as Dill told Bastan, that shipment had arrived in Alameda in December 1983, almost a year before – and just before Hilliard became a wealthy man. Rex was talking about a shipment that had only just arrived, and was still on the base.

There was only one reasonable assumption. If Rex was right, Hilliard had brought in two shipments of hash: one the year before; a second that was still on the base, awaiting collection.

For much of the rest of that day, a posse of NIS agents, rounded up by Dill, searched every corner of Alameda, looking for four crates of unusual dimensions. They found nothing. For Bastan in particular, it was a bitter disappointment.

It also raised questions. How reliable was Rex? What did Bastan know about him?

Practically nothing, Bastan admitted. But Rex had come to him highly recommended by Lawrence Ladage, the respected Special Agent in Charge (SAC) of US Customs in Portland, Oregon. Ladage had described Rex as a 'trusted' Customs informant with an impressive track record of providing accurate information on

24

European terrorists and illegal high-technology exports from the United States. Larry Ladage thought highly of Rex, and young Mark Bastan, with less than a year on the job, was in no position to challenge him.

And, over the next few days, some of the information provided by Rex did check out. For the umpteenth time, Dill searched through Hilliard's papers, and found they contained the telephone numbers of the two distributors Rex had identified. The phone records of the Alameda base revealed that Hilliard had called one of those numbers from his office. So Rex was right about that. But where were the crates?

They must be missing something, said Dill.

At his suggestion, Bastan went to the offices of American President Lines in Oakland, and searched the manifests of all ships that had arrived from Pakistan in the past few months with any large shipment bound for Alameda. Nothing.

Just a minute, said Bastan, what about shipments *due to arrive* from Pakistan?

American President Lines duly sent a telex to Forbes, Forbes, Campbell & Company in Karachi, requesting the details of any such shipments.

On 12 November back came the response: four crates of aircraft propeller parts destined for Alameda were on their way. They were expected to arrive in Oakland in a little over a month.

Bastan did not tell Rex the load had not yet arrived from Pakistan; he didn't have to. 'I'm sorry, the information I gave you was wrong,' said Rex the next day. He now knew the load was still on its way. It *would* arrive in California on about 14 December, he said.

It was extraordinary how easily Rex obtained his information. Whenever Bastan returned to the Marriott to ask a question that Rex couldn't immediately answer, the German would say, 'I'll make a call.' Moments later he would return from one of the pay phones in the lobby, armed with the information Bastan wanted, or a correction to something he had said before. It was as though he had a direct line to the other side.

The calls were made to Hong Kong – or at least that's what Rex told Bastan.

He said his source was a Hong Kong businessman. Quite how the businessman fitted into the picture, Rex did not say. He implied, however, that he and the businessman were engaged in some elaborate double game. The seizure of the hashish was only one of his objectives, Rex said. Equally important was his hope of persuading 'the terrorists' and their drug trafficking partners that someone inside their joint enterprise had talked. If they believed that, it would cause dissension and disruption of the pipeline – and that would be Rex's reward.

He was not interested in being paid, not even his expenses. He would, he said, go anywhere in the world, and do anything necessary, to accomplish his mission.

It occurred to Mark Bastan that private citizens are not usually so dedicated in assisting the war on drugs. Indeed, he came to suspect that Rex was not a private citizen at all, but one somehow connected to the American intelligence community, presumably the CIA.

That suspicion was reinforced when, during their third or fourth meeting at the Marriott, Rex revealed he had a partner, and introduced Bastan to an American in his mid-thirties who said his name was Ross.

Ross, like Rex, obviously kept himself fit. He seemed knowledgeable about law enforcement, and all of its paraphernalia and jargon. He invariably wore a bomber jacket, decorated with a seal of the United States.

Rex and Ross remained at the Marriott, meeting Bastan almost daily, providing him with fresh nuggets of information and a growing list of suspects who, they said, might have been involved with Fred Hilliard. Then, in mid-November, they told Bastan they had to leave California for another mission. They didn't say where they were going. They did say Bastan could always contact them through Larry Ladage at Customs' Portland office.

Looking back on the Dead Fred affair, it is striking how much of the information that Rex and Ross provided US Customs was either circumspect, dubious, misleading or just plain wrong.

For example, Dead Fred was most certainly dead. Contrary to Rex's claim, the hands of the corpse had not been amputated and, on 27 November, the FBI compared the fingerprints with those of Hilliard, held in its records. They matched.

Rex and Ross never told Bastan of Peter Combs's involvement in the conspiracy – indeed, never mentioned his name – though since Ross was, in reality, Thomas Sunde they most assuredly knew. They also never mentioned that Combs's partner in this enterprise was Howard Marks – though, again, they knew.

On the other hand, they did name as Hilliard's co-conspirators

26

people who worked inside the Alameda base – all of whom subsequently survived rigorous investigation by NIS and Customs.

But on one matter they were not wrong.

Oakland, December 1984

As soon as the S.S. *President Lincoln* had docked at Oakland, a Customs sniffer dog was taken on board and shown the four crates. It reacted the way all customs dogs are trained to when they detect the slightest scene of narcotic substances – with enormous excitement.

Disguised as a truck driver, discreetly escorted by fellow agents in undercover cars, Mark Bastan drove his precious cargo from Oakland docks to the Alameda base.

The crates were unloaded in Alameda's freight receiving area, next to the propeller repair workshop. For the next seven days, teams of agents, working shifts, concealed themselves in the area and waited. To bait the trap, a message was left on the telephone answering machine in the propeller workshop, saying the shipment had arrived. Nobody showed up to collect it.

On 21 December the crates were moved to the US Customs warehouse in San Francisco where, five days later, after the Christmas break, they were opened.

The opening was performed with due ceremony, recorded on videotape by a DEA agent. Inside each crate, protected by layers of Styrofoam, were three metal containers.

Each one contained 178 one-kilo packages of black Pakistani hashish, weighing a total of 407lb. Each package was wrapped in red cellophane, stamped with a logo that resembled the three prongs of a trident.

The total consignment weighed 4,800lb. At $1,000 a lb, the going rate for finest Pakistani black, it was worth $4.8 million, wholesale; five times that on the streets.

One hundred and fifty miles away in South Lake Tahoe, Peter Combs pondered his losses. They amounted to his investment in the load of some $300,000, plus more than $1 million in his share of the anticipated profits.

The news that the shipment had been seized came from Reiner Jacobi and Tom Sunde. They didn't tell Combs that, as Rex and Ross, they had given US Customs the information that had led to the load being seized. Instead they said that with the help of

27

the CIA they had penetrated the Alameda base – and had almost been caught by the waiting agents.

They told Combs that the DEA had made a videotape of the crates being opened. It wasn't until five years later, when Combs watched the video played in court, that he knew for sure that this much, at least, was true.

Peter Combs had been a fugitive for so long, he almost took it for granted.

That he had been able to evade capture was partly due to luck, mainly to preparation. As early as May 1974, the DEA in Los Angeles had no less than eight of Combs's aliases on record, which was nowhere near the total number. He could shed an identity faster than a snake sheds its skin – and, as the DEA knew to its cost, he always had a new one ready to move into.

They'd almost got him once in South Lake Tahoe, but Combs was tipped off by his high-priced lawyer that the arrest teams were on their way. Five minutes later he was gone, leaving behind his clothes, the house, his cars, and every scrap of identification in his current name. Before he reached the end of the driveway he was somebody else, equipped with new ID, on his way to a new house in Mill Valley, California that he'd rented for just such an occasion.

He was simply too elusive. In February 1975, a despairing DEA agent wrote a report summarizing recent leads on Combs, listing forlornly the places he might be: the Bahamas, Hawaii, South America, the Cayman Islands, Oregon, Mexico or Canada.

In fact he was in none of them. For the most part, Combs stayed in California, pursuing his career as perhaps the most prolific and successful dope smuggler on the West Coast.

Until finally his luck ran out. On 22 March 1985 – after eleven years, seven months and eight days on the run – Combs was arrested on the DEA charges at his South Lake Tahoe house.

The specific charge against him was conspiring to import seven loads of hashish into the United States from six different cities in Europe: Amsterdam, Dublin, London, Paris, Rome and Vienna. Each load was concealed in sound speakers of the type used by rock bands on stage. Since the speakers supposedly belonged to British rock groups on tour in the United States, they were imported into the country only temporarily – and attracted little attention from US Customs.

It was a clever scheme and might have succeeded indefinitely, except for bad luck.

In September 1973, twenty-nine speakers crammed with hash arrived at New York's John F. Kennedy airport from Amsterdam. Twenty-eight of them were airfreighted on to Las Vegas, Nevada. The twenty-ninth got left behind – and attracted the excited attention of another of Customs' sniffer dogs.

Combs had known in his bones that something was wrong.

'I don't like the feel of this,' he told Gary Lickert, one of his workers, who'd gone with him to Las Vegas to collect the speakers. 'Let's just forget about it.'

But Lickert was being paid $5,000 to drive the hash to Los Angeles, where Combs's partners, including Howard Marks, were waiting to sell it. 'What are you going to tell those people?' he demanded. 'You didn't get the stuff because you felt bad about it?'

God, thought Combs, now I've got the hired help telling me what to do.

Lickert asked what was the worst he would face if he got caught.

'You'd get five years; you'd serve two,' said Combs.

'What would you all give me if I went to jail?'

'Keep your mouth shut, you'd get paid a hundred grand a year.'

'Oh I'll go – to hell with it. For a hundred grand a year, I'll go.'

'All right, Gary, whatever,' said Combs, against his better judgement.

From the twenty-ninth floor of the Landmark Hotel, Combs watched through binoculars as Lickert drove a rented truck, loaded with the speakers, from Las Vegas airport on to the forecourt of a gas station. The idea was to allow Combs to establish if the truck was being followed. Of course it was.

'If I pass you, and I throw a candy wrapper out of the window, that means you're being followed,' Combs had told Lickert.

In a rented blue Plymouth, Combs carried out his part of the plan. So, too, did Lickert. Instead of leading the DEA agents to the rest of the gang in Los Angeles – as the DEA had hoped – Lickert drove aimlessly around Las Vegas, as though he were lost. Eventually, he pulled into the parking lot of Big John's Cocktail Lounge on Tropicana Avenue, which is where the DEA agents arrested him.

It was not part of the plan that Combs should give himself away. However, as he drove past Big John's – and took in the sight of

Lickert spreadeagled, with a DEA gun pointed at his head – two of the agents spotted him, and gave chase.

Combs drove the Plymouth to the Las Vegas Hilton, abandoned it at the front door, ran through the hotel lobby and out the back, and jumped into the car of a couple who were just leaving.

'Could I get a ride up to the Sahara?' Combs said to the driver.

'No problem. Lost all your money?'

'Yeah,' said Combs. 'I lost today.'

Combs made good his escape from Las Vegas in a new El Camino that he bought with poker chips, left over from gambling the night before. That should have been the end of it. With Lickert's lips tightly sealed by the promise of $100,000 a year, there was nothing to lead the DEA's investigation back to Combs. Or to Howard Marks who, hearing the news of the seizure on television, took the first plane out of Los Angeles.

But that reasonable hope foundered on the rock of a dogged and determined DEA agent named Harlan Bowe. The Californian Highway Patrol had turned down Bowe as a recruit, because he was too short. The DEA hired him because he was smart, and apparently indefatigable.

Nobody in Las Vegas had ever seen 820lb of hash before (the newspapers splashed it as the largest seizure of hashish ever made in the south-western United States), and Bowe became obsessed with the notion of identifying its owners.

Putting Combs in the frame was relatively easy. An alert fellow agent in Los Angeles sent Bowe a photograph of Combs, on the suspicion that nobody else could have handled a load so big. It perfectly matched the photograph on the driver's licence of 'Jonathan Ernest Kennedy' – the ID Combs had used to rent the blue Plymouth.

Then, over the next two and a half years, Bowe relentlessly pursued every possible lead. He checked out every phone number that Combs had called from his home or the hotels where he was known to have stayed. He visited houses and apartments Combs had rented, restaurants where he had dined, casinos where he had gambled. He tracked down Combs's friends, smuggling associates, girlfriends and lawyers – and, as often as not, subpoenaed them to testify before a grand jury. He traced cars that Combs had bought, always registered in different names. He even found an optician from whom Combs had ordered a new pair of glasses, and lay in wait in case Combs should call to collect them.

Gradually but inexorably he identified most if not all of Combs's partners in America and England, including Howard Marks, and slowly gathered the documentary evidence against them.

No detail was deemed unimportant or too much trouble to obtain. Needing evidence that the first shipment of speakers had been sent from Paris to Los Angeles on 8 March 1973, Bowe approached Trans-World Airlines for a copy of the waybill. TWA told him these documents were filed not by date but by the last four digits of the waybill number. Bowe, with another agent, sat down and sifted through more than 10,000 waybills until he found the one he needed.

Bowe expected no less from other agents in eight American states, and five European countries, from whom he requested similar evidence from airports, hotels, telephone companies, estate agents and car rental agencies.

By the time he was done, he'd logged 1,154 hours of unpaid overtime. In terms of arrests, he had precious little to show for it, but the case he'd built against Peter Combs and Howard Marks was practically flawless.

Even so, Bowe doubted that Combs and Marks would ever go to trial. Try as he might for years on end, he could not find Combs. And though Marks had been arrested in Amsterdam in 1973, a few months after the Las Vegas bust, he'd been released on bail in England and had vanished. Arrested again six years later, Marks had admitted his role in the Las Vegas business. Then he'd won his notorious acquittal at the Old Bailey on other drug charges, and had walked away virtually scotfree. Harlan Bowe had come to believe that Combs and Marks and their trafficking associates were too well organized, and too scattered, and too ingenious to be caught.

He didn't even have the satisfaction of being present when Combs was finally arrested in March 1985. By then Bowe was half a world away, serving as a resident DEA agent in Karachi, Pakistan.

Karachi, April 1985

One month after Combs's arrest, in Harlan Bowe's small and uncomfortable office at the US Consulate, Randall Waddell groaned with frustration. For three weeks, Waddell had pounded the streets of Karachi, pursuing any lead that might shed some light on the identity of the mysterious Mr Dennis, who'd sent the hash-filled crates on their way to Alameda nearly a year before. Waddell had almost nothing to show for it. He felt he had come to the last of several dead ends in what NIS still called the Dead Fred case.

Waddell's normal base was Subic Bay, the huge American naval base in the Philippines, some 4,000 miles away. But there were no NIS agents stationed in Pakistan, so Waddell had drawn the short straw.

He'd worked ten hours a day on the investigation, interviewing some 150 people through an interpreter, discovering that record-keeping in Pakistan was, to put it mildly, erratic. He'd sent a message back to his boss at Subic Bay in which he vividly expressed his sentiments: 'I'm still in Karachi. I appear to be reinventing the wheel.'

Waddell had spent much of his time trying to establish ownership of the blue Mazda truck which Mr Dennis had used to deliver the crates, and which still sat abandoned outside the offices of Forbes, Forbes, Campbell & Company. In the end, he'd concluded that the stated owner, a company called Gulf International, simply did not exist. As for the purchaser of record, one 'B.F. Khan', there were hundreds of thousands of Khans in Pakistan – and even if he did exist, Waddell had no idea how to distinguish him.

In a mood approaching despair, he spent two days at Forbes, Forbes, Campbell & Company, methodically interviewing the only people he knew who'd actually seen Mr Dennis.

From their memories, he constructed a composite picture. Using thin plastic overlays, each one printed with a different facial char-acteristic, he slowly built an 'Identikit' face.

'What did his eyes look like?' Waddell asked each of the witnesses, one by one. 'Was the chin broader than this, or narrower?'

It was a tedious process and not obviously rewarding. The composite that emerged showed a pale-skinned Westerner with modestly long dark wavy hair, crinkly eyes and a thick bottom lip; not somebody who Waddell had ever seen.

Footsore, weary and demoralized, he returned to his borrowed desk at the DEA's office in the consulate, where the agents were friendly and polite, but much too busy with their own assignments to worry about his.

'Still spinning it out, Randy?' said one of them.

'Sure. Three weeks' work and that's all I've got to show for it.' He tossed the composite picture on his desk.

Harlan Bowe walked over to the desk and glanced at the picture. Then he looked again, intently. 'Christ!' he said. 'That's Howard Marks.'

T W O

Howard Marks arrived at Balliol College, Oxford in 1964 to study physics, looking as though he had escaped from a time warp. He wore tight drainpipe trousers and thick crepe-soled shoes – both at least five years out of fashion – and a shirt undone to the waist to display amazing alabaster skin. In a pronounced Welsh accent, the likes of which had seldom been heard at Balliol, he'd tell those who asked about his background that he was the son of an illiterate Welsh coalminer, and that he'd walked barefoot to school. 'Did your family keep coal in the bathtub?' inquired one of his new friends. 'Oh, yes,' said Howard. That was typical of him: always, as one friend noted, 'magnificently extravagant with the truth'.

'He has no concepts of absolutes, and lives in a world of relative truths,' says Patrick Lane, Howard's eldest brother-in-law. 'Ask Howard where he got that wonderful suntan and he might reply, "Skiing with Bianca at Gstaad." He might be telling the truth. On the other hand, he might have got it crossing a high plateau on a Kurdish donkey train, bringing hashish through Syria. Or he might have got it at home using his new sunlamp. It wouldn't matter. All that matters is the telling of the tale, and whichever version he told, telling it would make it true.'

The truth is that Howard's upbringing was not romantically working-class. Although he was from a family of miners, his father, Dennis, was a ship's captain in the Merchant Navy, his mother, Edna, a schoolteacher. Howard was born on 13 August 1945, and

33

by the age of five he and his mother had circumnavigated the globe, accompanying Captain Marks on his voyages.

Then, when he was almost six, his sister, Linda, was born and Captain Marks left the sea for a harbour-master's job at the Welsh steel town of Port Talbot. The family lived in a semi-detached house in Waunbont Road in nearby Kenfig Hill, in relative prosperity. It was a world where Welsh was spoken, where attendance at the Baptist chapel was required every Sunday, and where the bright boys of Kenfig Hill were expected to go to grammar school, which Howard duly did.

He hated it. He was delighted when, at the age of ten, he developed glandular fever and could stay home in bed, being fussed over by his mother. Though he began to get better, he prolonged the symptoms for as long as he could. If his mother came to take his temperature, and then left the room to continue her housework, Howard would remove the thermometer from his mouth and flick the mercury to exaggerate the reading. Depending on whether his mother remained in the room or not, Howard's temperature would oscillate wildly. It looked as though he might have the more exotic undulant fever – so-called because of undulations in body temperature – which his father had contracted on one of his voyages to the Far East. Howard was taken to hospital where, to his astonishment, his temperature continued to undulate, unaided by trickery.

Hospital was where he discovered women. He became obsessed with the nurses and his own immature but powerful sexual yearnings. Back home, he now found distasteful the wrestling games he'd once enjoyed with other boys. What he wanted to do was wrestle with *girls*.

He no longer hated school but he still found it boring, and potentially damaging to his reputation. Lacking strength, he was hopeless at games or any kind of physical activity. On the other hand, he had a natural ability in every academic subject he took – except for art – and was in danger of becoming known as a swot, somebody who actually enjoyed study. To counter any such impression, he started running with a crowd of local toughs. He saw it as a means of self-protection.

There emerged two Howards: the one at Garw Grammar who passed exams with ease, and for whom the teachers predicted great things; the other, back home in Kenfig Hill, a rebel, deliberately mischievous, who drank under-age in pubs (and got caught), became the mascot of a notorious local small-time hoodlum, and affected the sartorial style of his great hero, Elvis Presley. Sundays were for chapel. Saturday nights were for dances at the Workingmen's Hall in Kenfig Hill, where villagers later recalled for the local newspaper that Howard 'was a wonderfully good-looking boy . . . a bit of a heartthrob'. Explaining his sexual precociousness by his early bout of undulant fever, Howard cut a swathe through the local womanhood; mostly salesgirls from Woolworth's, the only ones he knew in Kenfig Hill who would 'do it'.

When Howard thought about his future, which wasn't often, he assumed he would go to a local university, probably Swansea, like most of his schoolmates, and end up a teacher.

Howard's headmaster, however, thought he was extremely bright; bright enough, perhaps, to win a scholarship to Balliol, which was encouraging an influx of grammar-school boys. Howard went up there, with no great enthusiasm, to take the entrance exam. His mother, alarmed by her son's bizarre Presley quiff, insisted on a radical haircut which only confirmed his gloomy fears about the place. The Classics don who interviewed him, however, had hair down to his shoulders, the longest hair Howard had ever seen on a man. Howard thought, much less gloomily, that the place might not be so bad after all.

His Presley quiff fully restored, Howard nonethless arrived at Oxford with some trepidation. He had read about the 'effortless superiority' of Balliol, that the place – often described as being more of a cult than a college – revelled in its intellectual élitism. It was the home of the brightest. It had produced prime ministers Harold Macmillan and Edward Heath, politicians Roy Jenkins and Denis Healey, editor of *The Times* William Rees-Mogg, and Aldous Huxley and Graham Greene.

But for all that, Balliol in 1964 was in the midst of a social revolution. All the old mores and morals were collapsing. To those who were there, Oxford, and in particular Balliol, was the centre of the universe. It still mattered to be bright. What mattered equally, however, was the ability to have a good time, and Howard fitted the new-style Balliol like a glove. As one of his contemporaries put it, Howard was into sex, drugs and rock 'n' roll – though not necessarily in that order. He and Oxford were made for each other.

The novelties of his new life were intoxicating. He made the truly happy discovery that at Oxford, unlike Kenfig Hill, intelligent women and women who would go to bed with him were not mutually exclusive. Lynn Barber was in her second year at

35

Oxford when she spotted the Teddy boy with the alabaster skin in the quadrangle of Balliol. She resolved to meet him, and when, a few days later, she saw Howard again and approached to ask who he was, he invited himself back to her room. He seduced her, apparently, by saying not much more than 'Come here.' It was an effective technique, certainly with her – and with several dozen others to her knowledge.

He was, by all accounts, a considerate and romantic lover, if persistently unfaithful. To women and men he was also a seductive friend. 'There was instant sunshine wherever Howard went,' says John Nicholson, one of his Balliol contemporaries. He was incapable of any sort of malice or vindictiveness. His generosity was legendary. There was a roguish quality about him which people found endearing. A quarter century on, it is almost impossible to find anyone who did not (and does not) like him.

Howard attracted a retinue of friends who formed a sort of permanent party, who accompanied him everywhere, and on whom he showered pints of beer, affection, and always the gift of his undivided attention – even if that only lasted until yet another friend pulled Howard away for yet another party. ('The only place you could see him alone was in bed,' said Lynn Barber.) He was, in many ways, as addictive as a drug.

He'd been aware that Oxford had a drug culture – and that Balliol was the centre of it – but nobody offered him dope until his second term. The first time he tried it, there was no blinding revelation, though he liked the way it 'freed the mind of preconceptions and prejudice' – and, on a more practical level, didn't result in a hangover. By his second year he had become addicted to marijuana or, given the choice, hashish.

From that point on, cannabis dominated his life. Patrick Lane would later say that he'd never seen Marks without a joint, except in jail. 'As far as I am aware, Howard smokes hash twenty-four hours a day,' said Lane. 'There is no question but that Howard loves hash with a passion and that it is the central fact of his life. It is not love of money or love of power which drives Howard. It is a love of hash.'

At Balliol, Marks's room became the meeting-place for Oxford's drug sub-culture, where the latest music was played and seriously discussed. (Discussions about politics were tolerated, but with very little enthusiasm on Howard's part.) His main love was still rock 'n' roll, but he discovered soul music and a group of black friends, whom he met through the son of the president of Liberia, William

Tubman. They were all hip, they all smoked dope, they all had great record collections. They would scoop Howard up and take him to London to go dancing, and to the concerts of black soul singers. His expertise in music was acknowledged when he was chosen as entertainments manager for the Balliol Commemorative Ball, celebrating the 700th anniversary of the college.

More than anything else, what Howard really wanted to be was a singer, another Presley or a Mick Jagger. He made friends with the members of a college rock group, who would good-naturedly allow him to sing with them once in a while. There was rarely a party he attended where he did not insist on performing his interminable Elvis impersonation, causing people, as Lynn Barber remembers, to leave in droves. That was the problem. He looked the part (as Elvis, by stuffing handkerchiefs down the front of his trousers), he loved performing, but he couldn't sing in tune and he knew it. His taste in music was too good to allow him to tolerate his own mediocre voice.

He was equally frustrated by his academic work at Oxford – what little of it he did. He discovered that he hated physics. Spending eighteen hours a week in a laboratory 'swinging pendulums over buckets of water and timing them' seemed utterly pointless. He was, he decided, interested in philosophy. The Dean of Balliol was sympathetic and invited him to write a sample essay about the definition of Good. He tried, but he simply couldn't do it. With resignation, but no more enthusiasm, he returned to the pendulums and eventually graduated with a respectable second-class physics degree.

He settled on a career as a teacher. Meanwhile, and after the most exhaustive of surveys, he settled on the woman he would marry: Ilse Kadegis, a tall, spirited woman of Latvian descent who was a student at St Anne's College. They left Oxford together for London, where they both enrolled in teacher-training courses. It was not long before Marks discovered that neither teaching nor Ilse could satisfy his undefined but restless ambitions.

I was half-way through the postgraduate teaching course at London University, when I realized I definitely didn't want to teach. That was largely due to always being told by the supervisors that I couldn't have long hair. And what really turned me off was a primary school teacher giving us a lecture on school discipline and all kinds of weird philosophies and psychologies. It was a terrible lecture, really boring, and at the end of it, she said: 'Thank you, class dismissed.' Fuck this, I thought, so I gave up the course. But I

37

was still interested in teaching – you know, imparting something, getting someone to be better at something. I thought tuition on an individual level might be an alternative, so I enrolled with a number of crammer colleges which would find students who needed extra coaching. I did a lot of that and I quite enjoyed it. That wasn't so bad. The money was bad – a quid an hour, I think – but I quite enjoyed the way I spent my day.

I was living with Ilse at this point in Westbourne Grove in London. During my spare time I was reading more and more about philosophy and science, and then I thought: 'Oh, hell, let's go back to Oxford and do some postgraduate work.'

It was sparked off by picking up Russell's History of Western Philosophy. I read it and thought, 'Great!' Never really had heard of most of the names before, but I reacted to it much the same as other people react to political discussion. Definitely, that book gave me an interest at last. And so I applied to Oxford, got accepted and did an diploma in the history and philosophy of science.

When I read Russell I found I could anticipate what he was going to say. He would spell out Platonic arguments, and I would think, 'Hold on, Plato can't be right about this because . . .' And then Russell would say, in some instances, what I was thinking. I began to think, 'I might become a fan of this.' I knew I couldn't get into moral philosophy, like definitions of Good, because that was too difficult. But because of my scientific background, and what I'd got from Russell's book, I thought philosophy of science might be a suitable discipline for me. And for a while it worked. I knew enough about the terms in physics and science to be able to waffle on in an argumentative fashion with no trouble.

Everyone who took the course in philosophy of science had to give a lecture at All Souls. You could choose to a limited degree what to lecture about. I chose the contrast between Leibnitz's and Newton's theories on space and time, Leibnitz in many ways was a precursor of Einstein in that he didn't accept the idea of absolute space. He thought space should be relative, and that interested me. The lecture went down well enough. I mean, I got away with it.

Then I managed to get obsessed with paradoxes, and I really did find a genuine interest there, particularly in the paradox of confirmation as it applied to the growth of scientific knowledge. I did some creative work, and gave a good lecture. I summarized everything that everyone had ever written about it, and I managed to increase the field of knowledge a bit.

In order to understand the paradox of confirmation, you have to consider a statement like 'X is the same as Y' or 'All ravens are black', which is the one that they like to use. 'All ravens are black' is logically equivalent in every sense to saying 'All non-black things are non-ravens.' There's no difference in meaning between those two statements. If I say: 'All journalists are stupid' it's

38

like saying: 'All non-stupid people are non-journalists.' Again, the meaning is precisely the same in those two statements, and that process is called logical contraposition.

To test the hypothesis that 'All ravens are black' you have to look at a raven. If it's black that confirms that all ravens are black, at least to a small extent. If you look at thousands of ravens, and they're all black, that confirms it even more. If you look at every raven in the world, and every single one of them is black, that verifies *the hypothesis. But it's impossible to look at all the ravens in the world, so you never get better than* confirmation; *you don't get verification. You can't verify universal statements.*

Now, given that, a sensible way for a scientist to pursue or to test a hypothesis like 'X is the same as Y' is to look at examples of X and see if they're Y. But you could just as easily look at examples of Y to see if they're X. Equally, if 'All non-black things are non-ravens', why not look at non-black things to test the hypothesis? A brown piece of shit confirms the hypothesis that all ravens are black as much as a black raven does. And that's the paradox: why do scientists look at black ravens rather than brown lumps of shit when confirming all ravens are black?

You can, by intuitive means, explain that there are more non-ravens than ravens but when it comes to 'X is the same as Y', you might not know what the ratio is. You don't know if there are more Xs or non-Xs. If you don't know how many of these things there are in the world, you've got no guidance as to whether to look for ravens or pieces of shit. And I was just trying to solve that problem, basically. They liked that stuff, it all went down well. In fact, I wrote a paper which was called On Why Red Noses Confirm All Ravens Are Black, But Only Slightly.

But then, when I started reading the really heavy stuff, I found it difficult to follow. Maybe everyone does. Maybe all these disciplines are terribly difficult. I thought I really ought to brush up my mathematical logic. I did the first elementary courses in that pretty easily but then I got into areas which were mind-blowingly complicated. That's when I knew I couldn't contribute anything. I realized that the only thing I could contribute to the philosophy of science was the waffle stuff-pop philosophy if you like, which didn't impress me very much. I knew I could never be a Fellow of All Souls. I thought I might be able to swing it, but I knew I wan't going to be a genius at it. It was a bit like pop singing. I could get along, do a bit, but I wasn't going to make it very far.

In the meantime I was living with Ilse in Garsington near Oxford. It was when they started making it dark in the mornings by putting the clocks back, and I didn't like that, trying to wake up to the darkness. Ilse was having a very hard life. She had a dreadful job teaching at Didcot and she hated the travel. I was getting more and more pissed off

39

with my inability to work up a mathematic logic to solve the paradox of confirmation.

There was this chap at the University of Sussex called Jerzy Giedymin, a Polish logician, who had all this stuff at his fingertips. I could begin to understand his work and knew that he was very brilliant, and I thought that between us we might solve the paradox of confirmation. And Ilse was keen on moving out of Oxford to go to the seaside, so I thought I would give it a go down there. I applied to do a Bachelor of Philosophy course at Sussex university and got accepted.

We went down to Sussex, and Ilse started teaching at Worthing at a nice school and she enjoyed it, but I hated Sussex university. By this time I had a firm idea of what a university should be like. Sussex wasn't it at all. It was naïve and childish, and there's no romance about studying in the library. You couldn't sit back and think, 'Well, here's where the great philosophers studied.' It just didn't work at all. I couldn't study there properly. And Jerzy Giedymin was totally uncommunicative. I couldn't understand a word he said. He hardly spoke English, his writing was dreadful and there was no communication between us at all. And he wasn't concerned about solving the paradoxes of confirmation. He had other things that were concerning him, equally irrelevant.

The only good thing about Sussex was that I managed to buy my first-ever stereo system, with the headphones and everything. And I was very pleased with that. It was great. I thought, 'Fuck university.' For about three months I idled away my time lying in a horizontal position, smoking dope and listening to Led Zeppelin, wondering what to do.

Rock 'n' roll was out, academia was out. His marriage to Ilse was breaking up and he began an affair with Rosie Brindley, the wife of a maths lecturer at Sussex. They eventually decided to live together and moved to London where, without giving it very much thought at all, Howard Marks slowly but inexorably drifted into drug dealing.

Manila, the Philippines, 21 April 1985

At approximately the same moment as Harlan Bowe identified 'Mr Dennis' as Howard Marks, Howard was in the Philippines enjoying lunch.

'Call me Tony,' said Lord Antony Patrick Andrew Cairnes Berkeley Moynihan, the 3rd Baron Moynihan, as he welcomed Marks into his house.

40

It was inevitable the two of them would hit it off. After fifteen years in exile in the Philippines, the British peer still craved 'interesting company', and almost any fellow-countryman of style visiting Manila might find himself on the guest list of one of Lord Moynihan's renowned Sunday lunch parties. For his part, Marks collected extravagant characters like other people collect rare wine; to him Moynihan was irresistible, a connoisseur's item.

They had a lot in common. Both of them knew what it was like to live as a fugitive. Both had scant regard for other people's rules. Both were immodest about their formidable prowess at the game of Trivial Pursuit. (Later on Marks would claim, only half-jokingly, 'Tony never forgave me for beating him.' Lord Moynihan has no recollection of any such defeat.) Both were gourmets and *bon-vivants*. And, perhaps above all, both were irresistibly attracted (and attractive) to beautiful women.

Since Tony Moynihan inherited the title from his father in 1965, there have been three Lady Moynihans, none of them conventional. The first was a Pakistani exotic dancer who performed in nightclubs around the world under the name 'Princess Amina', occasionally accompanied by her husband on bongos. The second was a secretary in the Philippine Embassy in Pakistan, who went on to own and manage a number of massage parlours in Manila. The third, and present Lady Moynihan, is the exquisite-looking Editha, a Filipino twenty-seven years his junior, whom he first spotted and determined to marry when, aged sixteen, she modelled lingerie at a luncheon party.

It was women that, indirectly, brought Marks and Moynihan together.

Since quitting Britain and his seat in the House of Lords in 1969 – shortly before Scotland Yard was about to charge him with a number of complex frauds – Lord Moynihan had lived largely on his wits, parlaying his name and his innumerable contacts in the Philippines, and much of the rest of Asia, into business deals.

One of those deals concerned the Panache Health Centre, a massage parlour in the basement of what was then the Hyatt Hotel in Bangkok, Thailand. Moynihan had been offered the concession for the Panache, and had taken as his partner an expatriate Englishman named Phillip Sparrowhawk, who travelled on a fake Irish passport under the name of Brian Meehan. Since Sparrowhawk spoke with an east London accent, and insisted that everybody call him Phillip, it was not a convincing disguise. But Moynihan had himself been known to travel on a fake passport and was not concerned with such trifles, especially since Sparrowhawk put up the $100,000 necessary to refurbish the Panache.

Sparrowhawk had invested a further $125,000 in a run-down hotel in Manila's seedy Ermita district on which Moynihan had acquired a twenty-five-year lease. It was Moynihan's ambition to renovate the fifty-five-room hotel and equip it with a massage parlour of its own, called the Light of Dawn. Like the Panache in Bangkok, it would offer massage as part of room service. Whatever else the girls sold to hotel guests was not the management's concern.

Marks was not connected with either of these enterprises – though, for a joke, Sparrowhawk appointed him honorary 'procurement director' of the Panache. (Marks, delighted, had suitable business cards printed. He would hand them out to whoever he met on airplanes, urging perfect strangers to patronize the Panache 'and use my name'.) He was, however, a long-time friend of Sparrowhawk and described by him as a businessman always on the lookout for opportunities. Since Lord Moynihan was always searching for new investors for his hotel, that description alone was easily sufficient to win Marks an invitation to Sunday lunch.

Sitting on a pleasant shaded terrace, attended by Filipino servants summoned by his lordship's bellow, they greatly enjoyed the meal and each other's company. They didn't talk business; it wasn't necessary. Both of them knew that sooner or later they would come to serve each other's purpose.

Los Angeles, California, May 1985

International Offshore Operators, Inc. was established in business with an impressive-sounding address on Wilshire Boulevard, Beverly Hills. The incorporation papers, filed by a reputable attorney, named the president of the company as Gerald W. Livingston.

Mr Livingston did not exist, except in the imagination of Gerald Wayne Wills, who would fit most people's idea of a laid-back Californian. He was 6 ft 4 in tall, blond and blue-eyed, and he lived in a house overlooking the ocean at Santa Barbara.

Wills counted among his friends the very elusive Peter Combs, Howard Marks's partner and West Coast distributor. Like Combs and Marks, Wills was a dope smuggler of considerable experience. Unlike Combs and Marks, he drew no distinction between 'soft' and 'hard' drugs, and he also trafficked in cocaine. He was known in the business for his ingenuity; according to legend (and a DEA informant), he once employed a member of the US skydiving team to parachute a load of cocaine into the United States.

In May 1985, having incorporated his business, Wills and his wife, Wyvonna, flew to Hong Kong, where they checked into the Regal Meridien Hotel. Also staying at the Meridien was Howard Marks, who had been joined in Asia by his wife, Judy, and their two daughters.

On their return to California, Wills and Wyvonna began a series of complex financial transactions, opening accounts at various California branches of the Security Pacific National Bank and the Bank of America, depositing, transferring and eventually withdrawing what amounted to approximately $700,000 in cash.

While the cash accumulated, Wills, using the name Mr Livingston, went shopping for a boat.

Marks, Judy and the children, meanwhile, travelled from Hong Kong to Manila, where Howard renewed his new-found friendship with Lord Moynihan and gave him a copy of *High Time*. It was inscribed: 'To Tony, with much love, best wishes and thanks.'

Having given Moynihan the book, it was obviously necessary for Marks to explain himself and he did, telling Moynihan that *High Time* was the story of his earlier life, that he'd paid his dues, and that all that was behind him now, of course.

But Moynihan's abiding memory of the occasion was not the disclaimer about times past and now regretted: 'He made it sound as if the whole thing had been such fun.'

Karachi, July 1985

At Howard Marks's behest, George Lane and his wife, Assumpta, established the International Language Centre of Karachi in a building that once housed the American consulate. The original idea was to teach English to Pakistanis but, to the Lanes' surprise, they quickly attracted the foreign embassy crowd, a far more lucrative market. Advertisements for the school became ubiquitous: on the Lanes' yellow Toyota; on posters and billboards; even on the drinks coasters laid out on the tables of the American Club, one of the few places in Muslin Karachi where foreigners could buy a drink. Before long, impressively large chauffeur-driven cars were drawing up outside the school, depositing the wives and children of German, Dutch and other European diplomats. To Howard Marks's amusement, the clientele included the wife of at least one drug agent.

The school had been Howard's wedding gift to the Lanes – or at least that's how he'd presented it.

Of the small tribe of brothers- and sisters-in-law Howard had gained by marrying Judy Lane in 1980, George was perhaps the most complex. As a young boy he'd become fascinated with the nineteenth-century writer and explorer, Richard 'The Devil Drives' Burton. Burton's *Arabian Nights* provoked in him a love of Arab culture which survived even actual exposure to it. George hitch-hiked around the Middle East and discovered hashish and then opium, both of which he smoked in a hookah, sitting cross-legged on the floor. In Iran he learned Farsi and became an English teacher, sending back long, fascinating letters to his elder brother, Patrick, in which he predicted the fall of the Shah long before the name Ayatollah Khomeini became embedded in the public consciousness. For a while he lived in Jordan, then on a kibbutz in Israel where he met Assumpta, who was visiting from Belfast. They moved on together to Beirut, where they both worked for the British Council, teaching English, until the civil war in Lebanon forced them to reluctantly return home.

'Have you thought of living in Karachi?' said Marks at George and Assumpta's Belfast wedding in 1984. He told them his drug-smuggling days were over. He was going straight and wanted to invest in legitimate businesses. Marks offered to fund an expedition to Pakistan to allow them to evaluate the commercial viability of a language school. When they reported back from Karachi that the market was wide open, Marks sent them $25,000.

It was not an entirely altruistic gesture. The business was legitimate enough but it also provided Marks with excellent cover for his increasingly frequent visits to Pakistan. He told George and Assumpta to rent a large house to live in – large enough also to accommodate him and any of his 'associates' who might wish to stay.

The first to arrive in Karachi was Jim Hobbs, another connoisseur's item from Howard Marks's collection of eccentric characters.

Marks and Hobbs had met in the remand wing of Brixton prison in 1980, where they shared a cell while Marks awaited his Old Bailey trial. Hobbs was a 'Number One' in Brixton, meaning he was trusted to hand out soap and towels to new inmates. He was extraordinarily kind to his fellow-prisoners, comforting those who were depressed, tactfully borrowing tobacco and other necessities from those who had money to give to those who didn't. He was also blessed with a deprecating sense of humour, maintaining, for example, that his ill-fitting dentures had been stolen from a corpse. By the time Marks and the other prisoners found out that Hobbs was not in Brixton for fraud, as he had pretended, but because of his homosexual predilection for young boys, they didn't care.

Hobbs had once been in the music publishing business – and was a friend of Brian Epstein, manager of the Beatles – but those days were long over. On his release from Brixton he went to work for Marks, though not in any formal sense. Hobbs would undertake any odd jobs that Howard required, and Howard would give him money when he asked for it. The odd jobs included marrying Selina, a Chinese woman from Hong Kong who thus obtained a British passport, and who paid Marks handsomely for the privilege.

Quite what Hobbs was doing for Howard in Karachi was difficult to say. He hated the place; the climate and the food made him constantly sick. For more than two months he moped around the house and the school, seeming to do little more than keep a close eye on George (on Howard's strict instructions, in case his brother-in-law might resume his use of the hookah pipe).

In all probability, he was in Karachi as Howard's representative in case anything went wrong. For Marks and Combs were still very much in business, despite the loss of the Alameda load and despite Combs's arrest. Together with Gerry Wills, they were planning to export a new load from Pakistan, this one somewhat bigger than what they'd lost at Alameda. So in keeping Hobbs in Karachi as his eyes and ears, Marks was simply being careful. With $19 million at stake, who wouldn't be?

Early on a sticky July morning in 1985, Marks left the home of George and Assumpta Lane and, using a false name, took an internal flight from Karachi to Islamabad, the capital of Pakistan.

In the men's room of the Holiday Inn he changed into what looked like a pair of baggy pyjamas. He put on sandals, and a small cap on his head. With his suntan and that disguise, he could just about pass for a native of the North-West Frontier, which is where he was headed.

Waiting for him at the Holiday Inn were Saleem and Aftab Malik, an odd couple at least in appearance. Saleem, the older of the two (who preferred to be called Malik), was a tiny, undistinguished-looking man. His nephew Aftab, on the other hand, was well over six feet tall and strikingly elegant, with the looks of a young Omar Sharif. Together they ran a travel agency in Karachi. They also ran hashish and, occasionally, heroin.

In an American car that had seen better days, Marks and the two Maliks were driven north to Peshawar, which, thanks to the Russian invasion of Afghanistan, had become a boom town: a mecca for Afghan refugees and base camps for the *mujaheddin*; a gigantic arms bazaar, and the site of the greatest concentration of CIA agents in the world, who cluttered the road with their Jeeps.

By what seemed to Howard to be obvious pre-arrangement, their car was waved across the Pakistan–Afghanistan border without being stopped. Near the town of Barak, in barren, mountainous countryside, they finally reached their destination, a wooden stockade the size of four football fields. For Marks it was a magnificent sight: after fifteen years in the dope business, he was finally allowed his first look at something few foreigners ever see – a purpose-built factory dedicated to the manufacture of hashish.

Factory is, perhaps, too extravagant a word. Chopped-up tops of the *Cannabis indica* plant were stored in goatskins; black goatskins, as opposed to brown, to signify that they came from the first flowering of the season and were therefore of the highest quality. In pits dug into the ground, the tops were mixed with cellulose taken from the stem of the cannabis plant and then compressed into slabs or cakes with the aid of cantilever presses; two or three men at one end, a heavy stone at the other. Compression changed the molecular structure of the mixture, making it much more psychoactive than raw cannabis would be. Each slab was supposed to weigh a half-seer – or between half a kilo and one pound – but since there were no scales in the stockade, measurement was clearly a matter of guesswork.

Marks sat inside a crude shack, equipped with a wooden bench and, mercifully, an air-conditioning unit, surrounded by the first batch of the hashish he had ordered. The owner, a wild-looking Afghan with a beard and a turban, produced a hookah pipe and, in his smattering of English, invited Marks to select a large piece of any slab he chose. The hookah was lit and Marks inhaled a generous sample of what is known in the trade as Afghan black, the finest hashish there is. It passed with flying colours.

The heady effects of a concentrated dose of delta-9-tetrahydrocannabinol (THC) took two hours to pass. The Maliks, with little help from Howard, engaged their host in polite conversation about the Afghan war while they waited for food to be prepared, a ritual courtesy that could not be refused.

The food, when it arrived, proved to be exotic: the liver of a freshly-slaughtered lamb wrapped in fat. But Howard was beyond caring. He recovered sufficiently to propose that since hookah pipes were not common in the United States, the only fair test of the hashish would be for him to smoke a joint.

From somewhere in the stockade the owner produced a packet of Rizla cigarette papers. Once again the hash easily gained the Howard Marks stamp of approval.

There was just one other thing left to establish. In those pre-*glasnost* days, it was thought to be good public relations in the American hash business to show support for the *mujaheddin* by stamping the imports of Afghan black with some appropriately anti-Russian slogan: 'Crumble the Kremlin' was a favourite.

Drug trafficker though he was, Gerry Wills was an all-American boy at heart and fiercely anti-Communist. For this load, for which he was putting up most of the front money, he'd told Marks he wanted a special logo, something original. The real purpose of Howard's visit to Barak was to ensure that Wills got his wish.

It was easily achieved. With a broad smile, the wild-looking man in the turban promised Howard that each one of the 24,000 slabs of hash he eventually delivered would be stamped with a drawing of a pair of Kalashnikov rifles, underlining the legend, 'Smoke Russia Away'.

They didn't know about Howard's visit to Barak, but his frequent visits to Karachi, the setting up of the language school, and the lingering presence of Jim Hobbs, Howard's eyes and ears, did not go unnoticed.

Harlan Bowe of the DEA was convinced 'something big' was brewing. So, too, was Michael Stephenson of Her Majesty's Customs and Excise, Britain's Drug Liaison Officer (DLO) in Karachi, and the first British drug agent to be stationed overseas.

Stevenson, like Bowe, had taken one look at Randy Waddell's composite drawing of 'Mr Dennis', and identified him as Marks. Stephenson had an even better reason than Bowe to remember him.

During Marks's trial on drug charges at the Old Bailey in 1981, Stephenson had been subjected to a withering cross-examination by Lord Hutchinson, Howard's eminent and sagacious barrister. The point at issue was small but significant. It was part of the prosecution's case that Howard had visited an American attorney staying at London's Dorchester Hotel. It was part of the defence case that he had not. Stephenson knew perfectly well that Marks had been at the Dorchester because he was part of the Customs surveillance team; he'd seen him with his own eyes. But Lord Hutchinson's cross-examination technique, and Howard's gift for perjury, had combined to cast doubt on Stephenson's testimony and the jury, judging by its verdict, disbelieved him.

Stephenson might not have taken it personally, he might have shrugged it off as part of the game – though it's very unlikely. Within Customs he was known as a confident, aggressive investigator; something of a loner, perhaps, but driven by a determination that made him a highly effective agent, especially in the field (and in 1987 the British government would award him the Medal of the British Empire for his exceptional services in Karachi). Being made out to be a liar by the likes of Howard Marks was not something Stephenson would easily forget.

From London Stephenson obtained a photograph of Marks, which the employees of Forbes, Forbes, Campbell & Company said bore a strong resemblance to Mr Dennis.

That assertion, compounded by Howard's recurring visits to Karachi (and between February 1984 and August 1985 he was there at least sixteen times) could mean only one thing: dope. Bowe and Stephenson knew that Marks was very much back in business – though not for much longer, if they had anything to say about it.

Los Angeles, August 1985

Gerald Wills was a hard man to contact. Norman Ursin, who ran a seafood business out of Seattle, Washington, had been trying to get in touch with him for months, ever since Wills (or 'Mr Livingston' as Ursin knew him) had expressed an interest in buying Ursin's boat. It was called the *Axel D*, a two-masted, 103-foot, ocean-going fishing vessel, which trawled for salmon and herring in the northern waters off Alaska. Wills had said it suited his purposes just fine, and then he'd disappeared.

Despite its posh address, International Offshore Operators, Inc. did not respond to letters, and when Ursin called one of the many phone numbers Wills had given him, he found it belonged to a Mexican restaurant, or an answering service, or had been disconnected.

Then, suddenly, Mr Livingston was back in touch, paying Ursin $10,111 'earnest money' as a deposit. On 16 August he returned with a Bank of America cashier's cheque for $665,000, the remainder of the purchase price.

Three days later he paid Ursin $31,884 for the fuel left on board, and the deal was closed. Mr Livingston had bought himself a boat.

London, England, 31 August 1985

Long before the Cockney with the fake Irish passport arrived at Heathrow airport on a flight from Bangkok, Her Majesty's Customs and Excise were expecting him. In one very real sense Phillip Sparrowhawk, alias Brian Meehan, Lord Moynihan's partner in the massage business, was a marked man.

Though they won't readily admit it, Her Majesty's Customs are given the passenger list of every flight departing from and arriving at Heathrow. Some airlines are more efficient than others: the boarding manifests from transatlantic flights are transmitted to London by computer only moments after they close in the US while some Third World airlines merely deliver the passenger lists to Customs when the flight arrives at Heathrow.

Either way, by the time the passengers have passed through Immigration and collected their luggage, Her Majesty's Customs are ahead of the game. They not only know the names of the passengers but how they paid for their tickets, their precise routes, and who they are travelling with.

These tell-tale manifests are routinely matched against the 200,000 names and aliases contained in CEDRIC, the 'Customs and Excise Department Reference and Information Computer' – the master list of known and suspected drug traffickers.

A successful match can have one of two consequences. If the suspect is believed to be a courier, he or she might be stopped by uniformed officers as they pass through Customs and subjected to an interrogation that always begins: 'Is this your suitcase? Did you pack it yourself?' Bigger fish will usually pass through Customs unmolested but not ignored. It is always a fair bet that at least a handful of the hundreds of people thronging the arrivals terminals at Heathrow will be plain-clothes officers from the local Customs squad or from 'ID', Her Majesty's Customs Investigation Division.

ID has a methodology and a language all of its own. Suspects are called Tango One, Tango Two, Tango Three, and so on, depending on their supposed importance in their respective organizations. Tango stands for T, which stands for Target. Anyone waiting in the arrivals terminal to meet a Tango is designated a 'meeter or greeter' – and becomes immediately suspect themselves.

CEDRIC, like its American counterpart NADDIS (Narcotics and Dangerous Drugs Information System), is not constrained by technicalities such as proof. You don't need to be convicted of drug trafficking in order to be entered into either system. Mere suspicion is sufficient: guilt by association; the word of an informant; even the gut instinct of an officer – what British Customs calls 'the Revenue nose'.

Phillip Sparrowhawk was a Tango with a single digit number.

The official record might show he was a businessman who had graduated from selling imported T-shirts off a barrow on the streets of east London to running a number of successful and legitimate enterprises in Bangkok: among them, Sarco-Siam, which recruited Thai workers for manual labour in Saudi Arabia, and – in partnership with Lord Moynihan – the Panache massage parlour in the basement of Bangkok's Hyatt Hotel.

According to CEDRIC and NADDIS, he was a drug trafficker, pure and simple. He was listed as a major supplier of marijuana from Thailand to the dope dealers of both Britain and Australia, a profitable trade in which it was suspected that he enjoyed the protection of corrupt but highly placed generals in Thailand's military forces. The computers also listed him as a 'known associate of Dennis Howard Marks'.

Sure enough, Howard was at Heathrow to meet him. As ID officers watched and surreptitiously took photographs, Marks and Sparrowhawk – and Sparrowhawk's almost constant sidekick, Kevin Goulbourne – pushed a baggage cart loaded with suitcases to one of the airport's parking garages. They loaded the cases into Howard's red Mercedes station wagon (all he had to show for his collaboration in *High Time*), and drove off to his London home in Fulham – followed, discreetly, every mile of the way.

It is the natural tendency of drug agents to believe that when two or more dope dealers gather together they're either planning to bring in a load, or celebrating one that has already arrived. No experienced (and, therefore, by definition, cynical) narcotics agent would believe that Sparrowhawk would fly 6,000 miles for just the pleasure of even Howard's company. Nevertheless, it was not obvious what Sparrowhawk and Marks were conspiring to do.

Marks was known, first and foremost, as a smuggler of hashish, not marijuana – and if the information coming from Karachi was correct, he was already up to his neck in a major hash deal.

Sparrowhawk did not supply hashish, because Thailand did not produce it.

The *Cannabis sativa* plant that grows in such abundance in Thailand (and in the Philippines, Laos, Vietnam, Cambodia, Burma, Indonesia, India, Kenya, Malawi, Zaire, South Africa, Mexico, Colombia, Jamaica and the United States) is very different from *Cannabis indica*. *Sativa* is a gracious, lofty plant – unlike its scrubby, resinous cousin, *indica* – and most of its THC content is contained in the leaves. The markets for the two products are quite distinct: as a rule, hash smokers in the West mix their dope with tobacco; marijuana smokers take theirs neat.

So what were the two of them up to?

The next day the ID surveillance teams of Her Majesty's Customs followed Marks and Sparrowhawk to Denham Street in London's Soho district, which contains some of the city's seediest nightclubs, some of its finest restaurants, and the heart of Chinatown.

Among the 'suspicious characters' they were seen meeting were two men who turned out to be the Chinese ambassador to Britain and Peter Brooke, the local member of parliament – who also happened to be the government minister responsible for Her Majesty's Customs. The occasion was nothing more than the grand opening of the new offices of a travel agency, the Hong Kong International Travel Centre. Howard, looking for all the world like a respectable businessman, behaved as if he owned the place.

Seward, Alaska, September 1985

The *Axel D* had undergone something of a transformation. As local fishermen watched with idle interest, most of the commercial fishing gear was stripped from the decks, and the centre hold, meant for herring and salmon, was converted into an extra fuel tank. This addition meant that the boat could now remain at sea for two months, and maintain top speed, without refuelling.

The refrigeration compressors, which the former owner had spent several thousand dollars overhauling, were unceremoniously dumped overboard.

A new crew went on board – not local men, but Californians

who appeared to know little or nothing about fishing. On the last day of the month, the *Axel D* set sail from Seward, heading west.

Amsterdam, the Netherlands, October 1985

Jim Hobbs, his mission as Howard's eyes and ears in Karachi completed, had finally escaped the oppressive heat and unfamiliar food of Pakistan and settled by choice in Amsterdam. It was more tolerant than most cities towards homosexuals. It also had an extremely efficient telephone service.

Unaware that he had provoked the interest of the DEA and Her Majesty's Customs in Karachi, Hobbs took a small apartment on Jan Steen Straat, where he arranged for the installation of two telephone lines. He used one line for incoming calls, the other for outgoing ones.

Tipped off about Hobbs by the Dutch Drug Liaison Officer in Karachi, the Amsterdam narcotics squad tapped both of them.

It soon became apparent to the listeners that Hobbs was making and receiving a great many international phone calls. However, all the calls were in English – usually British, idiomatic English – which they had difficulty in understanding, even after they had been translated into Dutch by an interpreter.

The Dutch called on the British for help and Peter Nelson, an ambitious intelligence officer with Her Majesty's Customs, travelled to Amsterdam to listen to the tapes of Hobbs's conversations.

He had no difficulty in understanding them. Whoever Hobbs was talking to – in the United States, Pakistan, Spain, England and elsewhere – they were in the midst of a conspiracy to smuggle a large quantity of drugs.

Nelson also realized that Hobbs was at the centre of the web. He was operating as a 'cut-out', receiving messages from one part of the world and passing them on to another. Sometimes he would act as a switching centre, linking the two telephone lines together with some kind of device that allowed a caller in, say, the United States to talk directly to someone in Spain.

A lot of the calls that Hobbs made were to Spain, to telephone numbers 71-453350 and 71-450312. Via Interpol, the Dutch police asked their colleagues in Spain to identify the subscriber. The

Spanish responded that 71 was the area code for Palma, Majorca. The numbers were listed to a Judith Margaret Marks.

Meanwhile, in late October, the telephone tap on Jim Hobbs's phones revealed that someone called 'Gerry' from California was on his way to London.

London, 23 October 1985

The photographs they took of Gerry Wills when he stepped off the plane at Heathrow showed a tall, Nordic-looking man with a slight paunch, wearing a blazer, light-coloured trousers and a checked shirt. There was no 'meeter or greeter' waiting for Wills in the arrivals terminal, and he didn't seem to be expecting one. He cashed a travellers cheque at the airport bank, made a call from a payphone, and took a cab into town. The watchers followed the cab to 60 Cathcart Road, in south-west London – Howard's home.

Surveillance is the grunt work of the war on drugs. It is tedious, time-consuming and usually – apparently – unrewarding. It is also critical. So, tucked away in a south London back street, the Investigation Division of Her Majesty's Customs keeps a fleet of nondescript and often dilapidated vehicles from which its agents can keep watch. The vehicles are equipped with peep holes and portable chemical toilets which provide up to forty flushes.

At 10.00 p.m., four hours after Wills had arrived at Howard's apartment, the surveillance team saw him walking down Cathcart Road with two unidentified men to a Thai restaurant called Busabong. At about midnight he was seen heading for the West End, now in the company of a woman who ID thought might be a prostitute. (They were probably right. Wills was addicted to prostitutes, and told Marks that he spent an average of $150,000 a year on their services.) The surveillance was called off for the night, having produced what surveillance most often produces – precisely nothing.

But what makes it worthwhile, what keeps the watchers going, is the knowledge, based on experience, that sooner or later one Tango will lead them to another.

Wills led them to two. The first was a short, stocky American with reddish-brown hair and a full beard, later identified by the DEA as Ronald Allen, Wills's partner. The second was a tall, lanky man with long, ill-disciplined hair who bore a passing resemblance to Mick Jagger. He arrived at 60 Cathcart Road at 4.00 p.m. on the second day of surveillance, in an old London taxicab that was no longer licensed for public hire. He took Wills and Allen to a coin dealer in the West End and then to the Hollywood Arms, Howard's favourite London pub, where Howard was waiting for them.

The surveillance lasted for seven days, producing tiny threads of evidence that might later be woven into a tapestry of proof to convict Howard Marks: a description of a breakfast meeting of Marks, Wills and Allen, held at the Kensington Hilton Hotel; the contents of the waste paper bins of Wills and Allen, rescued by Customs from their hotel rooms after they'd checked out; the fact that their airline tickets were supplied by Hong Kong International Travel, the agency Howard appeared to own.

On 30 October, Wills and Allen were taken to Heathrow airport for a flight to Zürich by the Mick Jagger look-alike in his unlicensed taxi.

Marks travelled to the airport separately. He took a flight to Paris, but only to change planes. Like Wills and Allen, he was on his way to Karachi.

Karachi, 31 October 1985

'Meeters and greeters' are not permitted inside the arrivals terminal at Karachi international airport for security reasons, so George and Assumpta Lane waited outside in the hot night air. Harlan Bowe, with the benefit of his DEA credentials, waited inside. Four other agents – two American, one British and one Dutch – kept watch on the parking lot where the Lanes had left their yellow Toyota.

Howard arrived from Paris just after midnight, looking surprisingly formal in a grey business suit. As usual he had no luggage save for one small carry-on case. He'd long ago given up checking baggage on international flights because it always seemed to get lost or delayed – a consequence, he assumed, of his own notoriety. (Marks has a fantasy that somewhere, in some gigantic room, there are stacked piles of missing suitcases belonging to him and other dope dealers that have been filched from airports by drug agents over the years, in the hopes of finding something incriminating. 'What do they do with all that stuff?' said Marks.)

Shadowed by Bowe, he met the Lanes outside the terminal and headed for the parking lot.

'That's the bogies over there,' said George Lane, who recognized one of the men sitting in a nearby parked car as a Dutch agent and the husband of one of the pupils at the International Language Centre. 'I wonder if they're waiting for you?'

'Probably,' said Howard. 'The fuckers.'

He had been drinking on the plane and the combination of alcohol and jetlag made him reckless. He walked over to the agents' car, where Bowe was now standing, and crouched down by the driver's window.

'Hello, waiting for me?' he said.

'What makes you think we'd do that?' said Bowe.

At that point Marks lost his nerve, mumbled some excuse and returned to the Lanes' Toyota. George Lane thought the episode highly amusing. Assumpta did not, and she did not disguise her feelings. For better or worse, the Lanes' limited social life in Karachi, as well as their business, depended on the acceptance of the expatriate community. She did not entirely approve of her brother-in-law, and certainly not his behaviour.

But Howard is difficult to deter. Three nights later, Bowe and two other agents were eating in a Chinese restaurant that is, to say the least, intimate; it only has four tables. In the middle of their meal, Marks arrived with his own party. Coincidence? Maybe, thought Bowe.

Then Marks turned up at the American Club while Bowe was there. He was pushing it too far. Bowe sent over a waiter to ask him to leave. Marks refused. 'Ask Mr Bowe if I can buy him a drink,' said Howard.

As Assumpta feared, Howard's cheek had unfortunate consequences for the Lanes. Shortly after these episodes, most of their European clientele stopped attending the International Language Centre and its fortunes dramatically declined. The Lanes also found themselves socially ostracized.

For Marks, however, the consequences were not necessarily detrimental. Within days, the story went around the world that Howard Marks was a counter-surveillance expert. As other surveillance teams awaited his arrival at airports throughout Asia, they received urgent messages from the DEA advising 'extreme caution'. For years after, the reputation followed Howard wherever he went and, to a degree, it protected him. More than once the watchers stayed so far behind, they lost him.

The purpose of the Karachi summit, as it came to be called, was to allow Gerry Wills to satisfy himself about the quality of the merchandise for which he had put up most of the money. Howard's glowing reports from Bakar notwithstanding, Wills wanted reassurance before sending the *Axel D* into what he considered to be Pakistan's dangerous waters.

Somehow he managed to slip into Karachi unnoticed by the surveillance teams. But they were at the airport at five o'clock in the morning, along with Howard, when Wills's partner, Ronald Allen, arrived on a flight from Zürich. Allen was carrying a heavy aluminium suitcase and, given that he had come from London via Zürich, it was tempting to speculate that he'd brought the money to pay for the hash.

He had not. Though the agents in Karachi had no way of knowing it, another associate of Gerry Wills had already walked into the Hong Kong branch of the Crédit Suisse Bank with a similar suitcase and deposited $400,000 in cash into Howard Marks's account – the first of a number of payments that by the end of the year would amount to just under $1,300,000.

The agents didn't know, either, that Allen was in Karachi to inspect the load for Wills, 'quality control' being one of his areas of expertise. Through their surveillance they did identify Saleem Malik as the probable supplier of the hash, but they did not observe the occasion when Malik took Allen to see it.

After a week of considerable effort, the combined resources of the drug agencies of the US, Britain and Holland had produced practically nothing. Most of what had been learned came from Amsterdam, where Peter Nelson of Her Majesty's Customs was again listening to Jim Hobbs's phones. Even that information was infuriatingly imprecise.

The sum of $1,000 had been wired to Panama, presumably to register a boat. The boat itself had engine problems, and Marks had told Hobbs to get money wired from California to his Hong Kong account to pay for the repairs. The boat was, apparently, in Singapore. What it was called, when it would sail for Pakistan, and where it would go after that, were all imponderables.

On 6 November, Nelson overheard Marks tell Hobbs that he, Wills and Allen would be leaving Karachi the following morning for Bangkok.

George Lane drove them to the airport. As the surveillance team watched, Wills and Allen got out of the Toyota outside the domestic terminal. Ten minutes later, Lane returned and dropped Marks at the international terminal.

Of course, all three men eventually boarded the Bangkok flight, studiously ignoring each other. Whether the charade was prompted by the caution of counter-surveillance experts, or Howard's sheer devilment, was yet another thing the agents didn't know.

At Bangkok's Don Muang airport, a surveillance team comprising DEA agents and officers of the Thai Narcotics Control Board watched as Howard and his two companions arrived on the Karachi flight. They watched them pass through immigration control and customs, and walk into the arrivals terminal.

Then they lost them.

Manila, 24 November 1985

By the time he was twenty, Tony Moynihan had come to occupy a particular niche in Britain's popular newspapers. He was known as 'Rock 'n' Roll Tony', the wildest of the Mayfair set, and for a while he wrote a column in the *Sunday People* to perpetuate his own notoriety. 'British aristocrats of my generation have been accused of every possible irresponsibility and wildness,' his first effort began. 'I wish to state at the outset, categorically and without fear of contradiction: every word of this is perfectly true.'

Banished by his parents to Australia, after one particularly wild party had ended in police intervention, Moynihan absconded from the sheep farm owned by relatives of his mother for the nightclubs of Sydney, telling the readers of the *People*, 'I'm going to trim the Aussies – not their sheep.'

Back in Britain a year later, he became associated with the Condor night club in Soho, owned by Peter Rachman. To Moynihan, Rachman was 'nearer to a father to me than anybody I've ever had'. To most of the rest of Britain he was a seedy slum landlord whose name became synonymous with the brutal violation of tenants' rights. Moynihan also began a prickly relationship with the British police: prosecuted, though acquitted, for stealing a bed sheet; falsely accused, in a case of mistaken identity, of stealing a painting; eventually forced to leave the country, 'on my solicitor's advice', as the police were about to charge him with frauds that included buying a Rolls-Royce with a worthless cheque.

He moved to Spain, where the British government sought his extradition, and then on to the Philippines where, in due course, he was accused by an Australian Royal Commission of being a 'shadowy figure' involved with a gang of heroin traffickers known as 'the Double Bay mob'. Other, subsequent, accusations against

Moynihan included selling thousands of young Filipino girls into prostitution, and even murder.

In short, the 3rd Baron Moynihan has not led a sheltered life. Even so, it was not every day that he sat in his own dining-room discussing a proposition to turn part of the Philippines into a giant marijuana plantation.

Whose idea it was is a matter of dispute. What is not disputed is that the idea surfaced at the end of a long, liquid dinner as Howard Marks and Gerry Wills (and, according to Howard, Lord Moynihan) relaxed over joints of marijuana. The conversation turned to the inferior quality of locally grown marijuana, which Moynihan said he thought came mostly from Luzon, the most northerly of the 7,237 islands (at the last count) which make up the Philippines.

Might it be possible, somebody speculated, to introduce a superior strain of *Cannabis sativa* to the islands? Howard thought it was possible. He also thought that, given Moynihan's excellent connections to the government of Ferdinand Marcos, and the protection those connections might afford, they could grow marijuana on a vast, industrial scale.

'Well, that's going to cost quite a lot of money,' said Moynihan. 'Are you looking to lease or purchase the land?'

'Either,' said Howard. 'Money's no problem, Tony. Ten, twenty, thirty, forty, fifty million dollars – there are millions of dollars available.'

'Do you have that kind of money, Howard?'

'Don't worry about the funds, Tony, just worry about the land.'

Moynihan believed that every man had his price; his own was a great deal less than $50 million. 'Of course I will, Howard,' he said, 'no problem at all. I'll find you somewhere.'

Marks said he would pay Moynihan's expenses. They agreed that if they talked about the matter on the phone, they would both refer to it as the 'back-up project'.

There was a gathering of the clans in Manila. Phillip Sparrowhawk, still using his Irish alias and fake passport, turned his up with sidekick, Kevin Goulbourne. So did Bradley Weller, an associate of Wills who'd been ferrying money to Howard's Crédit Suisse account in Hong Kong. So did Jim Hobbs, who had abandoned the message centre in Amsterdam because it was no longer needed.

Trying to keep track of them all in Manila, Art Scalzo of the DEA had not slept for three days. At Scalzo's request, NARCOM, the Philippine Armed Forces Narcotic Command, was monitoring the phones of the Mandarin Hotel, where all of them were staying, and the hotel switchboard was monitoring their room-to-room calls. Even so, Scalzo had insisted on running a one-man surveillance operation at the hotel in the hopes of learning whom they were in Manila to meet. He felt lousy. In addition to fatigue, he was suffering from a heavy cold.

He had a room on the same floor as Marks. Content that his main quarry was, for the moment, at rest, Scalzo decided to go down to the lobby. As he entered the elevator so, too, did Marks.

Howard immediately struck up a conversation. He was friendly, perhaps suspiciously so. He was sympathetic to Scalzo about his cold and invited him to the hotel bar for a recuperative drink.

Was this Howard tweaking the tail of the elephant, letting the DEA know that, once again, he'd spotted the surveillance? Scalzo didn't know. He said, lamely, he'd have to take a rain check. What a shame, said Howard.

For three weeks Marks shuttled back and forth between Manila and Hong Kong, constantly watched – to no avail.

The Hong Kong police never established that the purpose of Howard's visits was to pay Saleem Malik in instalments – once in person, the rest by wire transfer – $1,030,000.

Similarly, while the Singapore police located and identified the crew of the *Axel D*, they never located or identified the boat itself. In December, once Malik had been paid, it sailed for Pakistan, where it collected its cargo unhindered.

After six weeks on the road, Howard was ready to go home, his job done. Pausing in Hong Kong to make one more money transfer – this, a modest $5,000 into his wife's housekeeping account in Palma – he flew back to London to spend Christmas with his family. He could well afford his celebratory mood.

Palma, Majorca, winter 1985

In Spain, members of the judiciary are referred to by number, not name. On 19 December, magistrate number three (*Magistrado del Juzgado de Instrucción número tres de Palma*) issued a warrant allowing police to tap two telephones located at Calle Fuego 3, La Vileta, Palma.

The request for the authorization came from Chief Inspector José Villar del Saz, known to his men as Pepe, the enterprising boss

59

of Madrid's undercover drugs squad. He said in his application that he was acting on a tip from an informant; Howard Marks, he believed, was in the process of importing 10 tons of hashish into Spain.

The products of telephone taps are not admissible as evidence in Spanish courts. They can only be used by the police as 'intelligence'. Nonetheless, phones in Spain are frequently tapped, and Palma police headquarters has a dedicated 'listening room' on the third floor; an odd-shaped triangular cell with unadorned concrete walls and bleak strip lighting, entered only with a key and the specific permission of the chief of detectives. Along one wall stands a bank of reel-to-reel tape recorders, whirring quietly away.

Beginning on 5 January 1986, when Howard and his family returned to Palma from their Christmas vacation in London, two of the recorders captured every call they made and received, clicking on automatically whenever they picked up the phone.

When each tape was full, it was handed to a police interpreter who translated the conversations from English into Spanish. The resulting transcripts were sent to Chief Inspector Villar in Madrid. Other than showing that Marks was talking to a lot of people, they were useless; they made no sense to him at all.

At the end of January, the Spanish police approached the DEA country attaché at the American Embassy in Madrid to ask for help. Specifically, Pepe Villar wanted Craig Lovato to fly with him to Palma to listen to the tapes.

Villar and Lovato were by now good friends. Earlier in his police career Pepe had been stationed in Palma for nine years, and he wanted to show Craig the island. He talked about the beaches, the restaurants and the friendly people. It sounded good: Madrid was cold in January. Palma, so the tourist brochures said, was where the sun took its winter vacation.

Lovato had never heard of Howard Marks. He knew nothing of Howard's frequent trips to Asia the previous year, or of his colleagues' fruitless and frustrating attempts at surveillance. He thought the Howard Marks assignment might last a couple of days.

THREE

The Lovato family emigrated to America from Spain about 250 years ago. Still, because of his appearance, some people look at Craig Lovato and assume he swam the Rio Grande yesterday, which gets to be offensive after a while. His father was so infuriated by similar discrimination that he refused to speak Spanish. Craig grew up in a Colorado town called Salida. He had no idea that *salida* meant 'way out' until he went to Bolivia for the DEA and saw the emergency exit signs on airplanes.

The Lovatos were given 97,000 acres of what became New Mexico in a land grant from the Spanish throne. By the beginning of the nineteenth century they'd lost most of it in lieu of back taxes. There was no money in Craig's family. While Howard Marks was dazzling his female contemporaries at Balliol, Craig was holding down three jobs in order to support the wife he'd married in high school and their two sons; a third son was born by the time he was twenty-two. ('No, contrary to popular opinion, she wasn't pregnant when I married her,' he said. 'We just told everybody she was so there would be no argument to us getting married.') They'd married in Salt Lake City, Utah, but there was no work there for non-Mormons who looked like they'd just arrived from Mexico. He'd hitched a ride to Las Vegas, Nevada, and got one job painting signs for a construction company, a second job managing apartments for a property company, and a third as a busboy at the Sahara Hotel, working the graveyard shift. In February 1968

61

he joined the Las Vegas sheriff's department as a deputy, primarily because it was the only way he knew to get a college education. (Thanks to an American government programme that allowed law enforcement officers to study part-time, he got a baccalaureate degree in criminal justice from the University of Nevada, and, later, a Masters in political science.)

He knew nothing about drugs. The Haight-Ashbury revolution, the seductive epistles of Dr Timothy Leary, the 'Make Love Not War' culture that swept most of America, had all passed him by. He didn't know how to recognize marijuana until one night, as a rookie patrolman in Las Vegas, he stopped a group of kids in a car and was hit by its pungent aroma. Until then, drugs to him were tobacco and alcohol, neither of which he used.

Yet after eighteen months as a patrolman, after he'd passed the detectives' exam, he found himself in narcotics, working under-cover, making hand-to-hand buys. The job took over his whole life. Day after day, he'd hit the streets of Las Vegas, unarmed and without a badge, attempting to infiltrate the drug milieu and persuade dealers to sell to him so they could be busted. The pressure was simply too much. He saw too many older and more experienced colleagues become drug addicts, or alcoholics, or crooks. After eleven months on the streets he requested and won a transfer to Homicide, which, he thought, was not bad for a twenty-three-year-old kid.

Again, he couldn't take it. At least in Narcotics he'd known that if he missed a suspect one day he'd get him the next, and not much harm would be done in the interim. In Homicide a mistake could cost somebody their life.

And he couldn't stand dead bodies. His first customer was a young woman who'd hanged herself, extending her neck by fourteen inches. He attended the death of a man who had blown his head off with a shotgun, leaving pieces of his brain on the ceiling. Another man died behind the Stardust Hotel in summertime and by the time they found him his body had putrefied and burst. The bodily fluids had drained into the pavement, attracting an army of maggots. The procedure in such cases was to take a knife, slice skin from a finger, and place it over one of your own in order to obtain a fingerprint. 'This is not my cup of tea,' said Craig, applying for a transfer out of Homicide after just three months.

What was his cup of tea was the Metro Squad, to which he was then assigned. Some people called it the 'goon squad'.

The idea was to target high-crime areas and what the police

termed 'major suspects', meaning persistent offenders who were generally too smart to get caught and who were listed in a black book. The job of the Metro Squad was to let these people know that their presence in the community was no longer desired – and if that meant bending the rules, so be it. Usually, after a second encounter with the Metro Squad, the suspects left the country. The crime statistics went way down. Most American sheriffs got themselves a goon squad just before election time – until the FBI began investigating a host of civil rights violations, and the US Supreme Court ruled that black books and goon squads were unconstitutional.

So, a year after quitting Homicide, Craig was back in a suit and a tie, this time working for the Burglary Squad. It was where he learned to be an investigator. It was also where he came to believe that, given the will, there is not a crime committed that can't be solved; not a crook alive who can't be caught.

I'll give you an illustration, what I call 'The Great Oleander Caper'. There were fourteen detectives in the Burglary Squad and we each had an area; mine was area 6, the south part of the Strip. We'd come in every morning and there'd be this stack of burglary reports, and we'd read them and throw them into one of three boxes. One was for crimes where we had a suspect: a physical description, or a licence plate on a car, or somebody left their fingerprints – there was something you would work with. The next box was for cases with no physical evidence but a modus operandi *that we knew. There were certain people in town we'd recognize because of the time of day, the type of forced entry, or the type of property taken. You'd say, 'Well, that's old Charlie', and you'd go and find him and put him back in jail. The third box was for cases where there was no evidence, no prints, no suspects, nothing. They'd just been reported to the police for insurance purposes. Every now and again, I'd reach over and pull out one of the reports from the third box and say, 'Well, let's see if we can solve this one.'*

One day I pull out this report which says that at such and such a time on such and such a date, fifty-nine oleander bushes were stolen from this cemetery. End of story. I look at this and I say, 'Who would steal oleander bushes from a cemetery?' Obviously someone who needed some bushes in their yard, right? Well, even oleander bushes deserve some protection from the law, so I decided to go out and find them.

Like most cemeteries in Las Vegas, this one was newly-made, way out in the southern end of the Valley. There was only one road leading out to it, and then there was a subdivision of several hundred houses beyond it. They were newly-constructed houses, and people were putting in new lawns and bushes.

Out of the fifty-nine oleander bushes that had been stolen, fifty-eight of them were red and one of them was white. Piece of cake. So I drive out there, and drive through the subdivision, and here's this guy whose entire house is surrounded by oleander bushes. He has old, mature plants, and in between each of the mature plants he has these brand new plants, and there's exactly fifty-nine of them. Fifty-eight are red and one of them is white. So I thought, 'This is going to be fun.' I got a search warrant for his house, and went and got soil samples from the cemetery, and went and took soil comparisons from his house, and submitted them to our laboratory. The nitrates were identical. I got an arrest warrant for the fellow and went out and picked him up. Case solved.

That's sort of silly, but it does show you. You can investigate any type of crime that's committed and solve it, if you dedicate the time and resources to it.

Basically, Howard Marks was out there, maundering around as long as he was because there hadn't been a collective effort to go after him. It was just a matter of somebody focusing their attention, and giving him a serious go.

Palma, 28 January 1986

Craig Lovato sat transfixed in the listening room at police head-quarters. Pepe Villar could barely drag him out of the place to eat or sleep; forget the beaches. Finally, after thirteen hours of listening to the reels of tape, he was persuaded to take a drink at Victoria's bar, a favourite police haunt. 'Pepe,' he said, raising his glass, 'it's a gold mine.' Four hours later he was back in the listening room.

As Lovato quickly discovered, Spanish phone taps leave a lot to be desired from an American standpoint. Before he arrived, the Palma police had recorded sixteen hours' worth of Howard's telephone conversations, on four reels of tape. They lacked any device to identify each recording with the date and time it was made. They also lacked any device to tell them where the calls had been made from or to. Since they had used two recorders to monitor Howard's two lines, there was no way to tell the sequence of the calls, except by deduction; for example, was call 3 on line 1 made before or after call 4 on line 2? And, because the recorders had not been constantly monitored, the tapes invariably ran out in mid-conversation.

Yet what the Spaniards lacked in high-tech sophistication, they sometimes made up for in human ingenuity. 'Very easy,' they said when Lovato asked how he could possibly tell which numbers Marks was calling.

They showed him how to do it. Every outgoing call began with the sound of the dial tone, followed by the high-speed clicks of each digit of the number being called. By re-recording those clicks at a slower speed, and repeating that exercise several times, they could eventually decipher each digit.

'OK, Craig, here's your number,' they said. Easy when you know how. After a bit of practice, Lovato found he could decipher the numbers almost as quickly as they could. With the aid of an international dialling code directory, he began to plot the far-flung whereabouts of Howard Marks's associates.

He had no idea whom the voices belonged to and words like 'drugs', 'marijuana' or hashish' were never mentioned. But every professional instinct told him he was listening to the details of a major dope deal going down. As he replayed the tapes over and over, and began to appreciate the global scope of the enterprise, he felt the hairs on the back of his neck stand up.

Some conversations were straightforward enough, although the British regional accents and vernacular were a problem. Lovato didn't know that 'Bugs Bunny' meant 'money' in Cockney rhyming slang, or that 'dog' meant 'phone', as in 'dog and bone'. But he had no doubt that Howard and his friends were talking in excruciatingly guarded terms.

These people, whoever they were, would say things like: 'And the guy who went down there has now returned here, and the one I was in communication with, he was quite happy when I told him.' (To which Marks replied: 'That's excellent news.') Different places around the world were referred to as 'Mac's place' or 'Jack's place' or, even more circuitously: 'It's very south, around the bend, half-way up the squiggly bit.' Craig heard the slight hesitations, as the callers thought out how to phrase certain points. He heard the change of intonation – a sudden underlying tension – when Marks asked someone, 'How's it going?' – and could tell that the importance of the answer belied the casual nature of the question.

Gradually, as he began to make some sense of the calls and familiarize himself with the voices, a cast of characters emerged.

Howard Marks, with his soft lilting Welsh voice, was easy to identify. 'Jim', in Lisbon, talked a lot about telephones and appeared to be having problems with his wife whose name, Selina, he couldn't always remember. Jim was in Lisbon with somebody named 'Mick', who called Howard 'the Boss'. 'Christine' and 'Old

John' appeared to work for Howard in London. 'Stephen', in Hong Kong, seemed to be a banker, trying to trace a missing $5,000 which hadn't arrived in Judy Marks's Palma account. 'Ron', in Manila, appeared to have something to do with a boat which had encountered problems but was now 'ship-shape'. 'Malik', in Karachi, also known as 'Mac', was always hassling for money, and sometimes Judy Marks would lie to him, saying Howard wasn't at home. 'Balendo', in London, seemed to be in the travel business but also passed on messages, most of them from 'Malik'. Then there was 'Mr Sims' in California, who might or might not also be 'Pete', celebrating his fortieth birthday and apparently on probation, awaiting trial. Also in California was 'Gerry', who seemed to be worried about the quality of something. And there was 'Phil' in Bangkok, and 'Mick' in London who, to judge by his Cockney cadences, was not the same fellow as 'Mick' in Lisbon.

Finally, there was 'Tony' in Manila, who spoke with an unmistakably plummy British accent. He especially intrigued Lovato because, though circumspect, he came the nearest to giving the game away.

'I've got somebody else here that I particularly want you to meet, on the project that you mentioned to me – with the laid-back fellow,' said Tony.

'Right, yeah, which we call the back-up project,' said Howard.

'I mean, it's already being done, you see.'

'Yes, yes, it doesn't surprise me. But is it done to any sort of significance?'

'Well, you see, that's why I need you. Because I'm offered the product.'

'Right, I see. Right.'

'And it looks great to me but I think the quality control is something you would have to know more about than me.'

'Yes, indeed, yes. That'd be essential.'

'I mean, I have some samples – some samples of some considerable size.'

'Oh, do you?' said Howard, his full attention now clearly captured.

'They're waiting for you.'

'All right. In that case I'll be accelerating.'

Piecing together the sixteen hours of conversations, Lovato built up a mental picture of Marks. Here was a guy sitting on an island in the Mediterranean, who had people working for him or with him in London, Lisbon, Karachi, Hong Kong, Manila, Bangkok and Los Angeles. He did at least some of his banking in Hong Kong. He owed money in Karachi which he could not yet pay. He was planning some kind of deal in Thailand; meanwhile there were samples waiting for him in Manila. There was a boat en route to somewhere, and there were people in California who were waiting for something to happen.

Listening to the tones of the voices, Lovato deduced that 'Jim', 'Mick', 'Ron', 'Balendo' and even the plummy 'Tony' deferred to Howard as the boss, whereas he seemed to be on equal terms with 'Phil', 'Gerry' and 'Pete'. Lovato began to see a world-wide organization – unmistakably illegal, given the guarded way they talked business – with Howard Marks as its centre. 'I don't know who this guy is,' he told Pepe, 'but it's heavy-duty stuff. Very heavy duty.'

The two of them agreed to forgo the pleasures of Palma and return to Madrid in the hopes of initiating a major international investigation into what they were already calling 'the Howard Marks organization'.

Before they left the island, however, there was one indulgence they could not resist. While listening to the tapes, Lovato had also listened to Howard's ongoing phone calls; any time the tape recorders had clicked on, he'd donned the earphones to overhear what Howard was saying. As a result, he knew that Marks planned to go to Palma airport to meet the London flight. 'Let's go and take a look at him,' said Craig.

In the early evening of 30 January 1986, Howard Marks went to Palma airport to meet Chi Chuen Lo, also known as Balendo, the manager of the Hong Kong International Travel Centre in London, of which Howard was a director. He took with him his two daughters, Amber and Francesca, and since they arrived early, they waited off the main concourse in a darkened cafeteria that had closed for the night. He was not aware of a couple of Spaniards greeting each other noisily, one taking photographs of the other in front of a 'Welcome to Majorca' sign. Craig Lovato, aiming the lens straight past Pepe Villar's out-of-focus right ear, captured his first impression of Howard Marks's face.

Back in Madrid, Lovato sent out requests to DEA offices in various parts of the world, and to DEA headquarters in Washington, asking for all and any information on Marks. The results were rapid and spectacular. Bells rang all over the place. In Lovato's words, the computers 'came up triplets'.

London, 6 February 1986

Nowhere did the bells ring louder than at Harmsworth House in Bouverie Street, London, once the command post of a newspaper empire, today the headquarters of Her Majesty's Customs.

Lovato went there directly from Heathrow airport, expecting to stay for a couple of hours. This was his first trip to London. He meant it to be brief. There was a lot to do in Madrid and he was scheduled to return there on an afternoon flight.

When he was met by Peter Nelson in the lobby of Harmsworth House, he was, therefore, in a 'Let's get down to business' mood. He'd brought along copies of the Palma tapes in the hope that Nelson, or one of his colleagues, could decipher the vernacular contained in the conversations, and identify at least some of Howard's British callers, if only by tracing their telephone numbers.

He did not know that Nelson had maintained his own vigil in Amsterdam, listening to the phone calls of Jim Hobbs. And he had no idea as to the sheer depth of knowledge that Her Majesty's Customs held on Dennis Howard Marks, his friends and associates, his past and his present.

Nelson did not immediately enlighten him. Instead he led Lovato to a large room on the second floor of Harmsworth House, from which it was just possible to catch a glimpse of the River Thames, and where other Customs experts on Marks awaited him. The room was not designed for comfort. The furniture was Civil Service functional: cheap imitation-leather easy chairs and a Formica-topped table on which sat the equipment and detritus of making coffee (instant coffee, of course, this being Britain), the only refreshment available.

After half an hour of listening to Nelson and his colleagues, Lovato wouldn't have cared if there had been bats on the wall. For the second time in not much more than a week he sat transfixed.

At nine o'clock that night Lovato was still there, any thought of returning to Madrid long gone. Nelson proposed they break for the night and resume the next morning. He offered to buy Craig dinner, but at that time of night, and in that part of London, the only establishment they could find open was a Wimpy Bar. Craig took his first bite of a British hamburger. If the rest of the day hadn't gone so well, British–American co-operation on the Howard Marks case might have ended right there.

As Lovato now knew, Howard Marks has first come to the attention of Her Majesty's Customs on 19 September 1970 at Heathrow airport, on his return from the briefest of trips to Germany. There were signs to warn travellers who had been out of Britain for less than twenty-four hours that they were not entitled to the duty-free concession, but Howard attempted to smuggle through a bottle of perfume anyway. A Customs officer found it in his briefcase, along with a toothbrush and a book, *The Philosophy of Time*.

'How long have you been out of the country?'

'Two days,' said Howard, displaying his own philosophy of time.

The Customs officer asked to see his ticket, which showed that he'd left London only the night before.

'You said two days.'

'Well, yesterday and today.' said Howard – but it clearly wouldn't do.

He was taken to a cubicle and searched. Hidden in one of his socks they found three £10 notes, which, under draconian regulations then in force to support the flagging British pound, was more than citizens were allowed to take out of the country. More important, in Howard's wallet they found a receipt which showed that he'd been to Germany to pay the court fine of a man named Graham Plinston.

Plinston was a contemporary of Howard's at Oxford and, by 1970, a significant British dope dealer. Howard, who was supposedly still wrestling with the paradox of confirmation at Sussex university, did not yet rank high in the Plinston organization. He was an occasional odd-job man whom Plinston would reward by saying. 'Hey, give Howard a weight [1lb] so he can make some money,' and Howard would make a few pounds selling the dope on the streets of Brighton. Nevertheless, by going to Germany to pay Plinston's fine (for running dope), and by getting stopped on the way home, he had crossed some imaginary line, both in his own mind and in a newly-opened file of Her Majesty's Customs, which identified Howard Marks as a 'known associate' of Graham Plinston.

Howard was not cut out to be anybody's underling. By the autumn of 1971 he had made himself indispensable to Plinston, and his equal in the dope business, when they travelled to Ireland, to the village of Ballinskelligs, County Kerry, to meet James

69

McCann: confidence trickster, thief, burglar and, by his own account, patriot, fighting for the Cause. Though the Provisional IRA constantly and vehemently disowned him, McCann would boast of his 'Provo connections', always adept at playing what he called 'the green card'. He assured Marks and Plinston that it would be 'no problem' to arrange for them to import hash into Ireland's Shannon international airport and, on this occasion at least, he was as good as his word. Posing as a reporter from *Fortune* magazine, McCann was allowed to inspect the inner workings of the airport. And, posing as a member of the IRA, he easily persuaded an Irish Customs official at Shannon to turn a blind eye to certain shipments arriving from Pakistan which, the Customs man was led to understand, contained guns for 'the boys in the North'.

It worked. The problem was that McCann lied as often as he drew breath, and Plinston couldn't deal with him. Howard, on the other hand, enjoyed McCann enormously. 'It doesn't matter if someone *always* lies,' he said. 'You know they're lying so you just make allowances for it.'

By the spring of 1972, the Marks–Plinston–McCann partnership had imported three loads of hashish into Shannon, and smuggled them into England. The first shipment weighed 200lb. The third shipment weighed a ton.

Howard was, as a result, a relatively wealthy man. Through his affair with Rosie Brindley, he'd fathered his first child, a daughter they named Myfanwy. He'd bought his first home and financed his first legitimate business – a clothes boutique in Oxford called Annabelinda. Despite those trappings of a normal life, it never occurred to him to go straight. Perhaps the thing he feared most was boredom.

Marks and Graham Plinston turned their attention to the United States market for hashish, which was obviously much larger than the British market and, in one sense, much more pragmatic. In Britain, none of their friends perceived Marks and Plinston as criminals. Criminals were bank robbers and people who used violence. Howard and Graham were, on the contrary, close to being folk heroes; people who risked their necks to keep others supplied in pot. The downside of this credulous assumption for Marks and Plinston was that none of their customers saw what they did as a business. None of their distributors expected to pay up-front for the hash they received. They took it on credit, and paid for it when they'd sold it, and if, in the interim, some of it got seized – well, that was Howard and Graham's bad luck.

In the United States the hash and marijuana business were managed very differently, on what was called a 'belly to belly' basis: 'Here's the dope, where's the money?' The word 'credit' was simply not part of the American doper's lexicon.

Their breakthrough into that lucrative market came about through Ernest 'Peter' Combs in Los Angeles, who toiled ceaselessly to keep the West Coast supplied with hash, and James Morris, a flamboyant Londoner and the road manager for various British pop groups, who first hit upon the ingenious idea of using speaker systems to import it. Introduced by a mutual acquaintance, Plinston and Marks agreed to supply the dope, still flowing into Europe through the ever-open door at Shannon international airport.

By his own account, Marks did not become actively involved in the scheme until the third load successfully reached America. He was certainly involved when the seventh load was detected in Las Vegas, on 14 September 1973, and Peter Combs was required to make his dramatic escape from town: Howard was waiting for Combs, and the dope, in Newport Beach, California, and learned what had happened from the television news. He fled to New York and, the next day, to Montreal. Back in London, he lay low, switching aliases as frequently as he changed hotels.

Two months later, he went to Amsterdam to meet Combs and, by misfortune, was visiting the house of a friend at the moment when Dutch police raided the house on another matter, and Howard was found to be in possession of hashish. By then Her Majesty's Customs knew a great deal about Marks's role in the sound speaker affair, thanks in part to the dogged detective work of the DEA's Harlan Bowe. The day after his arrest, two senior Investigation Division officers flew from London to interview him.

The interrogation was classic Howard Marks. For the first hour he bluffed, claiming to know nothing, attempting to gauge how much the opposition knew. Then, bluntly accused of lying, he sat in silence for a moment, looking at the floor. Then he smiled at them and said: 'All right. I had to try, didn't I?'

Then he said: 'I know your beliefs must be different from mine . . . I'm completely against cocaine and heroin but I regard hash in a different light. I think it should be legalized. However, I know that it's illegal in the States and England and it's even illegal here, although to be busted for a little piece and kept in custody is quite something. I know you've got your job to do and I understand that . . . I'll tell you now whatever you want to know . . . I'll help all I can.'

Then, of course, he did nothing of the sort.

The pattern is always the same. Trapped in a corner, confronted with the hard evidence against him, Howard dances a graceful pirouette, only occasionally brushing up against the truth. He lies by emphasis, minimizing his own role, exaggerating the role of others. And, just as he can embellish a suntan, gained from a sunlamp, into a convincing tale of 'skiing with Bianca at Gstaad', Howard can inflate any simple fact to extraordinary proportions, when circumstances demand. From acorns of truth he grows oak trees of lies.

He gave a hint of what was in store when he told the men from Her Majesty's Customs that before embarrassing themselves by arresting him, they might want to make a phone call. He gave them the London number of the British Secret Intelligence Service.

Hamilton McMillan, an Oxford contemporary, had recruited Marks to espionage, in part because of the formidable reputation he had gained at Balliol for success with women. In December 1972, McMillan asked Howard to seduce a woman from the Czech Embassy in London who was thought to be a spy for the KGB. The mission was aborted because the woman failed to show up for their date.

But Howard continued to 'serve my country' – as he would later put it. He agreed with McMillan that if his boutique, Annabelinda, opened up branches overseas, they could be utilized as cover by agents of the Secret Intelligence Service (officially, Department of Intelligence, Branch 6, or DI6, but better known by its former designation, MI6). He also agreed to supply DI6 with information on James McCann and his supposed connection with the IRA, though in the event he could reveal very little. In September 1973, McMillan, on the instructions of his superiors, broke off all contact with Marks.

From that acorn grew the towering myth of Howard Marks, secret agent. It was fertilized by the imagination of journalists. It grew unchecked because the British government would never publicly admit that DI6 existed and, thus, nobody came forward to deny even the most preposterous stories.

They began in May 1974, when Marks should have appeared for trial at the Old Bailey, on charges of conspiring to smuggle cannabis into the United States in sound speaker systems.

Howard, free on bond of £50,000, had vanished thirteen days before.

'WHERE IS MR MARKS?' screamed the front-page headline of the *Daily Mirror*, in the type size reserved for its most startling disclosures. 'A man who vanished before an Old Bailey drug-smuggling trial has been named to detectives as a link between an American drugs ring, the IRA Provisionals and DI6 – the British Secret Service,' the *Mirror* reported. It said that Marks had spied on the IRA for British intelligence. He had been taken away from his Oxford apartment by 'a tough-looking man with a London accent' and 'has almost certainly been abducted' by the Provisionals.

Not necessarily so, said the *Sun* the following day. Not to be outdone, it dominated its front page with 'MISSING AGENT – THE FIRST PICTURE'. Nevertheless, it downplayed the intelligence connection, speculating that Marks might instead 'have been murdered by Mafia drug smugglers'.

The more cautious *Daily Mail* wisely hedged its bets: 'INTELLIGENCE AGENT OR GANG VICTIM? MARKS RIDDLE GROWS'.

Before long, and inevitably, Members of Parliament hitched their horses to the wagon, after newspaper reports that a police inquiry into Marks's disappearance had been abruptly called off. Smelling a cover-up, they rose to ask questions in the House of Commons. The government, in its wisdom, did nothing to satisfy them, ruling the Marks case *sub judice* and therefore beyond discussion.

It was left up to the *Mirror* to resolve the matter, at least to its own satisfaction. In October 1974 the paper announced that 'Mirrorman Edward Laxton' had tracked down 'Mr Mystery' and could now reveal 'WHY THE MAFIA HID MARKS'. Laxton's report began:

> The Mafia made Howard Marks an offer he could not refuse.
>
> They bought his silence about a giant drugs racket in return for their protection.
>
> The price Marks must pay: a life in the shadows with the prospect of spending the rest of his days on the run.
>
> The tangled trail that led to Marks's hideout in Italy began at Oxford where he was living until he vanished earlier this year.

73

I traced the trail through London, Amsterdam and California to Milan, and finally to the ancient university town of Padua.

There Marks is living under cover as a student with a new name and a false passport, shielded and supported by Mafia gangsters . . .

Well, not quite.

Actually, Howard was enjoying the time of his life. He'd arranged for his own abduction. The tough-looking man who'd taken him away was a friend – a ruse designed to persuade the courts not to forfeit Howard's £50,000 bond, half of which had been put up by his parents. (It worked.) He went to Italy because he liked the place, and because his sister, Linda, to whom he was very close, was a teacher there. After returning briefly to England he moved on to America, where he joined Peter Combs. In New York he lived first near Maxwell's Plum and then in a riverside apartment in the Pavilion Building on East 77th Street. He became a regular at Régine's, Studio 54, and Nicola's restaurant, run by the former head waiter at Elaine's. He drove around New York in a limousine and was sometimes seen with beautiful women who did not know who he was: Sabrina Guinness and her sisters, Jane Bonham-Carter, and Lady Antonia Fraser's daughter Rebecca.

Marks also took a condominium in Miami on Brickell Avenue, overlooking Biscayne Bay, and all the while he and Combs continued to smuggle dope into America, mainly in 1-ton loads imported through New York's Kennedy airport.

He remained a fugitive for seven years, sometimes returning to Britain, where he attended parties or weddings. In 1979, for example, he audaciously appeared as best man at the wedding of two old friends from Balliol days, Dido Goldsmith and Peter Whitehead, a fashionable affair at London's Chelsea registry office. He posed for pictures with the couple and signed the register 'Donald Albertson'.

On such occasions he would do nothing to dispel the rumours of his involvement with DI6, the IRA and the Mafia. According to Dan Topolski, another Oxford contemporary: 'He'd crop up and you'd say, "Howard, are you all right? What's going on?" And he would just smile, and tell a little story, and you got the feeling that he was enjoying his bit of notoriety, he was enjoying outwitting people . . . He just enjoyed the fun of the chase.'

For much of his time on the run, Howard was accompanied

by Judy Lane. He'd first spotted her in Brighton when she was a seventeen-year-old schoolgirl studying for her A-level examinations: he was instantly attracted to her, he said, by the long blonde hair that fell down beyond her waist, and her irreverent sense of fun. Bright and hard-working, she nevertheless failed her exams because of him. Three years later, when Howard became a fugitive and Rosie Brindley (the mother of his child) declined to join him, Judy went instead. Their first child, Amber, was born in London in October 1977.

Together he and Judy indulged in a life of conspicuous consumption. Settling back in London, they rented a £500-a-month, five-bedroomed apartment in Hans Court, just around the corner from Harrods, where July did most of her grocery shopping. They ran up endless restaurant bills, and Judy bought silk dresses, jewellery and expensive furniture while Howard set about becoming a wine connoisseur.

Towards the end, he seemed to become increasingly careless in his habits, perhaps because he knew it could not last. 'There was going to be some point when I'd get done', he said. 'It was always on the cards, particularly as I wasn't very good at hiding'. In early 1980, Howard and Judy celebrated their engagement at the Hans Court apartment. There was nothing but 1967 Dom Perignon champagne to drink and Beluga caviare to eat. According to Judy's elder brother, Patrick, 'All of London, except Bianca, was there'. Howard might as well have taken out advertisements.

He was finally arrested by Her Majesty's Customs in May 1980 while ordering a dry sherry in a bar of the Swan Hotel in Lavenham, Suffolk. The charges against him included importing into Britain from the United States a massive load of 15 tons of Colombian marijuana – sufficient, according to media calculations, to provide every adult member of the population with a joint.

This time there was no question of bail. This time Her Majesty's Customs was entitled to believe Marks would have to pay his dues. The evidence against him was formidable.

But it should have been clear to them that his trial would not necessarily be decided by the facts. He hinted at what was to come during his interrogation.

'Shouldn't you have used your university training and, clearly, your high intelligence, in some worthwhile employment?' said one of the Customs men.

'Yes, possibly,' said Howard.

'Don't you feel it's been something of a waste?'

'Yes – but it's difficult to resist when you're flattered into believing your country needs you.'

Peter Combs, Howard's partner, blamed himself for Marks's arrest. The Colombian marijuana deal, which Combs had helped to organize, was probably doomed from the start because it brought into stark conflict the amateurism of the British dope distribution business with the much more demanding standards of the American suppliers.

The marijuana had arrived on the west coast of Scotland at the end of December 1979. It was vastly more than the British distribution networks were used to dealing with and it saturated the market. Marks was forced to drop the price, from £310 a pound to £260. Even so, it sold slowly. By the beginning of May 1980 the American suppliers had received less than $2 million – only a fraction of what they expected. They grew impatient, then suspicious. Against Combs's advice, they insisted on sending representatives to Britain to make an inventory of the remaining marijuana to ensure they were not being ripped off.

When Marks heard the news he was furious. He was already under great strain, for he had guessed (correctly) that the sensitive antennae of Her Majesty's Customs would have picked up the fact that the dope market was saturated, and would want to know why. As long as tons of the marijuana remained unsold, he knew he was at great risk. 'If they can't trust me, just forget it,' he told Combs. But Peter eventually persuaded him to accept that the Americans were entitled to reassurance.

Two emissaries arrived from America, one of them a prominent Miami defence attorney, and checked into the Dorchester Hotel. Their clumsy presence in London proved disastrous. Within days they'd attracted the attention of Her Majesty's Customs, which tapped their hotel phones. In at least one of the conversations Marks incriminated himself. While the conversation was not admissible as evidence (indeed, Her Majesty's Customs does not admit it taps phones), it placed Howard at the centre of the conspiracy and allowed the Customs men to trace and eventually arrest him. Combs blamed himself for that.

He exorcised his guilt by sending to London enormous sums of money – by his account, around $1.5 million. He arranged to pay the bills of Howard's London solicitor, Bernard Simons, and the fees of Lord Hutchinson, one of Britain's most eminent defence advocates. He also paid for Judy to buy the ground-floor apartment at 60

Cathcart Road, immediately above the basement apartment she already owned, and gave her the money to convert the two of them into a spacious maisonette.

Perhaps equally important, Combs also sent to London Tom Sunde, his ever-willing assistant. Sunde had not yet elevated himself to the ranks of the CIA but he behaved as though he had. Arriving in London with his German sidekick, Reiner Jacobi, Sunde told Judy Marks that they'd passed through Heathrow airport without pausing at either Immigration or Customs, their passage eased in advance by the British Special Branch. Sunde also told Judy that Jacobi had 'intelligence connections' that would allow Howard to mount a spectacular, if unorthodox, defence.

The first obstacle to overcome was the natural scepticism of Lord Hutchinson. Barristers of his stature do not knowingly go into court to present a defence that consists almost entirely of perjury, no matter how persuasive the client may be as to his or her innocence. Marks – awaiting trial in Brixton prison, where he gloomily considered the awesome weight of the case against him – knew that his only chance was to convince the jury that his undeniable association with drug trafficking had resulted from his work for DI6. First it was necessary to convince Lord Hutchinson.

Sunde and Jacobi apparently did that by bringing with them to London a man named Henry McNeill, who, in a private meeting, was able to satisfy the lawyers that he was a serving DI6 agent, based in Hong Kong. McNeill was not willing to testify at Howard's trial, for what he said were obvious reasons. He did, however, categorically state that Marks had been a DI6 freelance agent, recruited to infiltrate the IRA, and that he'd been abandoned by the intelligence service because of the public embarrassment caused by the *Daily Mirror*'s disclosures. Evidently, Marks's lawyers believed him.

There was more perjury to be bought with Peter Combs's money. Called on to explain a briefcase full of cash found under his bed, Marks claimed to his defence lawyers that, at the behest of DI6, he had also worked for the Mexican government, attempting to infiltrate a terrorist group financed by drugs. The money, he said, was what was left of the $150,000 the Mexicans had paid him. The story was ludicrous, but Sunde and Jacobi were able to produce a man who certainly looked Mexican, who said he was a member of the Mexican security police, and who confirmed to Bernie Simons that Howard's story was true. And, unlike Henry McNeill, the Mexican said he would testify at the trial.

While they waited for it to begin, Howard and Judy got married. She was by then pregnant with their second daughter, Francesca, and Marks was allowed out of Brixton prison for one day, escorted by two guards, to attend the ceremony at the Welsh Congregational Chapel in Southwark Bridge Road, south London and, afterwards, a champagne reception at a hotel near Harrods. To the friends and family who were there, Howard seemed remarkably cheerful for someone facing what seemed to be the near certainty of fourteen years in jail.

Patrick Lane, the eldest of the six Lane children, was nowhere near London when the trial began in September 1981 – which suited Howard. After Marks's arrest, Patrick had prudently left France, where he lived with his wife and two daughters, and moved to California at the invitation of Peter Combs. He was scarcely in hiding. The Lanes lived in Santa Cruz under their own names and Patrick published a newsletter, an offshore banking report, which he circulated widely. He did, however, cut himself off as much as possible from the events going on in London. His greatest anxiety was that his wife might find out what he'd done.

Natasha Lane, Judy's elder sister, was even further away from London – which also suited Howard. She was in a jail in Tijuana, Mexico, preparing to give birth to her first son, facing the consequences of the fact that when her sailboat had run aground off the Mexican coast, it had been found to contain 1 ton of marijuana.

Both had played some role in the conspiracy. Natasha had allowed her name to be used by Howard to rent a 'safe' apartment in London. And Patrick, recruited by Howard to help him dispose of his 'embarrassment of riches', had set up a system to pay the American suppliers of the marijuana, with the aid of a merchant bank in the City of London which wire-transferred the money to New York. (Patrick personally delivered the first deposit of £100,000 to the merchant bank in a suitcase. As he describes the occasion: 'The Bank was exactly what you would expect a discreet, old-school merchant bank to be like. There was a brass plate at the door, and inside the walls were panelled with oak. The directors had stepped from the pages of *Punch* magazine. They wore dark Savile Row suits and sported bristling white moustaches. Their accents were clipped and their eyes cold and restless. Nobody asked what I was for, and we all studiously avoided looking at the suitcase. We trooped upstairs to the Directors' Conference Room; four or five directors and myself carrying the heavy suitcase. We entered the room and stood awkwardly around a vast polished conference table. Conversation faded and all eyes turned in my direction. "What the heck," I thought to myself and, without a word, I opened the suitcase and spilled £100,000 in cash all over their polished table. There was a terrible silence in the room. Nobody moved. I did not dare even breathe. Finally, the chairman of the bank, his pink neck bulging over his stiff collar, moved slowly to the haphazard piles of banknotes. "Gentlemen," he said, his voice quavering with emotion, "*this* is what banking is all about."')

But what Patrick and Natasha had actually done for their brother-in-law bore little relation to the version of events given by the defence at the Old Bailey. In their absence, Marks had no hesitation in ascribing to them most of the roles he had actually played.

Thus, it was *their* Colombian marijuana deal, not his. The emissaries sent from America to carry out the inventory were *their* contacts, not his. Yes, he may have met the Americans but it was at dinner parties given by *Patrick*, in apartments that *Patrick* rented, not he. It was *Patrick* and *Natasha* who'd rented apartments and warehouses in false names. The only role Marks would admit to was that of an arbitrator, called in to audit the accounts when some discrepancies arose. He'd done that, he said, as a favour to Patrick – and because, in his role as an intelligence agent, he hoped to find out more about the drug suppliers.

The intelligence connection. It dominated and distorted the trial from the moment John Rogers, counsel for the prosecution, made the crucial concession that Marks had, as he put it, 'received a proposition from British Intelligence'.

Rogers sought to limit the damage by insisting that the connection had been severed in 1973, after Marks's arrest on the Las Vegas charges – but Howard would not compromise.

'Mr Marks, as a result of that charge, you were told in categoric terms that the Intelligence [sic] were dispensing with your services, were you not?' said Rogers.

'Absolutely not,' said Marks. 'What basis do you have for saying such a thing? Is that a suggestion from your own mind?'

'And you were told that you were being dispensed with because of your involvement in allegations concerning drugs?'

'No.'

'And that everything that you have said about being involved with Intelligence since that time – and your involvement had nothing to do with drugs – is quite untrue?'

'What *you* are saying is quite untrue. On two counts. My involvement with British Intelligence *was* concerned with drugs, and I *have* been involved since then.'

The only independent evidence that the jury heard in support of this claim came at the eleventh hour of the trial, when Tom Sunde's star witness turned up at the Old Bailey, apparently from Mexico.

He refused to testify in public, on grounds of 'security', and the court was cleared. He would not give his name. He refused to produce any credentials.

'Well, how am I to determine that you are who you claim to be?' asked the prosecutor.

'You have no way to do it.'

His testimony lasted for no more than ten minutes, and amounted to no more than the claim that Marks – using the alias Anthony Tunnicliffe – had twice provided 'useful information' about 'contraband of arms and drugs' for which he had been paid. In response to most of the questions he was asked, the Mexican replied: 'Sorry sir, I'm not able to answer that for security reasons.'

In his closing argument the prosecutor attempted to cut through the fog of deception with blunt common sense: Marks was a drug trafficker, nothing more, nothing less; his claims of being a secret agent were 'utter rubbish'.

But is was a lost cause. After a trial lasting about two months, the jury retired for two days and then returned a verdict of 'Not Guilty'.

Marks, being candid for the first time since his arrest, said he was 'relieved but astonished'.

It might be true, as Her Majesty's Customs insists, that its officers are too professional to take such defeats personally, and that they do not bear grudges.

It might be true – except for *that book*.

Howard had hoped that the British writer Piers Paul Read, author of *Alive*, might undertake the task of describing his life and times, but Read declined. Instead, from a list of writers who'd expressed an interest in telling his story, Marks selected David Leigh, a reporter for the *Observer*.

Leigh got a book contract from the London publisher William Heinemann, and an advance of £15,000 which he split with Marks. Leigh also agreed to split any further proceeds on a 50-50 basis and, anticipating a best-seller, Howard established a company, Stepside

Limited, to receive the profits. His accountant anticipated that they might be so substantial as to oblige Howard to move abroad, to avoid punitive taxation.

In the event, *High Time – the Shocking Life and Times of Howard Marks*, published in 1984, was not a great commercial success. It was, however, widely read in law enforcement circles in Britain, and almost universally hated.

It was bad enough that Marks was at liberty to describe his exploits, worse that he should boast about them, even worse that he should make money out of it.

At Her Majesty's Customs it was a book one did not admit to buying, subversive almost, 'rubbish' certainly – and 'Why put money in that bugger's pocket?'

Still, it's safe to assume that many Customs officers could not resist, and Peter Nelson certainly bought the book. In February 1986, at the end of what had turned into an exhaustive two-day briefing on Howard Marks, Nelson gave his copy of *High Time* to Craig Lovato.

Palma, 24 February 1986

There was an influenza epidemic sweeping the British expatriate community in Majorca, and all the Marks family had gone down with it. Lovato could hear it in their voices whenever they picked up the phone.

Getting permission to return to the listening room had not been easy. The two DEA agents in the Madrid office covered an enormous territory – Spain, Portugal, France and parts of North Africa – and Richard Dunnigan, then the DEA country attaché, was unwilling to lose half his manpower to the Marks inquiry. He'd tried bringing in a 'TDY' (a Temporary Duty agent) from Los Angeles, but that hadn't worked out. Finally Dunnigan relented: Lovato could return to Palma 'temporarily'. Neither of them had any idea that 'temporarily' would mean the best part of five months.

Thanks to Her Majesty's Customs, Lovato could now make much better sense of the conversations he was listening to. For one thing, he knew who many of the players were.

'Old John' – the man with the passing resemblance to Mick Jagger, and an unlicensed London taxi – was John Denbigh. His passport application said he was born in Petersfield, Hampshire, on 16 April 1940, and that he was an electrician. Curiously, when the passport was issued in 1980, Denbigh was living in Nepal. He now had an antiques business in London's Portobello Road.

'Jim' – the man with the wife whose name he frequently forgot – was Frederick James Hobbs, His passport application said he was born in Brighton on 15 December 1942, and that he was a salesman. Her Majesty's Customs told Lovato that Hobbs had run a 'telephone switching centre' for Marks in Amsterdam. He was now in Lisbon, trying to do the same thing, though he was still waiting for a second telephone line to be installed.

Of the two 'Micks', Customs had identified the one in London with the Cockney cadences as Michael Sidney Williams, 'a member of the Marks organization' but also a drug trafficker in his own right. Similarly, Customs said that 'Brian' in Bangkok, identified as Phillip Sparrowhawk, ran his own smuggling ventures to Australia and England but 'usually joins with Marks for bigger runs'. And what did Williams and Sparrowhawk have to do with a load of hashish going from Pakistan to the United States? Probably nothing. Her Majesty's Customs said it had 'information' that Marks was also up to his neck in two separate conspiracies to smuggle drugs into England: hashish from Morocco with Williams; marijuana from Thailand with Sparrowhawk.

'He enjoys having a number of deals in operation at the same time,' said Peter Nelson. 'Gets a kick out of it. Needs to fill in his time and mental space, otherwise he gets bored.'

'Tony' – the man with the plummy voice and 'samples of a considerable size' – was Lord Moynihan, wanted in England on fraud charges, Customs said.

'Gerry' was Gerald Wayne Wills, who had visited London with his partner, Ronald Allen, the previous October – and they produced the photographs the surveillance teams had taken at Heathrow airport.

The only major player Her Majesty's Customs could not completely identify was 'Peter', also known as 'Mr Simms' in California, though they knew from their informants that 'he considers himself, with Marks, one of the pioneers of marijuana smuggling'. They also knew from the Amsterdam phone tap that he had stayed at a hotel in Los Angeles with someone called Patti, and that he was probably on bail or probation for a drug offence.

Equipped with this partial list of the *dramatis personae*, Lovato reviewed the conversations that had been taped in his absence

Howard Marks: Graduating from Balliol College, Oxford, 1968

Howard Marks: The heart-throb of Kenfig Hill; with his daughter, Myfanwy; best man at the wedding of Peter Whitehead and Dido Goldsmith; *(opposite page)* with Judy at their wedding reception; at a birthday party for their two daughters; under arrest in Amsterdam; under surveillance in London by Her Majesty's Customs

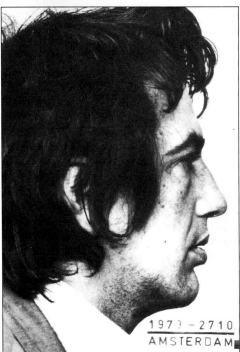

1973 - 2710
AMSTERDAM

The Howard Marks Organization: James Hobbs, messenger man; Gerry Wills, alias Mr Livingston, transporter and West Coast distributor *(below left)*; Saleem Malik, Pakistani hashish supplier

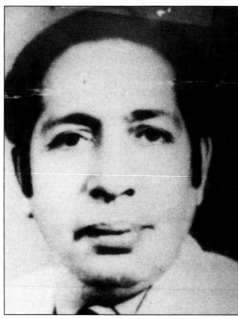

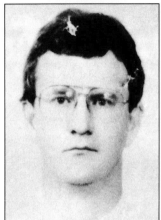

Roger Reaves, agronomist and
escape artist *(above left)*; Phillip
Sparrowhawk, marijuana supplier;
John Denbigh, 'the Vicar', under
surveillance in London and after his
arrest in Vancouver

Changing faces: Two of the California driver's licences of Ernest 'Peter' Combs, Marks's partner and pioneer

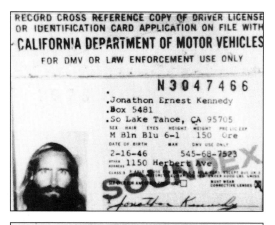

RECORD CROSS REFERENCE COPY OF DRIVER LICENSE
OR IDENTIFICATION CARD APPLICATION ON FILE WITH
CALIFORNIA DEPARTMENT OF MOTOR VEHICLES
FOR DMV OR LAW ENFORCEMENT USE ONLY

N 3 0 4 7 4 6 6

.Jonathon Ernest Kennedy
.Box 5481
.So Lake Tahoe, CA 95705
M Bln Blu 6-1 150 Ore
2-16-46   545-68-7523
1150 Herbert Ave

RECORD CROSS REFERENCE COPY OF DRIVER LICENSE
OR IDENTIFICATION CARD APPLICATION ON FILE WITH
CALIFORNIA DEPARTMENT OF MOTOR VEHICLES
FOR DMV OR LAW ENFORCEMENT USE ONLY

Ernest Franz Combs Jr
4175 Chestnut Ave
Long Beach Cal 90807

M brn blu 6-1 160 sgl Cal

1-17-46 25

4-30-71 Cls   Fs

Brothers-in-law: George Lane *(below left)*, on the run in Bangkok; Patrick Lane

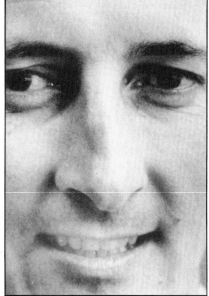

Rex and RW: Reiner Jacobi *(above left)* and Thomas Sunde. *(Below)*
Sunde on a beach with Marks and his youngest daughter, Francesca

Howard Marks: Behind bars in Miami

during February. For a lot of that time, it seemed, Howard had been preoccupied with personnel problems.

For one thing, he had lost his new communications centre in Portugal. Hobbs had been arrested on charges of kidnapping and sexually assaulting two sixteen-year-old boys. 'Fucking pervert', said Howard after receiving the news.

Meanwhile, Hobbs's wife-of-convenience, Selina, was stranded in London with not much more than her new British passport. She wanted Marks to find her an apartment and a job, and to send her money. Then she announced she was pregnant and demanded that Howard pay for an abortion.

For two days, Marks had been in Switzerland. He'd called Judy from the Hotel Savoy in Geneva, saying he'd 'withdrawn 10,000' and was making arrangements to withdraw more from Zürich – and Lovato, hearing that, asked the DEA office in Berne to get a list of Howard's calls from the hotel, in the hope of identifying his banks.

Other than that, things had been quiet. It seemed to Lovato that Marks was in limbo, waiting for something to happen.

Manila, 25 February 1986

It never occurred to Lord Moynihan that the Marcos regime could fall. In the eighteen days since Marcos had declared himself the winner of the (obscenely rigged) election, there had been protests in the streets but nothing Marcos couldn't handle, Moynihan thought.

Driving home from downtown Manila to his house on the outskirts, Moynihan saw a column of tanks heading for the city. He told his driver to stop.

'What's happening, whose side are you on?' he asked the officer in charge.

'The president's side, of course.'

'Fine, carry on,' said Lord Moynihan, fully believing that the army would re-establish the status quo.

Then suddenly Marcos was gone, air-lifted into exile on a US Air Force jet.

For Moynihan, as for everybody else in the Philippines whose ability to do business depended on contacts within the regime, it was a devastating moment; fifteen years of cultivating Marcos cronies all for nothing.

He knew he was now extremely vulnerable. It was not just his business he might lose; it was also his safe haven.

Newport Beach, California, 25 February 1986

Gerry Wills and his partner, Ronald Allen, checked into adjoining rooms on the sixth floor of the Meridien Hotel, south of Los Angeles, just off Route 1, 100 miles or so from the Mexican border.

Like Marks, they too had time to kill, waiting for their ship to come in. Wills occupied the interval making calls to numbers with a 900 prefix; 'dial-a-porn' establishments selling erotic conversation.

Palma, 26 February 1986

It was 6.15 a.m. when the phone rang in Howard's house, waking him up. To Lovato, the voice on the other end of the line was unmistakably that of 'Pete' – also known as 'Mr Simms' – in California.

'Wake you up?' said Pete.

'Yeah, almost.'

'Well, you'll be happy I did.'

'Oh, really?'

'Champagne in Mozambique!'

There was the slightest of pauses. Then Marks said: 'Really? Oh, fantastic!'

'So, it's no longer a four-twenty-type situation.'

'So everything's as it should be?'

'Yes, it's tucked away here.'

'Oh, great! Oh, that's good.'

'So, how are you doing, man?'

'Oh, all right, you know. I've been sort of ill a little bit, but I'm OK, really. I'm *very* good at the moment,' said Howard, sounding as though he meant it. Then he laughed.

In the listening room, Lovato replayed the tape over and over. The hashish had arrived in California; of that much he was certain.

But where? What was a 'four-twenty-type situation?' Where was

84

'Mozambique?' Pete had said 'It's tucked away *here*', so where was Pete? And for that matter, who was he?

Later on in the conversation, Pete had told Howard: 'Felt like I had to call. Didn't want to wait until it was in Connolly's, you know? I thought, because it's in Mozambique you'd love to know that'. So, they were going to move the stuff, from 'Mozambique' to 'Connolly's'; from one city to another, or between two stash houses? And when?

There was no way of telling.

'Anyway, I love you, man, and take care of yourself,' said Pete. 'Happy birthday! Merry Christmas!'

'OK, and thanks so much, you hear? I love you,' said Howard.

Yes, I'll bet you do, thought Craig.

He buried his frustration in frenetic activity, bombarding the DEA's California offices with a series of requests, clutching at straws.

He wanted to know if there was an airport or an airfield called Connolly anywhere on the West Coast, or, indeed, anywhere in the United States. Given that Marks had used airfreight to import hashish in the past, he thought that 'four-twenty' might be a flight number, and he asked the Los Angeles office to go through the *ABC Air Freight Shipments* manual – the size of a big city telephone book – to see if the code, 420, existed. Above all, he wanted to know about Pete.

Her Majesty's Customs had speculated that Pete was on parole or bond, and he seemed to confirm that on the tape: 'Let me tell you the worst thing of all, they have me on this testing programme, so I can't try it. That really pisses me off. I've got Patti but, I mean, *I* want to celebrate, you know?' And later he'd said: 'The pressure that they're putting on me! I have to call in and report to them every single fucking day'.

Lovato asked Los Angeles to check the NADDIS computer system for any known drug trafficker in that situation who'd used the alias 'Simms'. The answer came back almost immediately: Ernest Franz Combs, also as known as Nicholas Simms (among a great many other names) – a fugitive for eleven years, seven months and eight days – was out on bond of $100,000, awaiting trial in Las Vegas on 173 charges of importing hashish, hidden in the sound-speaker systems of non-existent British rock groups.

The Los Angeles office pulled a picture of Combs from its files and compared it to the picture Nicholas Simms had submitted with his application for a California driver's licence. They matched.

But where Combs was now, the Los Angeles office couldn't say. His home address was in Los Angeles, but there was no sign of him there.

There was nothing else they or Lovato could do but wait, and hope that Combs could call Marks again – and this time give some clue as to where he was calling from.

Howard Marks and Ernest Combs had both been in the dope business long enough to know that it was prudent to assume that their telephones were tapped. While the innuendo in their conversations was sufficient to raise the hair on the back of Craig Lovato's neck, they were never totally indiscreet. For example, they never gave out telephone numbers. They would say, 'Call me at Gerry's,' or 'I'll be at my other place,' or something equally obscure.

Occasionally, however, when the telephone number was new, they had to be more direct. Then they would use a code, which they called 'interstate'.

Two days after reporting 'Champagne in Mozambique', Combs called back to say he expected 'it' to be 'in Connolly's in about a week'. He told Marks he was using the name 'Mr S'. He said his telephone number was 'Interstate 218-8513'.

In the listening room, Lovato wrote down all the possible permutations he could think of on endless scraps of paper.

He tried reversing the digits, so that 218-8513 became 315-8812. He tried adding one to each digit, so that 218-8513 became 329-9624. He tried multiplying 218 by 8513, but the result was 185-5834 – and no telephone numbers in America began with a 1. He said to himself, maybe they've reversed all the digits between 1 and 9, so 9 becomes 1, 8 becomes 2, and so on. Nothing worked. After three days of tortuous mathematics, all the numbers he arrived at were either impractical, or, when he called them in Los Angeles, were not in service, or disconnected, or the people who answered the phone had never heard of Mr Simms.

Lovato is nothing if not persistent. He began again.

What if each digit was multiplied by the same number, and if the result was more than 9, he dropped the first digit? The multiplier couldn't be 2, or 4, or 6, or 8, because all the resulting digits would be even numbers. It couldn't be 5 either, because every resulting digit would be a 5 or a zero.

That left 3, 7, and 9 – the three multipliers that would give unique results.

He tried multiplying each digit of 218-8513 by 3. The result meant nothing. He tried again, this time multiplying by 7. The result, after discarding the surplus digits, was 476-6571.

It was the number of the Hotel Bel Air Sands on Sunset Boulevard, Los Angeles. And Mr Nicholas Simms, and his wife, Patti, were registered guests.

Los Angeles, 4 March 1986

Julie Desm had never felt so stupid. Under the bemused eye of the Bel Air Sands house detective – a moonlighting Homicide cop from the Los Angeles Police Department – she pulled champagne bottles from their crates and shook them, looking for non-existent traces of hashish.

'Craig, that's a dumb idea,' she said when he'd told her to check if there had been any recent deliveries of champagne to the hotel.

But Julie had been a DEA agent for less than two years. She didn't rank high on the totem pole; certainly not high enough to argue with Craig Lovato. He also had the advantage that when he called her – and he'd called her constantly for the last week – it always seemed to be three o'clock in the morning. She thought at first that he couldn't work out the nine-hour time difference between Palma and Los Angeles. Then she thought he didn't care what time it was.

She knew next to nothing about the background of the case. Until a few weeks ago, she'd never heard of Howard Marks. Even now, she couldn't really share Craig's obsession with the chase. It didn't help that her supervisors were not over-enthusiastic: in a city that had more major drug cases than palm trees, who cared about some Welsh pot smuggler sitting on an island in the Mediterranean?

Craig Lovato cared, that was for sure, and he was incredibly demanding.

As soon as Combs had been identified as Mr Simms, and traced to the Bel Air Sands, Craig had insisted that Julie place him under surveillance and follow him wherever he went.

Easily said. Craig apparently had no idea what it was like trying to drum up enough spare agents in Los Angeles to mount a proper surveillance. Or he did know and didn't care.

And, obviously, he'd never tried following somebody on a Los Angeles freeway where even the normal driving techniques border on the suicidal. Combs didn't drive by any normal rules. He'd take an exit ramp at high speed, and then swerve back on to the freeway at the last moment, oblivious to the chaos he caused. He would slow down or speed up for no apparent reason. He'd drive around in circles. Following him was a nightmare, and twice that day the surveillance team had lost him – the last time for good.

It was when they returned to the Bel Air Sands, in the vain hope of picking up his trail, that the moonlighting Homicide cop told Julie about the champagne. He said that at around the time Combs had checked in, the hotel had received a major delivery of California champagne – twenty-five crates. And Combs's room, the cop said, was next door to an unlocked fire escape that led to a secluded car park.

Was it possible? When Combs said 'Champagne in Mozambique' did he mean that hashish had been delivered to his hotel, hidden in bottles of California bubbly? No, said Julie's by now dispirited fellow agents, but she had to check. It was the least Craig would expect.

There were nineteen cases left in the hotel's storeroom; 228 bottles to shake. There was nothing in them but champagne.

'You might want to leave those corks in there for a while,' she said to the house detective as she left, feeling like a fool.

Palma, 9–18 March 1986

It had been ten days since Combs had called Marks from the Bel Air Sands; ten days of no news, anxious moments. Lovato, almost permanently in the listening room, found the waiting difficult to take. So too, evidently, did Howard.

The tape recorder clicked on as Marks lifted the phone and began dialling. To Lovato's now-practised ear, it sounded as though he was calling California.

'Hotel Meridien, may I help you?'

'Could I speak to Gerry Wills, please,' said Marks.

'What's the first name?'

'Gerry. I'm not sure if it's G or J. The last name is Wills.'

God bless you, Howard, thought Lovato. It was not every day that suspects were so thoroughly identified.

Wills was immediately reassuring. 'Everything is fine,' he told Marks. 'We've just had a lot of bad weather. I've been feeling guilty not calling you, but I didn't want to until I had something to say.'

'Right, but I mean everything is OK, yeah?' said Marks.

'One hundred per cent.'

*   *   *

Two days later:

'Thought I'd call and give you a report,' said Combs.

'Oh, please,' said Marks.

'Well, we've had real bad weather, you know, so we don't have anything from Mozambique yet. Our problem is, we're having to use a . . .' There was a pause while Combs searched for the right expression. '. . . An FP.'

'Yes,' said Howard, a little tentatively. Then more confidently: 'OK, yeah.' Understood.

FP? Lovato had heard them talk previously about a 'PS' which, from the context of the conversations, he'd guessed meant 'private ship' or 'private slow' – in any event, an ocean-going boat that they controlled. On that basis, FP could mean 'fast private', perhaps. A fast boat to make the final run from the mother ship to the shore? A private plane?

Combs was still talking: 'We were going to go on the highway you know, and then for the last thirty days there's been a major event there, where every once in a while they put on pressure, where they bother everybody.'

A highway in California where, from time to time, someone puts on pressure? There was one very obvious candidate in southern California: Interstate 5, which ends at the US Customs post on the Mexican border. So Mozambique was Mexico; it had to be.

'. . . We got this all together,' Combs went on, talking now about the FP, 'new parts and stuff because things had broken down on it, and then it started raining real bad, and then it was real foggy. It's driving me crazy because I want to get to work. It's kind of anti-climactic, if you know what I mean.'

'I know what you mean,' said Marks. 'What's the future look like? All right?'

'Everything's fine. There's no problem whatsoever. We just don't want to go all this time and then screw it up by being super-impatient.'

'Right,' said Marks. 'Just got to be patient and wait.'

You and me both, thought Lovato.

Finally, on 18 March early in the evening Palma time, came the moment they'd both been waiting for.

'I just got tickets to this play tonight,' said Combs. 'I just got them right now.'

'Oh, great!' said Marks.

'I mean the first, you know?'

89

'Right, sure. The first showing.'

'I just got it in my hands a half hour ago. Unfortunately I can't go to the show myself . . .'

'No, I figured not.'

'Because of my testing thing. Patti read it over, you know?'

'All right. She enjoyed it, yeah?'

'Yeah, loved it . . . Here, I'll let you talk to Patti.'

'Hi,' she said.

'Hi Patti, how are you doing?'

'Great.'

'So I can drink some champagne, yeah?'

'I think so.'

'Are you sure, now?'

'I forgot to get some myself. We'll have to go out. Yeah, drink up!'

Combs came back on the line. 'OK, I'll be in touch in a couple of days. Probably by the end of the week I'll be able to send you something.'

'That's fantastic.'

'By the way,' said Combs, 'good job. I'm really proud of you.'

Lovato transcribed the conversation as fast as he could and Telexed it in its entirety to the DEA's Los Angeles office, so it would be on Julie Desm's desk first thing in the morning. Then he called her at home and woke her up.

Afterwards neither of them could remember exactly what he said, only the gist of it.

Julie, the load is there! Ernie's got the stuff in his hands. They've flown it in from Mexico and they're sitting in some goddamned hotel room in Los Angeles and Patti's testing it. They're going to start selling it. They're going to be sending Howard money by the end of the week.

Julie, *find Ernie Combs*. Whatever you do, *find the load before they sell it*.

Los Angeles, 19 March to 3 April 1986

Easily said, Craig. Combs and Patti had long since checked out of the Bel Air Sands Hotel and they weren't at home. How do you find a man with any number of identities in a city

90

the size of Los Angeles? There are twenty-six pages of hotels and motels in the Greater Los Angeles phone book. What do you do, call them all? Ask if they've got a Caucasian male, forty years old, 6 feet 1 inch tall, 150lb, who might or might not have long hair and a beard, who might or might not be with a woman, who could be using any name under the sun? Sure, Craig.

The only lead Julie Desm had was the knowledge that Gerry Wills had been staying at the Meridien Hotel in Newport Beach, and that he told Marks in one conversation, 'Pete's been hanging around the neighbourhood.'

She went to the Meridien. Too late: Wills and Ronald Allen were long gone. She retrieved a list of the 124 telephone calls they'd made during their thirteen-day stay. Most of those that weren't made to dial-a-porn services were to switching centres of the kind that automatically direct messages to electronic pagers, and leave no trace.

She did not know what else to do. She told Craig they'd have to wait and hope that Combs called Marks again, and say where he was.

March became April, and still Combs didn't call.

Peter and Patti were staying at the Bel Age Hotel, forty-five minutes from Los Angeles international airport.

Their room was in semi-darkness, the curtains permanently closed. The air-conditioning was going full blast. It was so cold in there it made you shiver. Peter and Patti probably didn't notice because they spent most of their time in bed.

Wyvonna Wills did not want to be there. After five years of marriage she and Gerry had split up, and she'd only agreed to do him this favour because they were trying to remain friends, for the sake of their two young daughters. She'd agreed to carry money to London for him, and they'd stopped at the hotel on the way to the airport to pick it up.

Now they were all in this cold, dark room with this strange couple she'd not met before who were snorting cocaine – *in front of her children*. Gerry snorted some, too. She got so angry, she thought she'd explode.

Gerry told her to calm down. Then he took a brown paper bag containing stacks of dollar bills from Patti. He lifted up the cotton shirt Wyvonna was wearing and began stuffing the bills inside the top of her pantyhose.

That was more than she could take. She got out of the room as fast as she could. On the way to the airport, she and Gerry had a monumental row. Later she thought it was a miracle they didn't wreck the car.

On the plane to London, Wyvonna Wills transferred what she estimated to be $60–70,000 dollars from the top of her pantyhose to a brown envelope. She gave the envelope to Howard that night at his Cathcart Road home. He didn't open it while she was there. Instead he showed her his voluminous press clippings, carefully preserved in large dark brown folders, and videotapes of the television programmes he'd featured in. My God, she thought, the guy's a celebrity.

After two days in London, she flew to Palma with Judy Marks and called Gerry in Los Angeles from Howard's phone. 'Howard and Judy send their gratitude,' she said.

In the listening room, Craig Lovato had little doubt what they were grateful for. He called Los Angeles, and woke up Julie Desm again.

Los Angeles, 8 April 1986

Julie Desm lay full-length on the floor of room 620 of the Beverly Pavilion Hotel. By lying on her side it was possible, if uncomfortable, to keep one ear cocked to the crack under the connecting door leading to room 618. Sometimes, when they turned down the volume of the television, she could hear snatches of conversation coming from the next room, which she scribbled down as fast as she could in a stenographer's notebook.

She had four other DEA agents, all men, to help her and occasionally one of them would take a turn on the floor for a few minutes. But they complained it was uncomfortable. 'Julie, it's your case, you get to lie on the floor,' they said. She did so for the best part of ten hours.

They'd found Combs, as Julie knew they would, when he'd called Marks to report his progress, and gave the telephone number of his hotel in 'interstate' code. (The call was one of the more bizarre of the hundreds Lovato listened to. It began with Combs giving his (terrible) impression of the actress Carol Channing. 'Who the fuck is this?' said Marks. Combs's news was disappointing: the stuff was selling slowly, he said, because other dealers were 'dragging the price way down', to $800 a lb. Nevertheless he remained irrepressible: 'You take care of yourself, pilgrim. And if you need some help just call the cavalry and I'll come running, forty-fives in each hand, guns blazing'.)

The Beverly Pavilion was a small but classy hotel situated on one of the more expensive parts of Wilshire Boulevard. It was not an easy place to keep under observation from outside, because there was nowhere on Wilshire to park the surveillance cars. Inside, however, it was a dream. The hotel's management immediately agreed to rent the DEA room 620 – next to 618, where Combs and Patti were staying. The doors to the two rooms faced each other across a small vestibule. Each door was equipped with a spyhole, allowing the agents to observe easily any visitors that Combs and Patti might have.

And, as a bonus, there was the interconnecting door that allowed Julie to hear snatches of their conversations if she lay full-length on the floor – if they would only turn down the volume of their infernal television set. These were not the kind of circumstances they prepared you for at the DEA academy. This, Julie decided, was a lot more fun.

At 2.00 p.m., four hours after she had begun her vigil, Julie heard Combs talking on the telephone. He hung up and told Patti: 'Three-thirty.'

An hour later she heard Patti say, 'Got to get out of the central district, baby.' Combs said 'Nevada.'

At a little after 3.15 p.m., Combs answered the phone and said: 'Hi Rick, do you want to run by here so you don't have to carry it around?' He told Patti: 'Rick has ninety-three now.'

Ten minutes later, the two of them left room 618. Julie, watching them through the spyhole, used a hand-held radio to alert the surveillance team waiting on the street.

She went to the window of her room to watch as they emerged from the hotel and walked to the forecourt of a nearby Chevron gas station at the junction of Wilshire and Canon Drive. Almost immediately a black Jeep pulled up. The driver handed Combs a white plastic bag and then drove off at considerable speed.

'I think,' said Julie to herself, 'that what I've just witnessed is the commission of a felony.' She was certain that the plastic bag contained money; money that had paid for drugs. Then she stopped congratulating herself as she realized that Combs and Patti were not returning to the hotel. They were walking away with the evidence.

A proper surveillance, one that cannot be easily shaken, requires at least a dozen agents. Julie had four, and two of them had taken off in pursuit of the black Jeep. (They followed it to Century City, where the driver disappeared into an office block.) The remaining two were in vehicles, which they could not just abandon at the start of the rush hour, at one of the busiest intersections in Los Angeles.

Julie ran down six flights of stairs, out of the hotel, across Wilshire and on to Canon Drive. There was no sign of Combs and Patti. The street was lined with fashionable shops, any one of which might now contain them.

She chose Abercrombie & Fitch, the clothing store, trying to look nonchalant as she searched for her quarry among the racks. She couldn't find them (because they were in a changing-room). She returned to the hotel dispirited, wondering, not for the first time on this case, how Craig would take the news.

But half an hour later Combs and Patti returned to the hotel, carrying their packages from Abercrombie & Fitch – and, thank God, the white plastic bag. Julie resolved that they would not walk away with the money again. She didn't want to arrest Combs because, directly or indirectly, he might eventually lead them to where the load was hidden. On the other hand, she knew Patti was nervous (when she said, 'Got to get out of the central district, baby', she meant Los Angeles) and that they could take off at any minute. She determined to keep them on a very short leash.

For the next few hours she maintained her prone position on the floor. She heard Combs dial a number and ask by name for his attorney. It was a name that Julie, and every other DEA agent in Los Angeles, knew only too well. There are lawyers who represent what the DEA agents tend to call 'dirtbags', and then there are 'dirtbag lawyers'. The distinction is important, and not flattering to the latter. In just about every DEA agent's book, Combs's attorney was a dirtbag lawyer.

The traffic on Wilshire was now at the rush-hour peak. The subdued roar coming from six floors below allowed Julie to hear only fragments of what Combs said: 'I have partners as well . . . I have to take care of my commitments . . . Punish me for not showing up . . . I've never let you down when you asked me for something . . . These other guys fuck up my timing . . . I told him you had one hundred earlier and you were waiting for two . . . I said I had to take care of my commitments . . . Anyway, I have it right now in my hands . . .' He also said that the next day was Patti's birthday and he was going to take her to Las Vegas.

94

'I don't know when we're going to leave. We are just going to get up and go.'

Combs hung up the phone. It was quiet for a while, then Julie heard what sounded like bundles of paper being slapped down, one on top of another.

'This is forty-nine,' said Patti.

'These are five each,' said Combs.

'How much did Rick say he had here?'

'Ninety-three, that's what I've got.'

'A whole bag of money,' said Patti. 'I'm not parting with it easily.'

Wisconsin, where Julie Desm was born, and Santa Cruz, California, where she spent most of her childhood, were her idea of real America. When she first became a cop (in Fresno, California, in 1981) and volunteered for narcotics work, she imagined she would work undercover on tranquil student campuses. One month after she transferred to the DEA, and graduated from the academy, she was given her first assignment: Los Angeles. It was a city she had lived in briefly as a child and sworn she would never return to. She hated the place.

So, too, did Neil Van Horn, the most senior agent in her group. He'd spent the seventeen years of his law enforcement career in Portland, Oregon, the last eight of them with the DEA. He was more than content to stay there. DEA headquarters in Washington had decided otherwise, and sent him south.

Their mutual antagonism towards Los Angeles cemented the rapport between them. Van Horn was vastly more experienced than Julie but it was her case. She got to lie on the floor; she also got to call the shots.

'What do you want to do?' said Van Horn.

'Seize the money.'

'Sounds good. We're going to need a warrant.'

But before Julie and Van Horn could begin the laborious process of applying for one, Combs and Patti received a surprise visitor; surprising to the DEA, at least. They didn't know he was there until Julie heard a third voice, coming from the crack beneath the interconnecting door.

It was, they later discovered, the lawyer's son. He left room 618 with a white plastic bag slung over his right shoulder. He drove off in a black Cadillac which the surveillance team followed to his father's house in Canon Drive. Julie briefly considered then

95

rejected the idea of obtaining a warrant for the lawyer's house. He might be a dirtbag lawyer but he was also a prominent one, with good connections to the US Attorney's office in Los Angeles. Any raid on his home would require much stronger evidence than she had.

Instead she and Van Horn concentrated on showing 'probable cause' to justify a raid on the room next door to theirs at the Beverly Pavilion Hotel. Their application for a warrant ran to thirty-two hand-written pages, and at 3.00 a.m. it was duly signed by a federal magistrate wearing his pyjamas. It listed every reason they could think of to cast suspicion on Ernest Franz Combs; every reason bar one. Nowhere was it mentioned that the reason the DEA knew Combs was involved in a major drug deal was because of a telephone tap 9,400 miles away in Spain.

'Neil, I do not want to bust this man,' said Julie. She was furious, ranting. What was she going to do? What would happen to Lovato's case? Had she blown it? Why was Ernie Combs such a blithering idiot? She went on and on in this fashion, pacing her hotel room.

'What are your options?' said Van Horn after she'd vented her anger.

She thought for a while and then said: 'None, right?' It was true.

They'd found money in room 618: $44,333 in cash; less than they'd hoped but still a satisfactory haul. If that had been it, Combs would have been set free. He would have reported the loss to Marks, they would both have celebrated his narrow escape, and then – with any luck – he would have led the DEA to a much bigger haul.

Unfortunately they'd also found 576 grams of hashish, 270 grams of liquid Demerol (a brand of narcotic used as a sedative), fourteen syringes, a pipe used to smoke hashish, and a .38 revolver. Since Combs was already on bond on felony drug charges, all or any of the items were sufficient to make his arrest mandatory. Julie had no choice. She had to take him in.

And, having arrested Combs, she had no choice but to file a case report, known as a 'DEA 6' – a form that requires agents to detail the genesis as well as the outcome of their investigations. Writing a good DEA 6 is close to being an art form. It needs to be as explicit as possible, for the benefit of supervisors and other agents working on related cases. At the same time it needs to be as cautious as possible because, sooner or later, under the pre-trial 'discovery' rules, almost all DEA 6s end up in the hands of defence attorneys. All too often, they also end up in the hands of their clients, who can learn a great deal about DEA methods and sources from ill-considered disclosures.

Julie thought long and hard about how to describe the genesis of the Combs case. Finally she decided she had no choice but to state that her investigation derived from 'information developed by Special Agent Craig Lovato in Madrid'.

She thought her phrasing was sufficiently ambiguous to protect the phone tap. She also thought that by the time her DEA 6 got into the hands of Ernie Combs's dirtbag lawyer, the Howard Marks case would, surely, be history.

FOUR

The last time Patrick Lane had seen his brother-in-law was in 1982. Patrick was then living in Santa Cruz, California, in occasional contact with Peter Combs. Howard had recently been released from prison in England. They met in Vancouver, Canada – since Howard was still a fugitive from the Las Vegas charges, and dare not enter America – and spent four or five days catching up on old times. Patrick later calculated that Howard's real purpose in proposing the meeting was to re-establish contact with Combs, but at the time he was not so cynical. Howard brought with him to Vancouver as a gift a fine bottle of wine: a vintage year of Brunello di Montalcino, bottled by Biondi Santi, which Patrick had discovered, from reading the novels of Richard Condon, was a favourite of the top Mafiosi in New York. It turned out to be an extremely expensive present – expensive, that is, for Patrick.

Their reunion in Vancouver over, Patrick was refused re-entry into the United States on the grounds that he had previously overstayed his visitor's visa. The Canadians put him on the first plane to Europe, and he ended up in Amsterdam with very little money and no immediate prospect of rejoining his wife and children in California. His only option, he decided, was to take the cheapest flight to Mexico, and attempt to sneak across the American border as a wet-back.

In some ways the prospect appealed to him. As a young man, he'd been driven by a sense of adventure and what he described as 'the call of wild places'.

At the age of thirteen he cycled around England to find his 'wicked uncle Alan', his father's disgraced brother. At fourteen he spent the summer cycling around Europe – through the Ardennes, down the Rhine, along the Necker, around the Alps, through northern Italy and back through France, in time for the first day of school. At fifteen he went through Spain to Morocco, motivated by a desire to smoke hashish and unable to think of anywhere closer to find it. At sixteen he tried getting into Albania, and eventually reached the Turkish border with Iran. At seventeen, after leaving school, he went to America. He hitch-hiked around Canada, the USA and Mexico, getting as far as Guatemala. He sang in a night-club in Acapulco. He hung out with the then unknown Carlos Fuentes, who had just completed *Where the Air is Clear* and who turned him on to mushrooms and psyliciben and introduced him to Sybil Burton. In San Francisco he met all the Beats. Lawrence Ferlinghetti caught him stealing books from City Lights, but Patrick was able to introduce himself as a friend of William S. Burroughs, whom he'd met in Tangier – and, thus, forgiven, he smoked pot and dropped acid with Ferlinghetti. He spent three months painfully hitch-hiking from the Texas border to North Carolina through the deep south in 1965, just after Watts, with long hair and torn jeans, jeered at in every redneck town along the way. By the time he enrolled at Sussex university, where he met Howard, he had enough adventures to fill a book. And the travel continued: Asia always beckoned. In the university vacations he would head east along the hippy trail to Afghanistan, the Hindu Kush and the High Parmirs. He usually had no money and lived off the land, sleeping under bridges, eating what he could find. Despite the insanely dangerous situations he wandered into, no harm ever befell him.

Attempting to get back into the United States, Patrick Lane flew from Amsterdam to Mexico City, rapidly running out of money, and headed for the border at Tijuana. It took about three days, using tiny local planes, hopping from one fly-blown town to another.

In Tijuana he checked into a hotel 'of character' and phoned his sister Natasha, by now released from a Mexican jail and living in San Diego. He needed contacts who could help him cross the border. She recommended her friend Rodolfo, who could be found at the local jail. Rodolfo agreed to meet Patrick at the hotel. 'How will I recognize you?' Patrick asked. 'I'll be in black,' said Rodolfo.

Standing about 6 feet 6 inches tall, blocking the doorway, in black boots, black trousers, black shirt and a large black hat, Rodolfo was the baddest, meanest, most bloodthirsty-looking man Patrick had ever seen. (Later, he would say that he made Craig Lovato look like a member of the Vienna Boys' Choir.) 'I'm Rodolfo,' he said. 'If you're Natasha's brother, you OK people.' They sat in the bar while Rodolfo emptied a bottle of tequila and described how Patrick should cross the border.

The plan was for him to walk across the bridge that leads to the US as though he were a local American who had visited Tijuana for a night of heavy drinking and whoring. Rodolfo was to take all Patrick's possessions – passport, driver's licence, his accountant's pinstripe suit and the presents for his children – and transport them across the border later.

Wearing jeans and a shirt, smelling of drink, and with a hip flask of El Presidente brandy in his back pocket, he lurched towards the US border station.

'American citizen?' the guard asked.

'Do the Padres play ball?' he replied, and lurched on. Back in the US, he took a cab to Natasha's house in San Diego where, a few days later, Rodolfo arrived with his bag. He told Patrick it had been no problem getting it across the border: 'I hid it in the back of the pick-up, *amigo*, beneath fifty bales of marijuana.' He wasn't kidding: Patrick's bag reeked of the pungent smell.

The bottle of fine Brunello di Montalcino survived the long journey from Vancouver intact. Patrick let it stand for a couple of years. Then one evening – probably a wedding anniversary – he opened it. He decanted it carefully, and tasted it. It was undrinkable. He sorrowfully poured the precious liquid down the sink.

But Patrick kept the bottle as a memento and in time it became for him a potent symbol of his brother-in-law: well-travelled, great story, impressive label – an empty bottle which ended up costing him a fortune and left nothing but a bitter taste. Howard's gift.

Patrick resolved his problems with the American immigration authorities, eventually obtaining a green card that allowed him to live and work legally in the United States.

He got a job at $50,000 a year with the American International Financial Group and on 1 January 1986 moved with his family from Santa Cruz to Miami, Florida. He had an American Express card, a company car and a business card that said vice-president on it. He was joining the Chamber of Commerce, and his wife, Jude, got their rented house in Coral Gables ready in case he wanted to bring any fellow vice-presidents home after work. He was approaching his fortieth birthday. He felt he had finally 'made it'.

Then Howard called.

Patrick thought his relationship with Howard was unique. He felt very strongly that they shared a humour and a perspective that was exclusively theirs. Even after not seeing each other for a long time, as soon as they spoke, the closeness and understanding were immediately there. In many ways, the relationship was even stronger on the phone. They spoke their own private code (not because they knew Craig Lovato was listening but because that's how they communicated). The word and mind games they played were enhanced, Howard's constant laughter even more infectious. On the telephone, Patrick found himself pulled into a private and exclusive little world of magic, strangely exhilarated.

He'd always been stimulated by Howard. For fifteen years he had soaked up Howard's stories of dope dealing, fascinated not by the reality but by his own romantic images of 'the great game'; of Howard and his associates battling the 'grey forces' to keep the world supplied with pot. They may have been concerned with the net profit on the streets of London or Los Angeles. All he heard was the lapping of water against the dhow. He wanted to know what it felt like to sit there, under the stars, hands trailing over the edge in the warm waters of the Gulf. He wanted to know what they were thinking, crossing the mountain pass at night with a trail of mules: were they frightened? He observed it all through rose-coloured spectacles, imagining his brother-in-law as an intrepid adventurer, engaged in deeds of derring-do in exotic locales.

And, from time to time, he'd done his bit to help.

In 1968, having obtained an arts degree from Sussex university, Patrick quit drugs and decided to start a new life. He worked his way slowly through *Opportunities for Graduates*, rejecting everything through to and including Zoology. Then, following his father's insistent advice – 'It finally does not matter what you do, as long as you do *something*' – he went back to the beginning of the list and chose the first item on it: accountancy. He wanted something completely alien to the hippy, left-wing, student world of drugs. He donned a bowler hat and joined the firm of Price Waterhouse in the City of London. His work was mainly concerned with management organization and information flow, so the fact that he was almost innumerate scarcely mattered.

By the early 1970s many of his friends from university had set

101

up businesses and needed help. Many others had become dope dealers and were trying to set up businesses. Because of his expertise, they turned to Patrick for advice, and eventually he left Price Waterhouse, threw his bowler off London Bridge, and became, effectively, the office manager for a number of people – including Graham Plinston, Howard's original partner in the dope business.

He did not launder money for Plinston; there was no need, since Plinston had already set up his own numbered Swiss accounts. What Plinston wanted was an efficient business manager to run his British interests, which included a property company and a carpet shop in London. Patrick's job was to rent offices, pay taxes, hire workers, open up at 9.00 a.m. and close at 5.00 p.m. All the money that he worked with in London was already laundered. The legitimate British companies would receive legitimate loans from respectable Swiss banks, and pay interest.

But at least once there was more to Patrick's involvement than that. The Plinston–Marks organization faced a major crisis when one of its members was arrested with 20lb of hashish from one of the Shannon airport loads. Worse, his rented car was seized. It sat outside Hammersmith police station in west London, with a further 80lb of hash still undiscovered in the locked trunk. Patrick volunteered to rescue it. He called the AA, claiming to have lost his car keys, and a patrolman was sent to open the trunk. Patrick calmly removed two suitcases containing the hash, and hailed a cab.

It was entirely his own idea. Howard had merely called him to explain the problem. 'Are you sure, Pat?' he'd said when Patrick volunteered. 'You don't have to, mind. God, that would be really great. But you're sure, now? Don't do it unless you really want to. God! That would really save the day. Take care, now.'

Howard rarely asked people to do anything. His victims almost always chose their own fates.

Patrick Lane's formidable reputation as an international financial expert, a man who knew how to move money, stemmed from a gesture that was quintessentially Howard.

In 1973, Patrick and his wife, pregnant with their first child, moved to France, buying a dilapidated mill in the Dordogne. Patrick eventually got a job teaching at Dordogne College, and occasionally he and Jude would attend the cocktail parties of other British expatriates and listen to their grumblings about ruinous taxation rates and the need for trust funds in the Cayman Islands

102

and discretionary Luxembourg accounts. Patrick gradually decided that this was an area which fascinated him, and out of which he could make a living.

In the summer of 1977 – one of the wettest on record – he put Jude, pregnant again, and their daughter, Peggy, into their Renault 4 van and embarked on a grand financial camping tour of Europe. They visited Switzerland, Italy, Austria, Liechtenstein, Germany, Luxembourg, Belgium and Holland. They would pull up outside a bank or a set of law offices. Patrick would climb into the back of the van to change into his suit and tie, and then enter the wood-panelled offices as a wealthy English gentleman, considering opening up a trust fund. The biggest threat to his marriage came when bankers would take him out to lunch and Jude and Peggy would be left in the cramped and muddy van, peering through the steamed-up windows as he was taken off to a fancy restaurant. They would eventually drive to a muddy field to camp for the night, and move on to the next financial capital the next day. By the time they returned to the old mill, Patrick had acquired a small army of banking contacts and an impressive library of information.

Then Howard, who had been on the run since 1973, and Judy, who was also pregnant, returned to their lives. Howard was very interested in what Patrick was doing, and very encouraging. 'Here's ten grand,' he said. 'Go and check out the Caribbean.'

Patrick visited every single island between Miami and Caracas. Everywhere he went he opened bank accounts, depositing Howard's money in $50 chunks. Many of the banks gave him chequebooks; he eventually had a collection of forty or fifty. On each island he would grab phone directories and anything published by the local Chamber of Commerce. He would visit lawyers and bankers and talk to people in hotel bars and airports. He returned to France a walking encyclopedia of financial regulations in the Caribbean.

There seemed to be no point to it, other than Howard's fascination. It was like a game. Patrick would open a map of the Caribbean and say: 'Pick a country.' Howard would close his eyes and point.

'Saint Martin. French or Dutch?'

'Dutch.'

Patrick would transfer $500 of Howard's money to his account in the Dutch half of Saint Martin, and then order books from Brentano's on Fifth Avenue, paying with the Caribbean cheques. It worked. Books started arriving. When the account ran low, Howard would give Patrick more money and pick another country.

He would phone Patrick up and order lists of books and records, or the latest Japanese gizmo. It was an expensive and inefficient way to conduct his private banking but Patrick was truly learning about international banking; Howard, his willing apprentice.

By 1980, when Patrick moved to America after Howard's arrest, he really was an expert. He had expanded worldwide. He had accounts in Switzerland and in Vanuatu and the Marshall Islands in the Pacific. He read voraciously, and corresponded with people from Liberia to Uruguay. He had impressive contacts on Wall Street, and was welcomed there as an authority.

Patrick Lane was certainly a man who knew how to move money.

Palma, 13 April 1986

The disturbing news that Peter Combs had been arrested by the DEA was delivered to Marks by Gerry Wills in contorted code, though Howard seemed to have no difficulty in grasping what had happened.

'Our friend had a little problem,' said Wills.

'Oh, did he?'

'Yeah, that medical problem he had before, he had a little bit of a relapse. And the ambulance came and got him about five in morning and hauled him off to hospital.'

'Really?'

'Now, from what I understand it's not anything too serious, but I guess they're just going to keep him in there for a while. For observation.'

'Oh, dear, dear.'

'The doctor finally just moved in right next door and observed him for a while and said he needed to go into the hospital . . . A couple of them would have watched him for probably a day or two . . . They heard him talking about going on vacation. They just thought he was not healthy enough to do that.'

'How long is he likely to be there?' Marks asked. 'Like days and days?'

'Maybe a few months at least,' said Wills. 'That was the last thing I heard, that he wasn't healthy enough to be walking around . . . I think what they want to do is just hold him in there till his operation.'

'Jesus!'

*　　*　　*

Craig Lovato had not disagreed with Julie Desm's decision to arrest Combs. He was, however, alarmed by it; apprehensive that Marks, with his celebrated nose for trouble, might somehow realize that Combs was not the victim of sheer bad luck.

But Marks showed no sign of it. He seemed to accept Wills's assurance that nothing very serious happened – 'It's not like he's had a heart attack, or anything' – and that his arrest might even be a blessing in disguise. Combs's addiction to Demerol was so serious, Wills had been willing to take bets on how much longer he would live.

'The other day he like fish flopped and almost died in front of me and my family,' said Wills.

'God!' said Marks.

'He's very, very, very decrepit. Just to go over and see him sit in his bed in that room that's always real dark and real cold, and you go in there and he's in bed in his pyjamas, and just sweat pouring off his face . . . It's a very unnerving sight.'

But as they chatted on, oblivious to Lovato and his slowly spinning reels of tape, it dawned on both of them that Combs's forced absence presented a problem. Among other things, he was to have been responsible for laundering a large share of the profits. It was Wills who proposed a solution.

'I wouldn't mind getting in touch with Pat,' he said. 'With your brother-in-law. I don't know if he has entered into your plans.'

'Yeah, for sure. I mean, obviously now I'm not going to be able to use my friend. It's just occurred to me, I'm going to be stuck, aren't I?'

Lovato knew immediately who 'Pat' was. There were a dozen references to him in *High Time*, describing him variously as Graham Plinston's 'accountant', Howard's 'money manager' and 'a romantic poser with a plausible upper-class manner and dry wit'.

What he didn't know was where 'Pat' was – until Howard obligingly lifted the phone and dialled a number in Miami, Florida.

'I was just wondering whether you still do business?' said Marks.

'Sure,' Patrick Lane replied.

When the call came, Patrick's carefully structured new life in Miami was beginning to disintegrate. The American International Finance Group (AIFG) was not as solid or substantial as it sounded. Raoul del Cristo, the Cuban-American owner and Patrick's good friend,

105

had created an illusion, reinforced only by his considerable charm and energy.

They had met in the late 1970s when Del Cristo was a director of the Deak Perera brokerage firm and an *éminence grise* of Wall Street. He was a larger-than-life figure, with a silent interest in banks and various other companies, and he exuded a raw power. A genuine friendship developed between the two men: they complemented each other, and Del Cristo would entertain Patrick lavishly in the Wall Street dining clubs, or at one of his several homes. They basked in mutual admiration.

Then in 1984 Del Cristo's eldest and recently married son, Oscar, was diagnosed as having leukaemia and within seven months was dead, at the age of twenty-four. Del Cristo was inconsolable. His business affairs fell into chaos. Faced with the need to retrench and consolidate, Del Cristo decided to bring all his interests into a new holding company, AIFG, and to move to Miami where he had family, homes and offices.

Within months of joining AIFG Patrick discovered the business was in serious trouble. One of the outposts of the Del Cristo empire was European Smoked Fish, housed in a vast warehouse complex in Miami, which was haemorrhaging money, eating up Del Cristo's rapidly shrinking cash reserves.

Patrick was put in charge of turning the company around. He knew nothing about fish and was faced with dozens of hostile, unproductive employees and sub-contractors. Worse, he discovered they were buying condemned seafood, cleaning it up and selling it off to restaurants. Before Del Cristo could be arrested for causing mass food-poisoning, Patrick hired a gang of Haitian roofers, bodily ejected everybody from the premises, and changed the locks.

His plan was to sell off the plant and machinery, and forget about fish. But no one wanted to buy the fish factory – unless, perhaps, it could be turned into a going concern. And so, while Howard considered how to replace Peter Combs, Patrick abandoned his pinstripe suit, donned a pair of Wellington boots, and set out to learn everything there was to know about the business.

He was far too busy to listen to Howard's siren call. Yet he did.

In a series of telephone calls overheard by Lovato during early April, Marks told Lane that he anticipated receiving between $200,000 and $300,000 a week for ten weeks.

'Now is this yours, or are you acting on behalf of?' said Patrick.

'I suppose I'm about 25 per cent of it,' said Howard.

'Well, congratulations, brother.'

Marks said he wanted the money moved to 'the other side': most of it to 'Bruce's place', to 'my partner, for want of a better word'; the rest of it, 'my personal', to 'Deverner'.

'To be spent for eating and drinking,' said Patrick.

'Exactly.'

Patrick said he was not willing to take the responsibility for getting the money from the West Coast to New York; somebody else would have to do that. Once it was there, however, and if the amounts were 'not outrageous' there would be 'absolutely no problem'.

Palma, 16 April 1986

Nothing could now persuade Lovato to leave the listening room for more than a few minutes at a time. He haunted the place, willing the recorders to click on, waiting for the call that he *knew* would provide the breakthrough.

'Hello?'

'Oh, hello. How are you?' said Howard.

It was a bad line but the voice on the other end of it was unmistakable: John Denbigh, or 'Old John', or 'the Vicar', as Howard sometimes called him to other people. He was one of the more frequent callers because he took care of Howard's personal affairs in London. Most of his calls that Lovato had listened to were totally innocuous, concerning such things as the maisonette in Cathcart Road, domestic bills that needed paying, repairs to Howard's car. Not today.

'I'm on this air phone thing,' said Denbigh, meaning a cellular phone, perhaps to explain why the line was so bad.

'So I can talk OK, I can say anything, yeah?' said Howard.

'Yeah, I suppose so.'

'Right. You know my friend Pete?'

'Who?'

'Pete.'

'Pete?'

'Pete.'

'Pete? Oh, yeah.'

'Well, he's inside again, unfortunately.'

'Yeah? He's in hospital, yeah?'

'Yes. I mean it's his past catching up with him rather than anything present, but it means he isn't there to take care of my interests.'

'Yeah. So what's the problem?'

'Well, I just feel more strongly than ever that someone ought to go over there, you know?'

'Go over there?'

'Yes.'

'What, to get the money?'

'Yes.'

'Go out there and then come back?'

'Go out there and stay for a bit, about a week or so, yeah? Since Pete's gone it's just a bit worrying.'

'I can go for about a week, or two weeks. I can putter off down to . . . where is it? Down to . . . So, I'll take a holiday and go to Santa Barbara.'

'Right. Yes. Thanks a lot.'

'My goodness, it's been a while since I've been there.'

'I know. It's been a long time.'

'It's a wonderful place to go, isn't it?'

'Oh, yes.'

'It's a wonderful place to go. I'll ask to fly. What line should I fly? Can't go British Airways because they're in trouble now. You read that in the paper? Madness.'

'Yeah, we get the news.'

'[Margaret Thatcher] is speaking in Parliament today. About madness. I mean, of course she needs a lesson but the unions are totally out of hand.'

'I think so, too. I think it's the system.'

'OK, you take care,' said Denbigh.

'Thanks a lot,' said Howard. 'Have a good day.'

John Denbigh's wife, Elizabeth, and Howard Marks shared the same birthday. Marks and Denbigh seemed to have little else in common. Denbigh would not use illegal drugs, for example, and he was openly disapproving, even self-righteous, of the sexual promiscuity of some of Howard's associates (which is why they dubbed him 'the Vicar').

Yet Howard was immensely fond of Denbigh – as he was of Patrick Lane. Since he liked both of them, he assumed they liked each other. He was wrong.

Lane dismissed Denbigh as a walking cliché and an imposter. He believed that his rough-diamond, unpretentious, man-of-the-people persona, which so appealed to Howard, was a self-conscious sham. He tired of listening to his convoluted ramblings, his man-of-the-street philosophies, and felt that the effort required was finally not worthwhile. He had no doubt that Denbigh, for his part, saw him as the embodiment of every pansy-waisted chinless-wonder Englishman.

The last time they'd met was in London in 1985, when Patrick and his family went to England to collect their green cards. Howard had insisted that 'Old John' take care of them, and Denbigh had duly invited them to dinner at his house. It was a disaster. Denbigh was drunk; he insulted the Lanes and frightened their children. They fled the house, pursued by Denbigh, and he and Patrick came to blows in the street. Patrick's last words were: 'John, you are a drunken, bullying old bore.'

Marks was unaware of all that when he made his plans to fill the vacuum left by Peter Combs. On 23 April he flew to London where, observed by a surveillance team from Her Majesty's Customs, he made the final arrangements for Denbigh's trip to California.

Lovato took the opportunity to return to Madrid to visit his three sons from his first marriage, who were staying with him in Spain. He also made his own travel plans. He, too, was going to California. The time had come, he felt, to 'get this show on the road'.

Los Angeles, 4 and 5 May 1986

Patrick Lane sat in his room at the Westwood Plaza Holiday Inn on Wilshire Boulevard, waiting for a phone call. He was expecting to meet a man whom he and Howard always referred to on the phone as 'Mr Ecstasy'. He didn't know Mr Ecstasy's real name was Gerald Wills. He did know that Mr Ecstasy was a major 'investor' in Howard's latest load. He hoped to be able to persuade him to invest some of his vast profits in Raoul del Cristo's failing empire.

When the phone rang, a voice – an English Cockney voice – said: 'Are you in? OK, somebody's coming to the door in a minute.' Lane thought it might have been Denbigh. Whoever it was hung up.

A few minutes later there was a knock on the door. When Lane opened it there was nobody there; only a suitcase standing abandoned on the threshold. He took the case into the room and opened it. It contained ten manila envelopes with more cash than he'd seen for a very long time; about $100,000 by his estimate.

He waited for another call but it never came. He rang the telephone number Howard had given him for Mr Ecstasy – Wills's answering service – and left a message, but Mr Ecstasy did not call back.

As time passed, Lane's impatience and then his resentment grew. He realized there was not going to be any meeting with Mr Ecstasy, and no discussion about investments. He had fully expected to collect money for Howard and take it to New York. He had not expected to be treated like a menial courier.

The next morning he tried to reach Mr Ecstasy again, but none of his calls were returned. Heading for the airport, he decided to abandon the suitcase in a baggage locker but couldn't go through with it. Still unable to reach Mr Ecstasy, he accepted that he had no choice but to take the money to New York.

When his Pan Am flight was called he went to the security checkpoint, ready to place the suitcase on the belt that would take it through the X-ray machine. It was then that his indignation turned to alarm.

He'd belatedly realized that while he was going only to New York, the flight was going on to London and Zürich. Taking $100,000 across the country was not illegal; taking it out of the country, without reporting it, was. What if the security people – and there seemed to be a lot of them – thought he was going to Zürich? What if the X-ray machine detected the money? What if he was asked to explain where the money had come from? 'Somebody left it outside my hotel room' was not an answer they'd be likely to accept. He could not go through with it.

Lane returned to the main terminal and put the suitcase in a baggage locker. He noticed a lot of men with walkie-talkie radios who seemed to be watching him. Close to panic, he went to the men's room and hid the locker key in a toilet-roll holder.

He still could not reach Mr Ecstasy. He left yet another message with the answering service, this one much more urgent, and went to the Pan Am desk to book a later flight to New York. The ticket clerk seemed inordinately suspicious about why he'd changed his plans, and as to why he had no luggage. It occurred to Lane that the clerk thought he'd put a bomb on board the plane. He had visions of them recalling the flight, searching the cabin with sniffer dogs.

He assured the clerk that his luggage was in a locker, and that he was going to retrieve it. But when he returned to the men's room to get the key it had gone.

Pan Am said he would have to call security and get them to open the locker, for a fee of $15. The security men asked him to describe the suitcase, and its contents. 'Manila envelopes,' said Lane. Once they'd confirmed that, they let him take the case.

Finally, he reached Mr Ecstasy, put through by the answering service.

'I can't take it to New York, I think I'm being watched.'

'You are,' said Mr Ecstasy. 'I'm at the airport. I can see you.'

He told Lane to take the shuttle bus to the airport Hilton Hotel and to stand near the check-in desk as though he were about to book a room.

Lane did as he was told. As he stood in line, a tall, blond man came up behind him, picked up the suitcase, and walked away. Mr Ecstasy – he hoped.

Los Angeles, 6 May 1986

If Craig Lovato had learned one thing in his eight years as a DEA agent, it was the need for salesmanship.

Then, as now, the DEA was overwhelmed with cases and potential cases. The majority of drug traffickers in the US went largely unmolested by the agency because there were simply too many of them; they were, by some calculations, more ubiquitous than cab drivers. The DEA had to pick and choose its targets – 'prioritize', in the jargon. Some traffickers (the minor ones, hopefully) were left to other agencies or went free, in order that the big fish might be pursued.

So, when a DEA agent believed that a target was worthy of the DEA's full resources, they had to be able to sell that notion to other agents, and 'the suits' – the supervisors who command the field divisions, and those who occupy the decision-making seats at DEA headquarters in Washington.

Lovato sold his cases by putting together what he called a 'dog and pony show'. In the case of Marks his show would eventually consist of an elaborate presentation, illustrated by half a dozen large wall charts showing what he believed to be the hierarchy of the Marks organization and the extent of its worldwide dealings. In Los Angeles, however, the only visual aid he had was the obvious passion of his argument.

He gave his presentation on Marks to supervisors and agents

from the DEA's Los Angeles office in a conference room at the Hacienda Motel, a mile or so from Los Angeles international airport. (The choice of the Hacienda was ironic for, coincidentally, it was where Denbigh had first stayed when he arrived in Los Angeles a week before.)

His main objective was to win for Julie Desm much more support for her end of the investigation than she had so far received from the LA office. To do that he had to overcome the idea that, given the number of major dealers in Los Angeles, Marks was not very important: that 'when you're up to your ass in alligators, you don't worry about the mosquitos'. The thrust of his argument was that Marks was an alligator, not a mosquito. True, he sat on a remote Mediterranean island. He also sat at the head of a sophisticated and persistent cartel that has shipped and would continue to ship multi-ton loads of dope to Los Angeles until and unless they stopped him.

The conference seemed to go well. An Assistant US Attorney who was present agreed that there was sufficient evidence to prosecute the case against Marks in Los Angeles, provided they could come up with some proof of the load. But in the course of the discussion Lovato made an alarming discovery. For the first time he read Julie Desm's DEA 6, written after the arrest of Combs, and, to his horror, found his own name in it: '. . . information developed by Special Agent Craig Lovato in Madrid'.

'Jesus, Julie!' he said. 'Why not just tell Howard we're tapping his phone?'

She defended her decision on the grounds that she'd had no choice. Her supervisor told Lovato to 'calm down': there was no way any dirtbag lawyer would get hold of the DEA 6 for months, and they could always sanitize the report before handing it over.

Neither of them knew it was already too late.

The call began, unusually, with the sound of seven dollars'-worth of quarters being dropped into the slot of an American payphone. Then John Denbigh's voice came on the line. He did not waste time on formalities.

'Can you call back to Touch's number about eight o'clock or nine o'clock your time?'

'When? How many hours' time from now?' said Marks, sounding slightly puzzled.

'In the morning time. When you get up, before you take the kids to school.'

'Yes, I can, yes.'

'Yeah, but you must go out, you see?'

'Yes, of course.'

'I'll tell you why, because I think . . . You see, I think your dog is sick.'

There was a long pause. Then Marks said: 'Oh, really?'

In his room at the Hacienda Motel, Lovato sat bolt upright. Thanks to Her Majesty's Customs' crash course in Cockney rhyming slang, he knew that 'dog' meant phone. It wasn't very difficult to work out what 'sick' meant.

He'd arranged to call the Palma police station each night to review the tapes of Howard's conversations, recorded in his absence. Usually he was content to listen to a brief sample of each conversation. Not tonight. His phone call to the listening room cost more than $200.

'You know the married couple, and the old fellow went into hospital?' said Denbigh.

'Yeah.'

'We've had a report he's got a new complaint. And it would appear that besides having pleurisy he was most probably bitten by the dog.'

'Oh, I see.'

'So you phone that number in the morning, and tell where you're phoning from, and Touch will give you a tinkle and explain to you.'

'OK, fine. So I shall go somewhere and phone him tomorrow . . . Now, regarding the sickness of the dog, is he seriously ill do you think?'

'Well, it's a possibility that it is, because they've had a report here. Because the married couple, I saw the wife and he had pleurisy, didn't he?'

'That's right.'

'Right, so then the dog bit him and the dog's got rabies . . . They believe that here, anyway. And I'll tell you another thing. You know when it was your lady's birthday, around that period, you were all modelling together weren't you? It says you were all modelling together, you, Touch and some other people.'

'The report says that?'

'Yeah.'

'At the school, yeah?'

'No, no, no, not the school, your capital. There.'

'Oh, where I am now?'

113

'Yes, there or at the capital.'

There was another pause while Marks absorbed the implications. Then a new voice came on the line: Touch.

'Do you understand any of that?' said Gerry Wills.

'Most of it, yes, I think so,' said Marks.

'I think we need to have a good little talk . . . When you get up in the morning.'

'I understand that. I'll go out and call you. Is eight hours' time good?'

'Yeah, the sooner the better.'

They know that Howard's phone is tapped, said Lovato at the tense resumption of the Hacienda conference the next morning. They know that's how we got on to Combs. They know they've been under surveillance. And they know all that because they've got hold of Julie Desm's DEA 6. How?

There were no immediate answers. It would be some time before Julie would learn that the Assistant US Attorney originally in charge of the Combs case had given the prosecution's file to Combs's attorney, unread and unsanitized. It wasn't malicious. He'd quit government service to go into private practice. He'd just wanted to clear his desk.

Lovato left Los Angeles and headed back to Spain, angry and depressed. But at least he had a promise that the Los Angeles office would now commit the necessary resources to the Marks case. Somehow they would find John Denbigh and Gerry Wills. They would find what was left of the load or, if not, the money. Somehow.

Los Angeles, 8 May 1986

John Denbigh had a counter-surveillance technique of his own. He pointed his rented Mustang south on Route 101, pressed the throttle to the floor and kept it there. Crude but effective.

Until then Julie Desm had rather liked her government-issued Buick Somerset. It was small ('Just the right size for a woman,' they'd told her) but it was new, with a fancy digital dashboard. At 85 m.p.h., however, the instruments began flashing apocalyptic warnings of imminent engine seizure and worse. All she could do was bawl over the radio: 'Stay with him. I can't keep up.' Her male colleagues, their cars equipped with suitably masculine

114

8-cylinder engines, cruised smugly by the faltering Buick to take up the chase.

It was sharp-eyed DEA agents from Santa Barbara who'd spotted Denbigh's Mustang. They'd actually been looking for Gerry Wills, who they knew lived somewhere in the Santa Barbara area. They'd first seen the car in Carpinteria and followed it, alerting the Los Angeles office by radio. By the time Julie Desm, Neil Van Horn and a third DEA agent had made the 100-mile journey to Santa Barbara, Denbigh and Wills were sitting down together to lunch.

Now Denbigh was leading them all back to Los Angeles, apparently, at about 100 m.p.h. 'Let me know where he goes,' said Julie over the radio. 'I'll join you.' Eventually.

She caught up with Van Horn, sitting at a table in the piano lounge of the Sheraton Premier Hotel at Universal Studios. Denbigh and another man they'd never seen before sat two tables away, talking in an animated fashion. Desm and Van Horn strained to listen to the conversation – until the piano player came on duty and drowned out any possibility of that.

At 7.30 p.m., Denbigh got up from the table and went to the hotel elevators. Van Horn watched as the indicator showed he had travelled to the sixteenth floor, then followed. He arrived on the floor too late to see which room Denbigh had gone into.

'OK, there's only one exit out of this place,' said Julie. 'I'll sit up on the cliff and watch it.' She parked her car on a high promontory overlooking the hotel and waited for the Mustang to appear. It never did.

When they searched the parking lot, they found no sign of it. The Mustang and Denbigh were gone. They figured out that his ride in the elevator had been a ruse. He'd gone to the sixteenth floor, and straight back down again, and had walked right out of the hotel while they weren't looking – which is what happens when you have three agents running a surveillance instead of twelve.

They'd put an electronic tracking device on the Mustang when it was parked at the hotel, but it didn't work. Van Horn and another agent returned to Santa Barbara and spent the rest of the night looking for the car. They couldn't find it.

What is going on? said Julie. How can this happen to reasonably intelligent people? She was beginning to think the case was jinxed.

While he'd waited for Denbigh at the Sheraton Premier Hotel, Geoffrey Kenion had worked on sketches of a drainage system for

115

his new restaurant in Majorca, which he intended to call Wellies. He'd be able to pay for the work to be done now – thanks to Howard. He would be paid 10 per cent of however much cash he carried back to Palma, less his expenses.

'What he wants to do is build a septic tank,' Denbigh told Marks in apparent disbelief. Thereafter Kenion, once an actor on the London stage, became known as 'Mr Sewage' or 'the Sewage Engineer', even to his face.

While Desm and Van Horn tried in vain to overhear, Denbigh told Kenion that he didn't have the money yet. They arranged to meet in three days' time at the airport Hilton Hotel, a couple of hours before Kenion's flight was due to leave for London.

The DEA failed to find Denbigh in the interim, so there were no agents present when the two men met again and Denbigh gave Kenion $60,000 in 100-dollar bills and a further $40,000 in twenties.

It was almost twice as much as Kenion had expected to carry; a pleasant surprise since his 'commission' would also double. He didn't know where the money came from. He thought it might be prostitution, since he'd heard that Howard owned a massage parlour in the Far East. He didn't really care.

Wherever it had come from, he knew it was illegal to take so much money out of the United States without declaring it. He stuffed $60,000 in the waistband of his trousers, and $40,000 in his socks, and walked through Security, onto the London-bound plane.

Nobody gave him a second glance. He was now $10,000 richer, less expenses. Easy money.

Palma, 13 May 1986

The reels of tape still turned in the listening room, but most of the conversations they now recorded contained only the detail of domestic routine: Judy Marks talking to the plumber; Howard making arrangements to play tennis or to dine with friends; both of them arranging for playmates for their daughters. It was only foresight that allowed Lovato to continue monitoring at least some of Howard's more incriminating discussions.

Some three months before, Lovato had picked up indications that Marks occasionally used the office telephone and the telex of Justo Inarejos Urbana, a Majorcan friend who ran a travel agency in Palma. On 27 February 1986, the Palma police had obtained judicial approval to tap Justo's phone as well.

It was the product of this third tap that told Lovato that John Denbigh had moved from Los Angeles. From Justo's office, Howard phoned him at the Marriott Marquis Hotel in New York City.

The conversation was as ambiguous as Denbigh could make it. He was waiting for 'Straight'. He had to go and see 'the Executive'. 'The Sewage Engineer' was on his way. 'Bruce and his brother in New Jersey' were ready. 'The Chef' could call Canada. 'Touch' had told him to 'sign over the papers'.

And whatever had brought Denbigh to New York carried with it an element of risk. He told Marks: 'The people where I've come from were horrified. They shook my hand and said I must be raving mad.'

Close to midnight Spanish time, Lovato called the DEA's Manhattan office and cajoled them into setting up surveillance on the occupant of room 4010 at the Marriott Hotel.

New York City, 14 and 15 May 1986

John Denbigh had arrived in Manhattan on the 'redeye' flight from California.

When he eventually emerged from his room in the late afternoon, the surveillance team watched him go to the lobby and meet a man in his early thirties with blond hair and fashionable clothes, who said his name was Kevin. They both went to Denbigh's room. A few minutes later Kevin left the hotel and headed downtown, on a bicycle.

At just after 8.30 p.m. another man arrived at Denbigh's room, this one bearded and wearing a black leather jacket. He was carrying a bag of food. Denbigh re-emerged for another brief meeting with Kevin and then returned to his room. At 9.30 p.m. the man in the black jacket drove Denbigh to a house in Greenwich Village where he, and the surveillance team, stayed until four o'clock the next morning.

The surveillance team next saw him at 1.30 p.m. walking to a bar called Clarke's on Third Avenue. He met a woman and two men – one of them six foot tall with striking red hair. Denbigh stayed in the bar for three hours then left with the woman. They walked to a nearby garage, where they got into a gold-coloured Mercedes and drove off.

At which point the surveillance team was called off. New York, like Los Angeles, had more pressing matters to attend to.

The only lead the surveillance team produced was the tag

117

number of the gold-coloured Mercedes, 3526 ANN, which proved to be registered to a John Edward Francis at an address in Yonkers, New York.

The lead was not pursued any further. Had it been, it might have stimulated the interest of even the hard-pressed agents of New York.

John Edward Francis was listed in more than one law enforcement computer, and usually with the notation 'OCC'. The abbreviation stands for 'Organized Crime Connected'.

Francis, the man with the striking red hair in Clarke's bar, was a member of the Mob.

FIVE

The one thing Peter Combs could guarantee was that sooner or later he'd hear from Tom Sunde and Reiner Jacobi. They were the proverbial bad pennies in his life; they *always* turned up.

He was being held without bond in the federal penitentiary on Terminal Island, near Long Beach, when he received their inevitable letter. It said: 'We can help you with your problem. Add these two names to your visitor's list, Rolf Koenig and Werner Graebe.'

It was signed 'Your friends'. Friends!

The last time he'd heard from them was at the beginning of the year, after they had orchestrated yet another attempt to extract money from him. They told him they could get the 1973 Las Vegas charges against him dropped – if he would assist in a complex scheme to sell American microchip technology to Robert Vesco, the fugitive American financier then in hiding in Cuba. The details were far too Byzantine for Combs to absorb but he clearly saw the bottom line: 'Sounds like espionage to me,' he said. Sunde and Jacobi assured him that there was nothing to worry about since this, of course, was another covert operation on behalf of the CIA.

For once they produced some 'proof' of the CIA connection, in the overweight form of Greg Petragus, a large tall man in his early sixties with a shock of grey hair, supposedly the case agent from CIA headquarters in Arlington, Virginia, who Combs had met once before. Petragus flew to Los Angeles to see Combs, promising him the earth in return for his willingness to do his patriotic duty. Combs said he would do nothing until the case against him had been taken care of.

'OK, come to Washington,' said Petragus, 'and bring your attorney with you.'

Combs had more than one attorney, and one of them was not a dirtbag but an eminently respectable Los Angeles lawyer named Thomas Sheridan. He, too, spoke to Petragus, on the telephone to Virginia, attempting in vain to establish his credentials. He told Combs: 'We're not going to Washington if we don't know who we're supposed to meet, and what they want out of you.'

But Petragus bombarded Combs's father with calls, saying that everything had been set up and that Combs should travel to Washington as soon as possible.

Combs – not entirely able to shake the notion that Sunde and Jacobi *might* work for the CIA – called Petragus to say he would come.

'OK, but you need to bring some spending money,' said Petragus.

'What did you have in mind?' said Combs, thinking in terms of perhaps $5,000.

'Bring $200,000.'

Combs exploded. 'That's it!' he told Patti when she asked him what was wrong. 'That is the last thing I'm having to do with those guys – *ever*.'

Friends! In his cell on Terminal Island, Combs tore the letter into shreds. He meant it. He would have nothing more to do with them.

'Guess what?' said Patti when she next came to visit him. She was out on $10,000 bond, staying at a nearby Marriott Hotel. Sunde and Jacobi had checked into the same hotel.

They'd given her some disturbing news, she said. Their arrests at the Beverly Pavilion Hotel had not resulted from sheer bad luck. The DEA were working a major investigation, and they'd tapped Howard's telephone. No, she said, this wasn't another of Tom's stories because he'd shown her some transcripts and there was stuff in there that she knew they'd said on the phone. So it wasn't just a simple possession charge they were looking at. The DEA was trying to make a racketeering case against them.

But Tom and Reiner had a plan, she said. They'd got both of them new passports in fake names with their photographs and everything. No, they weren't lying. They'd shown her the passports and they looked absolutely genuine.

Anyway, the plan: Reiner knew how to fly a helicopter and they were going to fly in to Terminal Island and bust Peter out. All they needed was some money and . . .

'Patti,' said Combs, 'don't talk to them ever again. I mean it, I've really had it with those two guys. Just tell them to get the hell out of our lives.'

If only she had listened.

Maybe she was just out of her depth, or the drugs she and Combs were both addicted to had blunted her judgement. Certainly the responsibility she'd been left with after Peter's incarceration was a great deal more than she could handle.

The proceeds she held from the sale of just part of the Los Angeles load amounted to $1,191,000.

On Peter's instructions, she gave just under $800,000 of that money to his attorney (*not* the eminently respectable one), part of it to pay for his defence, the rest for safekeeping. She hid the remaining $394,000 – most of it owed to Howard Marks – in her father's house in the Sierras, eighty miles east of San Francisco. She couldn't think where else to keep it. Anybody who knew her well would have guessed that's what she'd do with it.

'The DEA thinks you've got money hidden in your father's house,' said Tom Sunde, who knew her better than most. He said the '*federales*' were planning a raid and that she should rescue the money immediately.

Sunde offered to accompany her on the eight-hour drive from Los Angeles. She collected the money from its hiding-place. As they were preparing for the long journey back to Los Angeles, she overheard Sunde on the phone to Jacobi: 'Yeah, we're leaving right now,' he said. She stashed the box containing the money in the back of her TransAm and locked the tailgate. Sunde climbed into the driving seat. 'I'll drive,' he insisted.

Just north of Bakersfield, Sunde pulled over into the parking lot of a large roadside restaurant.

'I've got to make a phone call. Let's get something to eat.'

'No, I'll wait here,' she said. 'Don't want to leave the money.'

'Come on! Who's going to bother with the car? It's all locked up. Let's go.'

So Patti, against her better judgement, went inside the restaurant with Sunde and waited while he made his phone call. 'The line's busy, we'll have to wait,' he said.

Twenty minutes later they returned to the car. The tailgate was unlocked, the money had gone. With a sinking heart Patti realized, belatedly, that a couple of days previously she had let Sunde and Jacobi borrow her car. She now had no doubt they'd taken the opportunity to get an extra key cut.

She confronted Sunde with the accusation but he denied it, countering with characteristic bluster. 'What are you talking about, you're crazy,' he said. 'I had my briefcase in there with presidential papers in it. I had important CIA documents in there. I'm gonna get killed for losing that stuff. Let's get out of here.' She didn't know what to believe. They completed the journey to Los Angeles in total silence.

It was a month before she dared tell Combs what had happened.

Meanwhile he was in 'the hole' – a solitary confinement cell deep in the bowels of Terminal Island. The prison authorities had received word from an anonymous informant of a plan to bust him out of the jail, by helicopter.

Portland, Oregon, 16 May 1986

Informants – 'CIs' – are the DEA's lifeblood. Without those willing to provide intelligence on traffickers and their operations, there would be few significant victories in the war on drugs. But informants also represent a great threat to the DEA. Since it is axiomatic that they must be close to the action in order to report on it, there is always the danger that some CIs will misinterpret or misrepresent their secret relationship with the DEA as a licence to operate. For that reason, the DEA has strict house rules governing the use of informants. Whatever the CI's motive – be it leniency, immunity, money or, very rarely, a sense of public duty – they must be identified, fingerprinted and documented. To protect their identity they are assigned a code-name (in fact a code-number) for use in reports, but the case agents *must* know who they are. And, at the end of the day, they must be willing to testify if necessary.

Julie Desm and Neil Van Horn arrived at Portland's airport from Los Angeles to meet 'Rex' despite that rule. They did not know his name was Reiner Jacobi. Indeed, they knew almost nothing about him, other than the fact he was highly recommended as an informant by US Customs.

Julie had initially refused to meet him. She'd first been approached by Mark Bastan, the Customs agent in San Francisco who had solved the principal mystery of the Dead Fred affair two years before, thanks largely to Rex. Bastan and Rex had remained in occasional touch: whenever Rex passed through San Francisco airport, he would drop in on Bastan and offer his latest intelligence – which recently had concerned the activities of what he called the Howard Marks organization. It was of little direct interest to Bastan since it had nothing to do with San Francisco. But when Rex told him that Julie Desm of the DEA in Los Angeles was investigating Howard Marks, he decided to do her a favour and recommend Rex as an informant.

Problem was, he told her, Rex would not be documented or even identified.

'Forget it,' Julie said. 'We can't do business that way.'

Neil Van Horn, however, with his much greater experience, knew that rules are made to be broken occasionally. Rex was strongly recommended to Van Horn as an informant by Lawrence Ladage of US Customs, whom Van Horn had known when they were both stationed in Portland.

'You should meet him. He knows a lot,' said Ladage, and, with the consent of his group supervisor, Van Horn agreed to fly to Portland for a rendezvous with Rex at the airport. Ladage told him to go to the meeting alone, but Van Horn would not do that – thought he did not tell Ladage. He invited Julie to go with him: 'It's your case,' he said.

They met in the airport terminal. If Jacobi was taken aback by Julie's presence he did not show it.

'This is Julie Desm,' said Van Horn.

'Ah, yes,' Jacobi replied, having introduced himself as Rex. 'I feel as if I know you. I've seen your name on so many Teletypes.'

Julie was stunned. Informants, even exceptional ones, did not normally have access to DEA Teletypes, which are regarded as highly confidential within the agency and are therefore sometimes extremely candid. 'Where?' she demanded.

'At the US Embassy in Bonn,' Rex explained, giving her the benefit of his most charming smile. It was possible. The Marks investigation was being conducted in more than a dozen countries and the DEA office in the West German capital might have been on the distribution list. Even so, that didn't explain how Rex had gained access to them. He wasn't inclined to tell her, dismissing her further questions with a shrug.

They went to a nearby hotel, where the three of them asked for rooms. Jacobi checked in under the name Rex Johnson, paying cash in advance, avoiding the need to show any identification. Then they went to his room to talk, so that Rex could tell them what he knew about the Howard Marks organization.

There was no doubt about it; he knew a lot. Desm and Van Horn listened carefully as he told them all about Howard Marks: his Oxford degree; his involvement with the British Secret Intelligence Service and James McCann of the Provisional IRA; his celebrated trial and acquittal. He said that Judith Marks had two sisters, one of whom had been arrested and jailed in Mexico on drug charges. Since the DEA agents had never read *High Time*, or even heard of the book, most of it was new to them.

Rex reeled off the names and duties of Marks's associates: Ernest Combs of course, and Gerry Wills, who were the West Coast distributors; Saleem Malik in Pakistan, the supplier of the hashish; John Denbigh, Howard's right-hand man; Patrick Lane, his brother-in-law and money launderer; Phillip Sparrowhawk, his marijuana supplier in Thailand, and more. He knew many of the codes used in organization's conversations – including the formula of the 'interstate' telephone code.

None of this was new to Desm and Van Horn – it was the same cast list and scenario presented by Craig Lovato – but they found it impressive that Rex knew so much, and had provided useful confirmation.

It was only the next morning, when the debriefing of Rex resumed, that he seemed less sure of himself. Pressed for precise details of the Los Angeles load, he confessed that he did not work alone. He said he had an associate he would identify only his initials, 'RW', who was the 'inside man' on this operation. RW was presently in San Francisco, he said. Rex volunteered to call him, to get answers to the agents' outstanding questions.

Thus, he was able to tell them that 'Mozambique', where the load had arrived, was Morro Bay on the Californian coast, 100 miles north of Los Angeles. A large part of the load still remained to be sold.

There was only one subject on which Rex would not volunteer any information whatsoever: his own and RW's identities. He said they had good reason not to trust the DEA – present company excepted, of course. He said it was vitally important that they did not write up a report about the meeting, the information he had given them, or even his existence.

Van Horn warned him that DEA informants had to be documented before they could be paid. Rex said they didn't want money from the DEA. He implied, though he did not say, that they were already on the payroll of another agency of the US government; an agency too secretive to be named.

About a week after the Portland meeting, Jacobi called Julie Desm at her office in Los Angeles. He said he was in town and needed to see her immediately. He refused to go to the DEA office on grounds of 'security'. He proposed a meeting at an outdoor café at the Bonaventure Hotel at Redondo Beach. She should come alone, he said.

Fat chance. There was no way she was going to meet Rex alone. Van Horn was not in the office, so she persuaded another agent to provide back-up and 'eyeball' the meeting from a circumspect but limited distance.

When she got to the café, Rex was not alone. His companion was Tom Sunde, of course, but he introduced him as 'RW, my associate'. Again Rex stressed the need for her absolute discretion; nothing in writing, please.

What they mainly wanted to talk about was Peter Combs's dirtbag attorney. They said he had laundered Combs's drug profits for years (a disclosure that no DEA agent in Los Angeles would have doubted) and that 'Connolly's' in the Marks organization code meant Los Angeles, because 'Doctor Connolly' was his lawyer's nickname. They said he had bought his lavish home in Beverly Hills with Combs's money. That favour notwithstanding, he had recently ripped off more than $350,000 from Patti Hayes. Since the money was owed to Howard Marks, and she could not pay it, there was some dissension within the organization.

Throughout the meeting there were more hints, heavier this time, that Rex and RW also worked for the US government, in roles they were not at liberty to discuss.

Julie thought this was nonsense, but she didn't challenge them. Her group supervisor had told her to 'play along' with whatever fiction they invented because, whoever they were, they surely had the goods on Howard Marks.

Afterwards, she phoned Lovato in Palma. 'God, Craig, they know everything,' she told him.

'Yeah, Julie, but who *are* they?'

Palma, last two weeks of May 1986

Sometimes Howard would get careless, or lazy, and make incriminating calls from home. Sometimes he would make or take calls in Justo's travel agency, and so Lovato would get them on tape.

But there was no denying that the flow of information covertly gained had slowed to a trickle. Marks knew Lovato was still listening to his home telephones, and he would sometimes lift the receiver and place it near to one of the speakers of his high-quality stereo system, and play music. He was into his classical phase at the time and the choice of music was always highbrow. He did it out of mischief rather than consideration, but Lovato appreciated the chance to expand his musical education 'That's nice, Howard,' he would say to himself. (In communiqués, Lovato always referred to Marks as 'Dennis Howard Marks', no matter how often it was repeated, as though the three names were inseparable. But Marks never used the name Dennis, and in conversation and in talking to himself, Lovato always called Marks 'Howard' – which is how he thought of him.)

Marks also suspected that Justo's office phone was tapped – or at least, he used it less and less.

Instead, John Denbigh would call Marks at home and say: 'How are you?'

'I'm fine,' Howard would say. 'I'm going out for a drink,' and he would give a time.

'OK, have a good time. 'Bye.'

And Lovato knew that Denbigh would be phoning Marks for a detailed talk at some prearranged number. This was confirmed when Peter Nelson of Her Majesty's Customs passed on intelligence information he had obtained from Bangkok about a telephone conversation between Marks and Phillip Sparrowhawk. Howard had told Sparrowhawk: 'You can ring me at home, but if I say I'm going out for a drink, then ring me back at my Spanish bar.'

Which bar? There were hundreds to choose from in Palma, Palma Nova, Portals Nous and Magaluf, all of which were within thirty minutes' drive of Howard's house.

Lovato knew he would somehow have to discover which phone or phones Marks was using. It was a matter of urgency. In Madrid the head of the DEA office said if Craig couldn't find the phones, and fast, the Marks investigation would be called off.

Once, in the middle of the Nevada desert, on the airstrip of an old abandoned gold mine, Craig Lovato had stood with a man named Bernie Lawrence, staring at a mess of tracks in the sand. Craig, who had quit the Las Vegas sheriff's department for the state drugs agency – the Nevada Division for the Investigation of Narcotics (NDIN) – learned nothing from the tracks. As far as he was concerned, they could have been made ten minutes or ten weeks ago.

Bernie Lawrence, who had been a lion hunter and tracker in Mexico for forty years until he retired, looked at the same set of tracks and described the events that had caused them as if he'd been there to see.

'Well, Craig,' he said, 'you had 450lb off-loaded from a Piper Navajo here last night, between eleven and two o'clock. The day before that you had the airplane come in, but they didn't off-load anything, all they did was take on fuel. There was a young tall guy and an old guy here in a truck, delivering the fuel and picking up the load. The guy you want to talk to is the old guy because he's the one who will talk to you. He'll give up the whole shit.'

'You pulling my leg? How do you know all that?'

Very patiently the old hunter explained. He knew the plane was a Navajo because of the width of the tracks left by the wheels on the undercarriage. He knew they'd unloaded 450lb because he'd counted ten distinct markings made by the gunnysacks and, traditionally, Mexican marijuana came in 20-kilo bales – of approximately 45lb each.

He knew the plane and the truck had been to the airstrip twice, and he could distinguish between the separate tracks they'd left on each occasion, because a brief rainstorm in the interval had left markings on the older tracks.

He knew they'd come in the middle of the night to collect the load because of a crushed desert flower that only blooms when the heat of the day has dissipated.

He knew one of the men was tall because his stride was thirty-three inches long; twenty-seven inches is average for somebody six foot tall. He knew the other man was nervous, and liable to crack under interrogation, because in the sand where he'd stood waiting for the plane there was a mound of half-smoked cigarette butts.

'OK, I'll buy all that,' said Craig, 'but how do you know he's an old guy and the other one's young?'

'Simple. Look at the flower, look at the tracks. Old men walk around flowers. Young men step on them.'

The hunter turned out to be right in almost every detail. At the subsequent trial of the marijuana smugglers, the defence attorney became so fascinated by Bernie Lawrence's account of his methodology that he forgot to cross-examine him.

'Bernie,' said Craig, 'teach me how to hunt.'

Howard and Judy's house in La Vileta stood protected behind high stone walls and wrought-iron gates opposite the church on Calle Fuego, which was a street just wide enough for two cars to pass. It was not possible to keep the house or even the street under surveillance without being seen. Indeed, there was nowhere in La Vileta where the watchers could wait unnoticed, with the possible exception of the Bar Luis on the town's tiny central *plaza*. Unfortunately Howard was an early riser, and the bar did not open until late in the morning.

So like any good hunter, Lovato waited for his quarry to come to him.

There was only one road out of La Vileta. A mile and a half out of town, the road passed by a large municipal sports centre, set on a hill. Sitting on the hill, on an old stone wall, under the comforting shade of an olive tree, Lovato would wait for Howard's grey Ford Sierra to come into sight and then alert other watchers, Palma detectives, waiting further down the road.

They sat in an unmarked car at a strategic junction where the road from La Vileta split into two. One fork led directly into Palma; the other to a freeway which in turn led to Palma Nova, Portals Nous, Magaluf and beyond. They were under strict instructions not to follow Howard. Lovato said the risk of him spotting surveillance was too great. They were merely required to observe and report: did he go straight on for Palma, or turn right for the freeway?

Most of the time he turned right, so Lovato moved his own observation post to one from where he could observe the freeway to see which exit Howard would take. Usually it was the exit to Portals Nous, so Lovato moved there the next time, and waited for Marks to arrive.

Before very long he had identified Howard's pattern. In the morning he would take his two daughters to school, then drive to a club in Portals Nous where he played tennis while Lovato watched from a safe distance on the club's terrace, sipping coffee. His tennis partner was a fellow British expatriate and after their game Howard would frequently go to his house.

He ate lunch in a restaurant in La Vileta owned by a fellow-Welshman, or at one of a handful of restaurants in Palma Nova.

In the evening, after the children were home from school, he'd leave La Vileta once again and take a different route; not right towards the freeway, but straight on towards Palma. More often than not he would stop at the Bar Ca's Cunyats, just a couple of doors down from Justo's travel agency.

Howard's bar? It seemed very likely. On 21 May, acting on information suppled by Lovato, a Palma magistrate gave permission for the police to tap three more telephones, including one at the home of Howard's tennis partner and one at the Bar Ca's Cunyats.

The phone in the bar rang once.

'*Si, digame?*'

'Hello, Howard Marks, please.'

'Just a moment, please. Hold on.'

It was Gerry Wills calling from Los Angeles. He told Marks that John Denbigh – 'the Vicar' – was with him. He said they were still 'in the middle of things' and that 'everything is doing real good'.

'I'm leaving in about forty-eight hours,' said Marks. 'I'll be in Zürich overnight . . . I'm going to Elena's place on Saturday, and staying with Brian there for at least five or six days.'

Wills said he hoped to join Marks in 'Elena's place'. Meanwhile, Marks should look up Elena and 'give her a little money before I get there'.

'So she's in good order when you arrive?' said Marks.

'Yeah, right,' Wills said.

'OK, I'll do that with pleasure. You want me to test her out?'

'No, no, no. She wouldn't, anyway.' Both of them laughed.

When Denbigh came on the line, Marks repeated his itinerary then added: 'Then I'm going out to Bruce's way. I'll be hanging about there for a bit, then going to Pearl's place. And then I'm going to give the Chef as much as I can.'

'Yeah, by that time everything should be OK,' said Denbigh.

'Well, that's what I'm hoping . . . Please look after yourself, now. Thanks for calling.'

Zürich certainly; he'd been quite open about that. 'Brian' was what they called Phillip Sparrowhark, so if Marks was meeting Brian

129

in 'Elena's place', Elena's place must be Bangkok. 'Out Bruce's way?' Lovato guessed that meant Hong Kong. 'The Chef' he knew was Saleem Malik, the supplier of hashish, so 'Pearl's place', he guessed, must be Karachi.

Lovato sketched Howard's journey on an imaginary map and began firing off requests to the DEA offices in all four countries – and, to be on the safe side, Manila as well – urging the tightest possible surveillance.

He was certain that money from the Los Angeles load was now flowing into one or more of Howard's accounts in Switzerland and Hong Kong, and that Howard was on his way to collect and disburse it.

The tone of his requests was singularly urgent, as though he was saying that this was the last chance. He did not mention it, but he'd just received disquieting news from the Assistant US Attorney in Los Angeles: unless the DEA came up with a substantial portion of the dope or the money, it was unlikely Howard Marks could be prosecuted.

In Zürich the Swiss police tapped Marks's phone at the Hotel Central – to no effect. He called nobody of any consequence from the hotel. The most suspicious thing he did during his eighteen hours in Zürich was to leave the hotel and walk to the nearby railway station, where he made liberal use of the pay telephones. Who he called from the pay phones they could not say, since those phones were not tapped. According to the watchers, he went nowhere near a bank.

When he left Zürich, on a flight to Bangkok, Swiss police disguised as security workers thoroughly searched both Marks and his luggage. Actually, to avoid raising his suspicion, they searched every passenger on the Bangkok flight. They found nothing that might help them.

Arriving in Bangkok, Marks claimed on his immigration card that he was employed as a 'researcher', which covered a multitude of sins. There was nobody at the airport to meet him. Watched by the Thai police surveillance team, he made a call from a payphone but received no answer. Shortly after, Phillip Sparrowhawk arrived at the airport to greet Marks, somewhat breathless. Two DEA agents were close enough to overhear Sparrowhark apologizing to Marks for being late.

They drove together to the Hyatt Hotel, from where Marks phoned Judy in Palma. Lovato overheard him complain that the

'FDs have not arrived', and that he did not have one cent to give to Saleem Malik.

The next stop, the next day, was Manila. Marks and Sparrowhawk flew there together, to be met, covertly, by another small army of watchers. Marks checked into the Mandarin Hotel where, once again, he called Judy in Palma to complain about the missing 'FDs'. Fortunately, he said, Saleem Malik was being 'very understanding'.

Well, to some degree. Downstairs, in the lobby of the Mandarin Hotel, Marks and Malik were seen talking together. Two Filipino detectives got close enough to them to hear Malik say that he was leaving Manila the next day for Hong Kong, to 'collect my 300'. He was to be disappointed. For two days after Malik flew to Hong Kong, just about all the listeners heard was his complaints to Marks, or Marks complaining to other people, that there was still no money to pay him.

Lord Moynihan turned up at the Mandarin Hotel to see Marks, and the two of them had dinner in the hotel restaurant with three other unidentified men. Art Scalzo of the DEA managed to get a table close enough to them to overhear parts of their conversation. So far as he could tell, it had nothing to do with drugs. Nevertheless, Lord Moynihan's home telephone was also tapped.

In Hong Kong, Saleem Malik waited for his money for three days. Suddenly, he made plans to return to Karachi. Had he finally got paid? The DEA proposed to the Hong Kong police that Malik be searched at the airport upon departure. Sorry, said the Hong Kong police, they had no grounds to justify a search. Carrying money – even drug money – out of the colony was not illegal.

Marks was not so fortunate. Four days later, standing in line in the immigration queue at Hong Kong airport, Howard experienced a worse-than-usual attack of the flutterings. He *knew* he was going to be stopped. He was travelling with David Embley, his tennis partner from Palma, who had joined him in the Far East for an exotic vacation. 'Let me go first,' said Marks. 'If I don't make it through, give me a day and then call Judy.'

They barely looked at his passport before taking him away. He was held for an hour until a Hong Kong police officer (a fellow-Welshman, as it happened) arrived to interrogate him.

'It's my old record catching up with me, is it?' said Marks.

'Oh, you've got a record here in Hong Kong, have you?' said the cop. 'No, this is just routine.'

Sure. They searched him and his luggage thoroughly, taking

away every single item they found – to be photocopied, Marks was certain. Then they returned every item and sent him on his way.

Throughout it all they were immensely polite. Nevertheless, Marks was badly shaken. Lovato could hear it in his voice when Howard telephoned Judy in Palma to tell her what had happened.

'You can't believe what a relief it is to talk to you,' he said, sounding as if he was almost in tears. Then he told her: 'I can't say too much because I know they're bound to be listening at both ends of this.' He did make it clear, however, that he was very worried. 'I hope I don't get a problem leaving,' he said.

He did not. Three days later, Marks left Hong Kong for Bangkok without being stopped, though he was closely observed. Three days after that, he flew to Rome and then on to Palma. He had been on the road for twenty-one days, spied on and listened to for every single one of them.

The Madrid office of the DEA sent fulsome messages of thanks to all the agents and all the local detectives who had taken part in the mass surveillance operation. It was not their fault that they had nothing to show for it.

Palma, 19 June 1986

By any standard, the international co-operation the DEA had received in its pursuit of Marks was extraordinary. The performance of almost all police agencies is measured by statistics: the crime rate, the number of arrests made, the amount of property recovered, the amount of contraband seized. All too often, the statistics affect the budget and decide careers. It was therefore remarkable that so many police forces in so many countries were willing to pursue Marks and his associates when few of them would have anything to show for it in terms of statistics; no 'bodies' to improve the arrest statistics, no seizures of drugs or money.

So why had the British done this to him? thought Lovato. Why were they being so bloody-minded?

In London Her Majesty's Customs had arrested Michael Sydney Williams. Lovato heard of the arrest not from Her Majesty's Customs but from senior Spanish police officers in Madrid, some of whom were extremely angry.

There was supposed to have been a deal. The Spanish had been able to justify their considerable contribution to the Marks investigation on the grounds that this was not a wholly American affair.

The phone taps had revealed, and Her Majesty's Customs had confirmed, that, in league with Williams, Marks was also attempting to import a load of Moroccan hashish into England through Spain. For Lovato this was a sideshow, but he had dutifully transcribed every telephone conversation between Marks and Williams and passed them on to both the British and the Spanish police.

As a result, in March, Spanish police had trailed Marks to Malaga, in southern Spain, where he met Williams and two other men to search the nearby coastline for possible landing spots for the hashish. (Howard had spotted the surveillance while standing on a beach. Despite having the 'flu, he did what all British tourists are believed to do when anywhere near even the coldest of oceans: he took off his clothes and jumped in.) The Spanish expected the hashish to be driven across Spain on its way to England, and they expected to seize it.

But the British had other ideas. While Lovato was investigating Marks, Her Majesty's Customs was running a parallel but discrete investigation into Williams. In their case they wanted both the bodies and the dope.

They waited until the load reached England and then seized more than 500lb of hashish – and 24oz of heroin – near Bristol. Williams, and four other men, were arrested. The Spanish got none of the prize and little of the credit.

Lovato called Peter Nelson, his main contact at Customs, to complain that the British had not played fair. He also said that as the unofficial middleman, he had been placed in a very difficult position with his Spanish hosts.

Nelson said the load was nothing to do with Marks, and was therefore not part of the deal with the Spanish Police. Lovato had learned his first but not his last lesson that international co-operation has its limits.

Los Angeles, late June 1986

Now Julie Desm was certain the case was jinxed.

In an attempt to trace the ever-elusive Gerry Wills, she asked DEA technical agents – experts in electronic surveillance – to place a 'pen register' on the telephone lines of Unlimited Communications, the answering service he habitually used. A pen register would automatically record every phone number dialled out, *and* the originating phone number of every incoming call, allowing her to follow his movements. At least, that was the theory.

The tech agents scratched their heads, consulted with the phone company, and reported: 'No can do.' Unlimited Communications had so many lines, they said, it would take them a month to assemble and install the necessary equipment. Monitoring the results would be a nightmare. Forget it.

Then she was forced to abandon her case against Peter Combs. His attorney had cried foul, claiming the DEA must have gained evidence against Combs by illegally tapping his car phone – otherwise how did they know were to find him? Not so, said the government in all honesty.

But the government couldn't provide a proper explanation without revealing the full extent of the DEA's worldwide operation against Marks. Howard knew his phone had been tapped. He did not know how long it had been tapped, or why, and the government was not about to tell him.

The prosecutor explained all this to the judge in a private meeting. The judge was not impressed: 'Sounds to me like you have to disclose it,' he said. Rather than do that, and hear Craig Lovato go ballistic, Julie dropped the possession charges. Her one consolation was that Combs remained on Terminal Island, awaiting his long-overdue trial on the 1973 Las Vegas charges.

Her only bit of luck was in finding John Denbigh. He was, thank God, a creature of habit. She'd asked the car rental agency on Sunset Boulevard, where he'd got his Mustang the last time he was in Los Angeles, to let her know if ever he returned. On 23 June they called to say he was back.

'Stall,' she said. 'Keep him there as long as you can.'

But the traffic was impossible, and by the time she reached Sunset they'd run out of excuses and had to let him go. Still, she knew he was driving a tan Caprice. She also knew where he was staying: the Hacienda Motel. She went there alone and took the room opposite his. Then she called for help.

This time the Los Angeles office did not deny her resources. Julie was assigned ten agents, almost her entire group, to maintain round-the-clock surveillance. The first agents had not long arrived at the Hacienda when Gerry Wills turned up, knocking on Denbigh's door. This time, said Julie to herself, you're not going to lose us.

And they did not – though John Denbigh had vastly expanded his repertoire of counter-surveillance techniques. He made unexpected and illegal U-turns. He stopped in the middle of the road, forcing the vehicles behind to pull around him. He dodged on and off freeways with absolute abandon. (Curiously, however, he never seemed to notice the surveillance cars doing many of the same things. Like Combs, he never looked in the mirror. It was as though he drove that way by rote, not because he seriously thought he was being followed.)

Wherever Denbigh and Wills went, the surveillance teams stuck with them: from the Hacienda Motel to the Hilton at Anaheim, to the Westwood Marquis, to the Le Parc Hotel in West Hollywood, to a house in Willow Glen; to the Kirkwood store on Laurel Canyon Drive, where they made abundant use of the payphones; to a cycle shop where they test-rode the stock; on seemingly pointless drives around the block.

The agents put them to bed at night and were waiting for them first thing in the morning. So far as they could see, Denbigh and Wills met nobody, made no deliveries, took no collections. By the end of the second day, Julie had a near-mutiny on her hands. 'There's *nothing* going on, Julie,' said one of the agents in frustration.

She was by then extremely tired. In addition to running the surveillance during the day, she was working nights at the office, from midnight to 8.00 a.m., manning the emergency phone and the radio.

Wills and Denbigh were at the house in Willow Glen, and seemed to have settled in for the night. She agreed to call off the watch, but she wanted the surveillance team back on duty first thing in the morning. One of the agents said that was 'dumb': they could easily get an LAPD patrol to run by the house in the morning and see if the car was still there.

'Listen,' she said, 'you get your fanny out of bed and *you be here.*'

They stood there in the middle of a darkened street, in the high-priced hills of Los Angeles, arguing like sailors. She insisted on getting her way. She drove away, heading for the office, thinking unattractive thoughts about DEA agents in general; male agents in particular.

The surveillance units were on duty bright and early the next morning – to watch Denbigh and Wills repeat their apparently profitless routine: moving from one hotel to another; visiting the payphones and the cycle shop; then back to the hotel. Agents do not join the DEA to sit in cars and watch people do nothing. Talk of mutiny grew.

The only breakthrough came when one of the agents overheard

135

a receptionist at the Le Parc Hotel tell Wills, 'Your friend Dave Oas is here.'

Oas. Full name: Luther Daniel Oas. Profession: sea captain. The skipper of the boat that had delivered the load?

Late that night, the surveillance team led by Julie followed Luther Daniel Oas to a house in Long Beach, south of Los Angeles. He remained in the house for no more than five minutes, emerging with a box that appeared to be heavy. He put the box in the trunk of his car and looked up and down the street. There were four cars in sight, all of them belonging to the DEA.

He drove away slowly, the DEA cars in careful pursuit. Then he made a sudden U-turn and retraced his progress down the street, accelerating wildly towards them. It was almost midnight and there was no other traffic. They could not follow him, unless they did it openly with flashing blue lights. He left them, literally, in his dust.

They found him the next morning at the Westwood Marquis Hotel and followed him to the airport. There was no sign of the heavy box. He carried nothing but a slim briefcase. He flew out of Los Angeles on a one-way ticket to Denver, Colorado and they never saw him again.

After he'd gone, Julie had his rental car examined by a sniffer dog. If a box full of drugs had recently been carried in the car the dog would react, its handler said. He said the same applied to a box full of money – since *most* of the currency in circulation in the United States carries the traces of illegal substances. The dog did not react. The car, the handler said, was clean.

Julie's group supervisor called off the surveillance. He said the Los Angeles office had better things to do.

There was one last chance, one final opportunity to retrieve something from the ashes.

The day after the surveillance in Los Angeles was called off, Craig called Julie from Palma to tell her that Geoffrey Kenion – 'the Sewage Engineer,' as Denbigh called him – was on his way back to Los Angeles. All the indications suggested that he was coming to collect more money for Howard. Seize it, said Lovato. Whatever else you do, Julie, seize it.

She knew she would never be able to find and follow Kenion without the help of a surveillance team. She knew the chances of getting a surveillance team were zero.

But she also knew that Kenion was due to fly back to Europe

from Los Angeles over the 4 July weekend. That is when she would find him, she decided – if she had a little help.

'How would you like to spend the weekend out at the airport?' she said to Peter Shigeta, one of the agents in her group and a man with valuable contacts at the airport. He knew people from US Customs who might be willing to stop Kenion, and seize the money, and make it look like his sheer bad luck.

'It's the 4 July weekend,' said Shigeta. Even the war on drugs stops for Independence Day weekend.

'Please,' said Julie.

Eventually Shigeta agreed, on one condition: 'You owe me,' he said, 'your first-born child.'

They waited at the airport for most of the weekend, checking every flight to Europe. Kenion never appeared.

'Sorry,' she said. She eventually paid the debt: Shigeta became godfather to her son.

It had been Kenion's idea to drive across the country, from Los Angeles to New York. He'd held romantic notions about 'the great adventure': the freedom of the road, the magnificence of the scenery, the changing face of fifty nations rolled into one. Now he wasn't so sure.

Certainly the scenery was magnificent, and John Denbigh was an amiable enough companion, except that he was . . . well, odd. He talked disjointedly, in staccato monologues that were interesting but not at all easy to follow. At night, when the stopped at motels, he would haul two heavy blue bags from the trunk of the car into their shared room but never open them. Whenever he made a phone call, he insisted Kenion left the room. 'Business,' he would say.

Kenion could no longer doubt that he was mixed up in something very serious.

Howard had promised to loan him $20,000 so that he could complete the building work on his restaurant. Then, when he'd asked for the money, Howard had said he would have to return to America to collect it. 'That's where my money is,' said Howard. Kenion had been annoyed, then suspicious, no longer sure that Howard was a *retired* drug smuggler. But he needed the money and the first time had been so easy. Just once more, he'd said to himself, and that's it.

But this time wasn't so easy. He was nervous as soon as he arrived in Los Angeles, persuading himself that if he flew straight back to Europe as planned, he might attract attention. Hence his decision

137

to drive across America and fly to Europe from New York. 'Wait a couple of days and I'll come with you,' said Denbigh, and Kenion couldn't really refuse.

It took them five days to reach the East Coast, and by then Kenion was up to his neck in the conspiracy.

The moment of truth, the casting out of the last doubt, came in a motel in Colorado when Denbigh made yet another of his business calls. He thought Kenion had left the room. Instead he was in the bathroom, and able to overhear at least some of what Denbigh said: 'It's 1.3 million in the bag instead of the 1.6 we were expecting.' For the rest of the journey Kenion could not look at the two blue bags again without imagining what they contained.

New York was his last opportunity to back out, to refuse to carry the $100,000 of drug money, in 100-dollar bills, that Denbigh gave him to carry back to Palma. He thought about it, briefly. Then he went out and bought a box of plastic sandwich bags and a roll of sticky tape. He divided the money into bundles small enough to fit inside the bags and taped them to his body, underneath his shirt, and around his legs. It seemed a lot more professional than stuffing it into the waistband of his trousers.

Unfortunately, New York in July is hot, and 8 July 1986 was the hottest day in New York for a quarter-century. At Kennedy airport Kenion waited in the stifling departure lounge for his flight to Spain – which was, of course, delayed: not daring to remove his jacket; watching the sweat drip from the end of his nose on to the book he was pretending to read; waiting for security to arrest him as an obvious terrorist suspect.

On the plane, and once it was airborne, he rushed to the lavatory. He removed his jacket and shirt and peeled off the tape holding the sandwich bags to his torso. In his haste he dropped the bundles of cash into the open toilet bowl. He had to retrieve them. Not-so-easy money.

Palma, July 1986

Craig Lovato knew he'd lost as soon as Marks began using his home telephones again with almost no reservations. Perhaps he'd just got lazy, but he seemed to be saying there was no need for further caution. It was all over. Let them listen. It no longer mattered.

Gerry Wills called Marks at home and said: 'Since I don't owe you anything I don't hear from you any more.' He said Denbigh 'can have a job with me anytime'. Wills joked bawdily about an eye infection Marks had picked up, and how he might have received it. Wills said: 'Everyone thinks I made a lot of money. We know that you've made it all.' Both of them laughed loudly. They were clearly in excellent spirits.

Marks called Denbigh in New York to receive an accounting, as though he was calling his stockbroker to get the latest ticker prices.

'Straightback is one four hundred,' said Denbigh. 'The other man was one two seven six five five zero. Touch's missus was fifty. Bruce, 165. Sewage, 200. My friend Jay was 52.5. The flat, 57.5. Thirty for the drink. Ten for the ping. Now that's exactly, totally where we stand at the moment.'

Marks thanked Denbigh for 'putting all this effort into it'.

'Yeah,' said Denbigh, 'well, you've got to.'

Two days later Denbigh told Marks he was heading home, flying from New York to Madrid and then on to Palma for a brief visit before returning to London. At Lovato's request, DEA agents covertly searched Denbigh's luggage at Kennedy airport. They found nothing to satisfy them.

Wills also flew to Palma, bringing with him an associate and a woman. For six days he met Marks frequently, apparently to celebrate, before flying off to the South of France in a private Lear jet.

Lovato did not give up. When he wasn't keeping Howard and his friends under surveillance, secretly taking their photographs, he was in the listening room recording yet more tapes of Howard's conversations.

And there was certainly no official admission of defeat. Peter Nelson of Her Majesty's Customs flew out to Palma from London to 'clarify overlapping areas of responsibility' – and to help smooth ruffled Spanish feathers. Lovato took him to the club at Portals Nous to watch Howard play tennis. 'Want to challenge him to a game?' he said.

But the game was effectively over. At the end of July, Lovato's two-year stint in Spain came to an end and he was recalled to the United States to take up a new assignment in Miami. He took with him the tapes of Howard's conversations, which was about all he had to show for six months of inexhaustible persistence.

After he left, the Palma police discontinued the taps on Howard Marks's phones.

ACT TWO
The Middle Game

By its very nature, the chess trap is a form of combination. As a rule, it consists of the offer of a baited unit – anything from a Pawn to a Queen dipped in poison. More often than not, the trap is supported by a play on the adversary's predatory instincts and hope and a prayer.

I.A. Horowitz, *All About Chess*

S I X

Douglas is a dusty one-horse town on the Arizona border with Mexico, about fifty miles south-east of Tombstone. It's famous now, as small Arizona towns go, because in 1989 someone shifted 300 tons of earth to build a tunnel under the border, linking Douglas with its Mexican neighbour, Agua Prieta. Until federal agents found the tunnel, in May 1990, the bad guys shipped God knows how much cocaine along its 200-foot, concrete-lined length while too many of the townspeople – and, rumour has it, more than one local official – looked the other way. Now the townsfolk sell T-shirts and baseball caps and other souvenirs with logos celebrating this small engineering triumph. Their town and their tunnel have become minor tourist attractions.

In 1973, when Craig Lovato first arrived in Douglas, the town was less commercial but still dependent on its historical bonds with Agua Prieta based on the three Cs: Copper-mining, Cattle and, most of all, Contraband. It was marijuana in those days, rather than cocaine, and they didn't need a tunnel to get it across the border; they just drove it over in trucks.

Lovato went there as sheriff's deputy because one of his informants in Las Vegas had got himself into serious trouble in Douglas. He was no more than a kid. Before he got involved in drugs, he was a member of the junior wrestling team that Craig ran at the Las Vegas YMCA. Then he smoked marijuana, dropped acid, popped amphetamines and graduated to cocaine. He was caught near Douglas, crossing the border with 60lb of marijuana in his backpack. Facing two years in jail, he appealed to Lovato to go to Douglas and help him cut a deal.

The experience was one that Lovato can never forget because he'll always bear the scars. They act as a permanent reminder that marijuana trafficking is not, as some would argue, a benign occupation. Sometimes it is deadly.

Francisco Cornejos was the biggest marijuana dealer in Douglas, which was saying a lot. He owned houses all over town and a fleet of twenty cars, and the DEA agents from Phoenix told Lovato, 'Listen, if your informant can get so much as one marijuana cigarette out of Cornejos, the kid's not going to have to do one day in jail.'

So the informant set Cornejos up, introducing Craig as Johnny Luna, a hot-shot dealer from Las Vegas, looking to buy a ton of dope. Cornejos, being cautious, agreed to sell him 70 kilos for $30,000 as a first instalment. The hand-over was supposed to take place on a motel forecourt on the edge of town, but at the last moment Cornejos said he didn't like it: one of his people had been busted at that motel before, he said, and it gave him 'bad vibes'. He insisted the hand-over take place several blocks away at the parking lot of the local drugstore.

'Fine, wherever you want to go,' said Lovato, 'but just let me tell my wife.'

He went to the motel room where the DEA agents were hiding, waiting for the deal to go down, and told them of the change of plan. Don't worry, they said, we'll be at the drugstore.

But they weren't, because as soon as Lovato and Cornejos left the motel two carloads of Cornejos's men turned up and mounted guard in the parking lot. The DEA agents were trapped inside the motel, unable to move without giving the game away.

Though he didn't yet know it, Lovato was on his own.

In this job you don't survive if you can't read people. When you look into a person's eyes you learn to read their character, because that's what's going to make a difference between life and death. When you're undercover, what the bad guy is telling you is totally irrelevant because he's lying. I mean, you're telling him a total lie and he's telling you a total lie. So you stop listening to words and you start reading eyes. I knew that Cornejos was a desperado, I could see it in his eyes.

We're walking towards his car, where his lieutenant is sitting, and all I can hear is the wind in the telephone lines. I'm waiting for the pitter-patter of friendly feet. When you're undercover, you always hear your guys come in. There's this scraping of shoe leather on the pavement and you hear the running and, 'Police officer, don't move! Freeze! Everybody, hands in the air!' A lot of commotion takes place and you're used to it because you do it all the time.

But I'm not hearing anything except the wind in the telephone lines and I'm thinking, 'Holy shit, something's wrong here,' I don't know what's wrong, but something's wrong. It's just me and Cornejos and his lieutenant, and these are real desperadoes.

And the other thing was, I'd never worked with the Feds before, not these Feds anyway, and the young agent who had brought the flash roll, the $30,000 down from Phoenix, had said, his last words to me were: 'Remember, whatever you do, don't lose the money.' And you're impressionable when you're a young local agent, and you think the Feds know what they're doing. When you get to be a Fed yourself, you realize they don't always know what they're doing, but at that time I thought they did so I'm thinking to myself, 'God, don't give him the money, protect the money.' But I know that when I don't give him the money he's going to start shooting because he's going to sense – he goes by his senses, too – he's going to realize there's a problem, and he's going to shoot the shit out of me and then get himself to Mexico. And it gets really quiet out there when things are going wrong.

I knew I was going to have to take him down myself, so I reached into my pocket and took out this little .32 calibre semi-automatic the Feds had given me. I grabbed him by the back of the shoulders, walked him about a foot and a half farther, and I slammed him on to the hood of the car and said, 'I'm a police officer, you're under arrest, don't move'. Well, while I did that, he'd already pulled his gun, and he's over the hood of the car with his gun in his right hand, looking up at me. And I could see in his eyes he was going to shoot. It didn't matter a shit what I told him, he was going to go for broke. And I said, 'Drop the gun or I'll shoot you.' Well maybe he thought I didn't have a gun, or maybe he didn't care. Maybe he had made up his mind that if he was ever arrested he'd rather die than go to jail. He had this mind-set. I could see in his eyes that this was a situation where I had to kill him before he killed me, but I'm thinking – and these are very quick thoughts – 'Craig, if you shoot this man, you're going to have to shoot him in the back of the head. How are you going to justify that at the coroner's inquest? They're going to say he was assassinated.' Then I say to myself, 'Craig, if you don't shoot him, he's going to shoot you,' and just then he fired three rounds right in my face. I saw the muzzle flash and heard this deafening sound. I threw one arm up to protect my face and I took a round through the elbow.

Now, I used to practise what I called instinctive shooting, which is common practice now but was pretty innovative in those days. I was always amazed at how violators and cops could get into shoot-outs within seven to ten feet of one another and never hit one another. That happens consistently in shoot-outs. I remember a cop named Hal Creeton who went into a bar in Las Vegas, half hour before midnight, and the place gets robbed by a young kid with a gun. The kid goes off down a narrow hallway, and Hal goes after him, and they fire twelve shots at each other. They're just a few feet apart but all that happens is, Hal gets a bullet hole through his tie, and the kid was nicked in the head. Now how can that happen? You ask yourself and then you realize that when you're frightened, you don't pay any attention to where you're pointing your gun.

So, I had trained myself to do instinctive shooting, which is to instinctively bring the weapon up to whatever you're looking at, lock the elbow and the wrist, and fire. As long as the arm's straight, the elbow's locked, the wrist's locked, the hand's going to be level with your eyeline and the bullet will go where your eyes are looking. If you're looking at your target, you'll hit it. That's what they teach now, but they didn't teach it then. And that's what I credit with saving my life, because I fell backwards, I fired instinctively and hit him in the neck.

I fell down on one side of the car, and I could see his boots underneath the car, pointing directly at me. I thought, 'God, he's probably standing there waiting for me to stick my head up so he can shoot me between the eyes.' Now, strange thoughts go through your mind in situations like this. I'd seen a movie with Frank Sinatra called The Detective, *and Frank was this detective and the bad guys were going to assassinate him. He's in this garage and they shoot at him and he falls down by his car, and he sees the guy's feet and he shoots the guy in the leg. The guy falls down and Frank kills him. So I think 'God, shades of Frank Sinatra, I'll just shoot this guy in the leg and he'll fall down and I'll take him out.' So I go boom, and he goes 'Ow, you son of a bitch,' and he comes around the car and he's really pissed off, and he's popping round after round at me, and these explosions are going off. A round would hit the car door and sound just like a sledgehammer. I shoot again and hit him in the chest.*

The car was what we called a low rider – slung low on the suspension, really popular in those days. You can't get under a low rider, but I did, and came out on the other side, and he'd put a bullet hole through the back of my shirt. Now I don't know to this day how that could happen, any more than I can explain the bullet hole in Hal Creeton's tie. I mean, if you have a bullet hole in the back of your shirt, it's logical you have a bullet in your back, but I didn't. All he did was hit me in the other arm.

As I came out on the other side of the car, his lieutenant, who's been sitting in the driver's seat, gets out with a Colt .357 Magnum and looks down at me, and I reach up and I shoot him in the chest. It hits a nerve centre and he goes over backwards, down for the count.

Then I ran like hell for the side of the drugstore hoping to find some cover there. But there was no cover at all. When the Feds had given me that little gun I'd popped the clip, and I knew there was a full clip, but now I'm thinking, 'God, how many rounds does this gun hold? I've shot three, I've shot four, it can't hold much more than seven.' So I'm getting down to the nitty gritty here. And this guy's madder than a bear. There's no place to hide so I've just got to turn around and shoot it out with him, and assume I've got another four rounds to do the job. I turn around and, thank God, I see him limping off in the opposite direction. Then I hear the sirens.

By the time the Feds turn up and go after Francisco, he's already gotten home and his brother has busted the border and put him into a Mexican hospital. I sort of wanted to meet him later and talk to him because I had a certain amount of admiration for a fellow who comes from a socio-economic background where, unlike Howard Marks, he had no education and no opportunity to better himself. Where this fellow came from you can eat beans the rest of your life, earn two cents an hour, or you can die. Francisco decided he'd become a desperado knowing he would pay for his actions – and he did, because later on he was killed – but in the meantime his family, his relatives, and the people round him would benefit. He was a basic man. He had no intelligence. I mean, unlike Howard Marks he wasn't educated, he didn't have a high IQ, but he had character and I respected him for that.

I can respect Marks's intelligence but I have nothing but disdain for his character, because he has no character.

The city of Las Vegas was reluctant to pay Lovato's medical bills for the treatment of his gunshot wounds because he incurred them in Arizona. Arizona wouldn't pay because he worked for the city of Las Vegas.

Eventually the city did pay, but it also imposed a new rule that sheriff's deputies would henceforth do their work only within the boundaries of Clark County. Lovato, aware that drug dealers were not constrained by lines drawn on maps, looked around for a bigger arena in which to operate. The DEA would not hire him because the wound he had received in his gun arm while in their service made him technically disabled, so he joined the state narcotics division.

On his last day of service for the city of Las Vegas, Lovato found himself in a trailer home, looking down the barrel of another drug dealer's gun, this one a sawn-off shotgun. This time he did not hesitate.

At the coroner's inquest he was asked by a woman juror why he had not waited before opening fire.

'Ma'am, I made that mistake before . . .'

By the time he joined the DEA in 1978 (having proved that, disabled or not, he could score 300 out of a possible 300 on the target range), Craig Lovato had acquired very set views about drug traffickers. There was, in his view, no such animal as a 'good doper'.

There were drug dealers who were less violent than others, and some, like Marks, who weren't violent at all. There were those, like Marks, who dealt only in pot, refusing to have anything to do with heroin or cocaine, or the hallucinogens, or lethal stimulants such as methamphetamine. But, according to the Lovato philosophy, uncomplicated and widely shared in his profession: 'A doper is a doper is a doper.' It didn't matter that marijuana was medically less dangerous than cocaine and heroin (and perhaps tobacco and alcohol for that matter); it was just as illegal and, because of that, highly profitable. Money, vast sums of money, drove the marijuana business just as surely as it drove the cocaine trade, distorting economies and corrupting everyone it touched: from the generals and politicians who took bribes in the supply countries to the bankers and lawyers and estate agents who benefited from the dealers' profits – and everyone in between. Drug money was drug money was drug money, whether the traces it carried were from the cannabis or the coca plant, or the opium poppy.

And it didn't matter to Lovato that Howard Marks was personally not a violent man. Somewhere down the cannabis pipeline, *every* cannabis pipeline, there were men ready to use violence to protect or enlarge their share of the profits. Lovato had the scars to prove it.

So he would not accept the notion that Marks was unimportant – some old hippy left over from the sixties, still shipping harmless dope while other more urgent targets flooded America and Europe with cocaine. He saw Marks as the clever, unprincipled and incorrigible head of an organization that was as sophisticated as any cocaine cartel, and, in a subtle way, just as deadly.

The distinct possibility that Marks would be left alone on his

Mediterranean island, celebrating his last load, planning the next one, was, to Lovato, simply intolerable.

Darwin, Australia, 19 August 1986

First it had been 'Find the load, Julie.' Then it was 'Julie, find the money.' Then it was 'Julie, find the boat.' Well, that at least she had done.

It was the middle of the night but from her car she could see the *Axel D* clearly. It sat in dry dock, elevated on ramps. For a boat that had crossed the North Pacific Ocean with a multi-ton cargo of hash, it looked very small.

This was just a dry run. They had to know if anybody stayed on board the boat at night, and Steve Austin had volunteered to find out. He was a DEA electronics surveillance expert from San Diego, who was more than willing to demonstrate that 'tech' agents also knew how to handle themselves in the field. They'd asked what he was going to do if he got caught. 'What do you think?' he said. 'I'm going to run like hell.'

He was dressed from head to foot in dark clothing, with a cap to prevent the moonlight reflecting off the bald patch on his head, but he was still visible in the lights on the dock. Julie watched him climb aboard the boat, wondering what he would say if he was challenged. Trevor Young of the Australian Federal Police, who shared her vigil, kept watch through binoculars, waiting for the first sign of trouble. He had men standing by in case Austin could not run fast enough.

For most of its length the deck of the *Axel D* was flat, except at the stern where the ship's accommodations were contained in a superstructure topped by the wheelhouse. If there was a watchman on board, that was where Austin would most likely encounter him. It was also where he would most likely find what he needed: a place to hide a Satellite Tracking Device. Not much bigger than a couple of cigarette packets, the 'sat-track' would transmit a signal to satellites of the US National Security Agency (NSA). Bounced back to earth, those signals would allow the DEA to pinpoint the precise location of the *Axel D*, wherever the ship went.

Austin slowly climbed the companionway leading to the bridge and vanished for a moment inside the wheelhouse. Then he re-emerged, and Desm and Young saw him climb up on to a platform on top of the bridge where the ship's stout main mast stood, bristling with antennae and radar and navigation equipment.

Within twenty minutes he was back at the car, pleased with himself. There was nobody on board – or if there was, they were not on watch. And he'd found the perfect place to hide that sat-track. A third of the way up the mast there was a compartment which he could just reach by standing on the rods designed to diffuse a lightning strike. The compartment was there to provide access to the electrical cables running inside the mast and it would be opened rarely. Even if somebody did look inside the compartment, they would probably think the sat-track was nothing more than a relay box.

They returned to the *Axel D* the next night at 2.45 a.m. to install it. Austin was gone a little longer this time, about an hour. 'It's done,' was all he said when he returned. Back at their hotel, Austin telephoned the El Paso Intelligence Center, known as EPIC, in El Paso, Texas.

When EPIC started in 1974 it consisted of a handful of agents from the DEA and the Immigration and Naturalization Service, housed in a borrowed conference room, who were trying to keep track of illegal immigrants and brown heroin crossing the Mexican border. Now it had a staff of 240, drawn from eleven government agencies, housed in a secure and purpose-built command centre in the middle of the Fort Bliss army base. It operated around the clock, 365 days a year, receiving intelligence from around the world – and above it; signals from sat-tracks like the one placed by Austin.

EPIC reported it was receiving a perfect signal from the *Axel D*. For the first time in a long time, Julie Desm had reason to celebrate. She also had reason to thank Rex and RW, she supposed, though she didn't feel at all grateful towards them. She felt mad.

Her relationship with Reiner Jacobi and Tom Sunde – or Rex and RW as she still knew them – had not improved with the passage of time. She'd met them half a dozen times since May and found them patronizing and constantly infuriating, particularly Rex.

They were not as smart as they thought they were. At the third meeting they'd asked to be provided with fake identities by the DEA so they could 'go undercover' to better investigate the Marks organization, as they also called it. Neil Van Horn, Julie's partner, had said, 'Fine,' and persuaded them to go into the DEA's Portland office on a weekend, when nobody else was around, and where the DEA had a Polaroid camera and other equipment to manufacture fake Oregon driver's licences. Rex and RW had posed for the Polaroid. They were unaware, apparently, that the camera automatically made *two* copies of each print. They didn't know it, but they were now on record in the DEA's files.

That small victory aside, Julie felt increasingly uneasy about the two men – particularly Rex. Accidentally on purpose, the German had let both her and Van Horn see that his briefcase contained copies of DEA Teletypes. The fact that he had them was an appalling breach of security, but there was nothing they could do about it at the time.

For Rex and RW claimed to have 'inside information' that the Marks organization was already planning to bring in the next load, again by sea. They'd said the boat was in Australia being readied for the voyage; they didn't yet know the name of it, but they were on their way to Sydney to find out.

Absolutely not, they were told. They had no authority or authorization to go anywhere on behalf of the DEA. They said they were going to Australia anyway, as private citizens. Fine, but they were on their own and they were not to claim any affiliation with the DEA under any circumstances. Of course not, they said. Nevertheless, Van Horn thought it prudent to tell the US drug liaison officer for the Australian Federal Police about Rex and RW, just in case.

Which was just as well, because as soon as they landed in Sydney, Rex and RW told Australian Customs they were 'working with the DEA' on the Marks investigation. The Australian government, which liked to be advised before foreign agents operated on its territory, lodged a protest with Washington, and Julie had caught some of the flak.

Still, to give them their due, they had come up with the name and location of the *Axel D* – though, naturally, they would not tell her how. She'd worked it out for herself when she got to Sydney. The solution she came up with did not improve her opinion of Rex and RW.

When the *Axel D* had arrived in Darwin in May (after delivering its cargo to Mexico two months before), it had failed to clear Customs. The ship was boarded and searched and though nothing illegal was found, the event had been recorded in an official report, along with the names of the skipper and crew. Rex, in his guise as a DEA informant, had been shown that report, among others, by Australian Customs.

So he knew that the captain of the *Axel D* was Luther Daniel Oas. It was a fair guess that he also knew, from Julie's DEA Teletypes, that Oas had been seen in Los Angeles with Wills and Denbigh. He'd simply put two and two together, which was enterprising but alarming. It only served to re-emphasize the persistent question in her mind, how? How was Rex able to get his hands on copies of the Teletypes?

And, for that matter, how had he known she was coming to Australia? He and RW were in Sydney when she arrived with Austin (who took an immediate dislike to Rex, as did Trevor Young of the federal police. The AFP did some checking on the pair and discovered that RW stood for Ross Woods). When the three of them flew to Darwin, Rex followed, calling her hotel to ask how the investigation was going. Julie finally agreed to meet him for a drink, determined to confront him with her most crucial question.

'Where did you get the Teletypes?' she said. 'You never did tell me.'

Rex responded with an extraordinary outburst of Teutonic anger. Forget the damned Teletypes, he said. He'd destroyed them. It didn't matter where he'd got them from. He was sick of her attitude. He'd given the DEA all this help and all she'd done was complain. Well, he'd had enough. If she didn't 'wise up' and 'get with the programme' he was going to break off relations with the DEA. He was also going to give her name and the story to his newspaper buddies in Washington DC. These were powerful people. She and the DEA would not like to read the kind of story he could get published.

She calmed him down as best she could and left, believing their relationship was over. It was like ending an unhappy love affair: liberating.

Julie Desm and Steve Austin had been back in California no more than a few days when EPIC reported that the signal from the sat-track on the *Axel D* had abruptly ceased. The battery attached to the device was supposed to last for six months. Either the battery was dead or the sat-track had been discovered and destroyed.

Austin returned to Darwin to find that the *Axel D* was at sea undergoing trials. This time he went aboard openly, from a cutter, disguised as an Australian Customs officer, albeit one who was mute. While genuine Customs men kept the crew of the ship busy, he re-climbed the mast which, in the interim, had been re-painted.

His box of tricks was intact and there was nothing wrong with the battery. Instead, he discovered somebody – probably the painters – had neatly coiled the thin wire that served as the sat-tracks's antenna and placed it inside the mast, making it useless.

He easily fixed the problem. Then, for insurance, he added the second battery pack he'd taken along as a replacement, doubling the sat-track's transmitting life to one year.

Los Angeles, September 1986

Craig Lovato flew into Los Angeles just as Julie Desm was preparing to fly out. It wasn't exactly what he had in mind.

He arrived with a briefcase containing cassette copies of the 433 phone conversations recorded in Palma and the firm conviction that, with a lot of work, they could assemble a prosecutable case against Marks.

He was under no illusions about the size of the obstacles in their way. For one thing, they would have to verify every statement on the tapes, and every assumption made by Craig, with documentary evidence. It was not enough to stand up in court and say, 'On this date John Denbigh called Howard Marks from the Hacienda Motel and gave the telephone number in interstate code.' They had to *prove* beyond doubt that Denbigh was at the Hacienda when he made the call. They needed a copy of his hotel bill; the credit card slip he'd signed; with any luck, a statement from a receptionist or room service waiter who could identify him; a printout of the telephone numbers he had called. Following that kind of paper trail would take months of foot-slogging work.

And that was only half the battle. Even before the paper chase could begin, they had to get the US Attorney's Office on board. However immaculate the supporting evidence, their case would still be what is known in agents' jargon as a 'no dope historical'. As a rule, prosecutors do not relish no dope historicals. The drug cases they want to take to court are those where there is 'powder on the table'. They want to be able to say, 'Here's what was seized,' because the sight of a small mountain of dope or a million dollars in cash has an electrifying effect on jurors. A mountain of paperwork, on the other hand, is liable to send them to sleep.

Lovato knew that the sat-track on the *Axel D* might eventually provide them with 'powder on the table', but he wasn't willing to depend on it. He intended to put Marks behind bars the old-fashioned way, by investigating him to death. That, after all, was what detectives were supposed to do.

To succeed he needed Julie. Technically, it was her case, not his. Los Angeles was where the load had been delivered and sold, so Los Angeles had jurisdiction – 'venue' in their jargon – over the crime. His new management in Miami had let him to California without making too much fuss, but only on a strictly temporary basis: two weeks maximum. Then Miami wanted him back for, God knew, Miami had pressing problems of its own. So Julie was going to have to do the bulk of the grunt work. That, at least, was Lovato's view.

She saw things somewhat differently. Her plans did not include sitting down with Craig Lovato and his wretched tapes for two weeks, compiling an endless list of things for *her* to do. Howard Marks was his obsession, not hers – and he was certainly not an obsession of the LA office.

She was willing to pursue the investigation, but on a different tack. She flew out of town with Neil Van Horn to do that, leaving Lovato – not very pleased – to his tapes.

New Orleans, Louisiana, 28 September 1986

The DEA was not the only US government agency with a stake in the Marks investigation. US Customs also had an open file on Marks, dating back to the Alameda case when he had been identified as the mysterious Mr Dennis, the renderer of the crates delivered to Forbes, Forbes, Campbell & Company in Karachi.

Their role in the investigation had not amounted to much, other than recommending Rex to the DEA as an informant. But Customs had been kept informed of developments, and they had a legitimate interest in the outcome, so it was not unreasonable that they should invite Julie Desm and Neil Van Horn to a conference to review progress. It was held in New Orleans because Lawrence Ladage, Rex's mentor, was now the Special Agent in Charge of that office.

Almost as soon as they arrived in New Orleans Neil and Julie knew that something was very wrong. They were sitting in the lobby of their hotel with a handful of Customs agents, preparing to go out for the evening, when suddenly there among them, large as life, was the smiling Ross Woods – RW.

He was clearly at home with Customs, very much one of the party. Julie was surprised, even shocked. The DEA rule that said informants must be fully documented was followed by another rule which said: *never* socialize with informants. Obviously, she thought, US Customs lived by a different set of rules.

When the party set off to find a place to have a drink, RW tagged along, following at Van Horn's heels, peppering him with questions about the Marks case. Van Horn did not like RW (or Rex, for that matter). He thought he was like a puppy dog, always anxious to please but always getting in the way. He particularly did not like being asked questions by RW. Informants were supposed to provide information, not demand it. 'I'm not going to answer your questions,' he said. 'What we know isn't available to the public.'

'Neil, what is this guy doing here?' Julie whispered as they sat in a bar watching RW dance with a female Customs agent.

'I don't know,' said Van Horn, 'but I don't like it.'

They found out what he was doing the next morning when they walked into the Customs conference room. RW was sitting at the table. He was there as a delegate, Customs's in-house expert on the Howard Marks organization. They hadn't yet given him a badge but it was probably only a matter of time.

Van Horn asked RW to leave the room for a moment. Then he bluntly told his Customs colleagues: 'Listen, the stuff he knows about, if it makes you feel better to have him in here and tell it, fine, that's great. But there's a whole bunch of other shit that we know, that he's not going to know because we are not going to discuss it while he's in the room. It's that simple.' The message was implicit: either he goes or we go.

Van Horn and Julie went to see Lawrence Ladage to repeat their threat. Van Horn and Ladage were hardly of equal rank in their respective organizations but they were contemporaries and they went back a long way in Portland, where they had worked at the same time – and, anyway, Neil Van Horn is not easily intimidated. He greeted Ladage like an old friend and then said: 'Get that man out of here.'

They reached a compromise. RW remained at the conference only long enough to give his presentation on the Marks organization – which contained nothing the DEA agents didn't already know. Then he was politely shown the door.

At Ladage's request it was tactfully done. He'd told Julie and

155

Van Horn: 'I don't care if you get rid of him, but don't hurt his feelings.'

London, October 1986

Howard and Judy Marks were in London for the birth of their third child – a son, Patrick – when Sunde turned up unannounced on the doorstep of their home in Cathcart Road.

He brought with him a gift: detailed notes of many of Howard's telephone conversations which, he said, had been recorded in Palma and transcribed by the DEA. He said he'd got them from the DEA. He told Marks that the names of the agents he should worry about were Craig Lovato and Julie Desm.

Glancing at the notes, Marks realized for the first time the sheer scale of the DEA operation against him. Until then he had believed that Peter Combs was the DEA's main target, and that his own phone had been tapped only incidentally. The notes that Sunde brought him shattered that comfortable illusion.

There was more.

Sunde took him to see his partner, Reiner Jacobi. Marks knew that Jacobi had helped fabricate his defence at the Old Bailey trial in 1981 but he'd never met him. They went to the Kensington Hilton Hotel in west London, where the German met them at the entrance, wearing a tracksuit. He said they would have to excuse him: he had an appointment with his contacts from MI6. He would meet them in an hour at another Kensington hotel.

When he arrived, promptly, at the Kensington Palace Hotel, he was cordial but elliptical. He was very much the senior executive, there to talk in broad terms, not detail. 'Tom,' he said, 'will explain everything to you. Keep doing what you're doing. Bear in mind we are only here to help you.' Then he excused himself; a busy man.

In the car, on the way back to Cathcart Road, Tom Sunde did indeed explain everything. He told Marks that the DEA had planted a Satellite Tracking Device inside a compartment on the main mast of the *Axel D*.

Howard had known Tom Sunde for almost ten years without deciding quite what to make of him.

He'd first met him as Peter Combs's dogsbody, sent over to London occasionally when Peter and Patti could not tolerate his suffocating presence in California any more and needed a break.

156

'Go and see Howard,' they would say, and Sunde would arrive in London or wherever Marks was, ever willing to do whatever Howard wanted.

He'd been in London in 1980 when Howard and Judy got engaged, and he'd taken over the organization of their engagement party. He'd spent endless afternoons with Howard at the Caviare Bar in Knightsbridge, careful never to indulge his considerable cocaine habit in his presence – though Howard was fully aware of it. During the preparations by the defence for Howard's Old Bailey trial, he was tireless; the main assistant architect of the tower of perjury that Howard built.

By the time Howard was released from prison, Sunde had undergone his metamorphosis. He was drug-free and, as Marks could testify, very much into personal fitness.

Howard and July's eldest daughter, Amber, was then a pupil at Putney High School in London and she was insistent that her father uphold the family honour at the school's sports day by competing in the fathers' race. Howard, after twenty years of inhaling tobacco and dope, wisely declined. He sent along Tom as his ringer, and Sunde won the race, even though his opponents included Nigel Havers, then in superb condition from preparation for his role as the Olympic gold medallist in *Chariots of Fire*.

Sunde claimed that he owed his splendid physical prowess to the training regimes – unarmed combat, endurance tests, and the like – imposed by his new employers, the CIA. Howard who, of course, knew a thing or two about exaggerated claims to an intelligence connection, did not necessarily believe him. Still, one never knew.

The first load Howard had sent to the US after his release was on behalf of the CIA – or so Sunde and Jacobi claimed. Yet again, they had promised Combs that the 1973 Las Vegas charges would be dropped (and this time they'd showed him a letter to that effect, typed on Justice Department notepaper) if he would import a load into New York and donate 30 per cent of the profits to the CIA for 'off the book' activities. Greg Petragus, the supposed CIA case officer, made his first appearance on the scene to say that 'the Company' would ensure the load got through.

So Combs asked Marks to find a supplier in Pakistan, and Marks found Saleem and Aftab Malik, who agreed to send more than 4 tons of hashish to New York in four separate containers. They were consigned to the AT&T telephone company, which was considered sufficiently reputable to preclude a search by US

157

Customs. The consignment was air freighted, via Paris, in January 1984. It vanished, apparently, off the face of the earth.

Sunde and Jacobi claimed it never arrived in New York. Combs assumed it had been seized by Customs, but he could find no reference in any of the news media to what would have been a significant bust. Greg Petragus said he had made an analysis, and the only possible conclusion was that Marks had diverted the shipment as it passed through Paris – an accusation that Combs did not believe and Howard angrily denied. The only certainty was, Combs had lost $1.2 million in front money.

Whether or not Sunde and Jacobi worked for the CIA, however, it was now impossible for Howard to deny that they had extraordinary access to official information. The DEA transcripts of his telephone conversations were sufficient evidence of that; the transcripts and the alarming news about the *Axel D.*

On learning about the sat-track from Sunde, Marks immediately called Gerry Wills to tell him that his boat was bugged.

'Yeah, I know,' Wills said. Sunde, it transpired, had already tried to sell the information to Combs. Though Combs had told him to 'get fucked' – this time he *really* meant it – he had passed on the information to Wills. But Sunde had not told Combs precisely where the sat-track was hidden. Wills took the details from Marks, though he said it wasn't worth paying for.

'Well, look, maybe they can come up with some more information,' said Marks. 'I think you ought to pay them.' Reluctantly Wills agreed.

'Peter says to be careful of them because they work for the DEA.'

'Of course they work for the DEA,' said Marks. 'How do you think they know what they know?'

They discussed the sat-track some more and how it might affect their future plans for the *Axel D*. Wills said he would have it taken care of in due course. In the interim the boat would be sent on 'a vacation'.

'Mozambique might be nice,' said Howard.

The signals received at EPIC from the *Axel D* became distorted. It was no longer possible to pinpoint the precise location of the ship. The best they could do was place her somewhere in the Indian Ocean; somewhere near the East African coast. Six months to the day after the sat-track was first installed, the signals ceased.

In San Diego Steve Austin couldn't understand it. The second battery pack he'd added should have kept the signals coming for a year.

Jim Hobbs, finally released from jail in Lisbon, the charges against him of kidnapping minors dropped, was once more working for Howard Marks. It was the only thing he wanted to do. He once said he would spend a year in jail just to spend one week in Howard's company.

In Hong Kong he collected $250,000 from a courier sent from California, and handed it over to Tom Sunde, as instructed. It was not his job – or his desire – to ask why.

Manila, December 1986

The MacArthur Hotel (proprietor: Lord Moynihan) was not exactly the Mandarin, but through a lot of hard work and the financial resources of a number of partners (each of whom would, invariably, fall out with Lord Moynihan and be replaced by a new investor), the place had been refurbished to a decent standard. The most luxurious accommodation it offered was called the Howard Marks Suite. Howard, however, insisted on taking a room at the Mandarin because, unlike the MacArthur, it offered direct international dialling.

'Look,' said Howard when they met for dinner, 'I've got an associate of mine who is going to be here for a few weeks or days, I'm not sure which. I want him taken care of. Everything's on me, right? Just take care of him.'

'Well, how's the bill going to be taken care of?' said Lord Moynihan.

Marks said he would provide an advance of $50,000, which seemed more than generous. Moynihan wanted the money paid into an account outside the Philippines, to avoid the irritating government regulation that required residents to convert their foreign currency into pesos. Unfortunately he didn't have an overseas account, an omission which Howard said was 'stupid'. He instructed Moynihan on one provision of Marks's Law: 'Never make it difficult for people to pay you.'

Lord Moynihan's wife did have an overseas account, in Hong Kong, and they settled on that, and a week later the money arrived – at approximately the same time that Howard's guest turned up at the MacArthur.

He enjoyed the hospitality of the MacArthur for the next few weeks – 'Just the necessities, mind you,' Howard had said, 'he's not a champagne guest' – apparently in limbo. He said he was a boat captain and complained to Moynihan that his crew were stuck in Hong Kong without money. He said he didn't understand it: Howard Marks was normally so reliable.

'Well, stay as long as you like,' said Moynihan. With $50,000 on hand, the captain could stay in the MacArthur until it fell down.

But Marks, though exceptionally generous to his friends, was not a fool either when it came to money, and he was expecting a good deal more for his money than second-rate hotel accommodation. He went to Europe for the long Christmas and New Year vacations, and then returned to Manila on 21 February on a flying visit.

He told Moynihan it was time to proceed with the 'back-up project'. He said he would be back in a couple of days' time with an agronomist, 'the world's greatest expert' on the cultivation of marijuana.

'Jesus. Oh, Jesus, Jesus,' Moynihan said to himself. 'What the hell am I going to show him?'

Since the 'back-up project' had first been proposed fifteen months before, Moynihan had done almost nothing to turn the Philippines into a gigantic marijuana plantation. He had introduced Marks to an Australian mobster (one of his investors in the MacArthur Hotel) who'd produced samples of Filipino dope, but nothing had come of it. He had not, as he had promised, scoured the islands for somewhere suitable. And though the fall of the Marcos regime had temporarily made him vulnerable, and provided a reasonable excuse for inaction, he seemed to be surviving quite well under the Aquino government. ('He's such a turncoat, you know,' Marks had told Wills on the phone.)

No, he didn't have an excuse that would wash, he decided. If Howard was going to return in two days' time, he'd better have something to show him. Fortunately, as he would later say, 'One has influential friends.'

By the time Marks returned to Manila with his agronomist – a laconic American named Roger – on 25 February, Moynihan had found two private islands for sale, both of which had ample fresh water supplies, he hoped; Howard had said it was a basic requirement for marijuana cultivation. One of them, Hermana Minor, was distressingly close to the American naval base at Subic Bay, but Moynihan saw no reason to mention that. The other, Fuga, was in the extreme north of the Philippines and, thus,

160

close to international shipping lanes, which Moynihan thought might be useful.

They set off on a tour of inspection the next morning, flying in a small chartered plane. Hermana Minor ('Little Sister'), viewed from the air, turned out to be blessed with freshwater lakes and even a dam.

'Water, Howard. There you are, water, water. I mean, there's water coming out of your ears,' said Moynihan, milking this lucky discovery for all it was worth. 'It's taken me months to find,' he claimed, though he had never even heard of the island until two days before. 'All this water . . .'

His reverie was interrupted by the radio: 'This is Subic. Identify yourself,' said an official-sounding American voice. Roger did not react well to this intrusion. He had an accent honed in the deep south of the United States that Moynihan found incomprehensible, but on this occasion he had no difficulty in understanding what Roger wanted: 'Let's get the hell out of here.'

They flew on to Fuga, which was not scanned by American radar and which also had water. It had another potential advantage: it was in Luzon province, still solidly pro-Marcos and therefore less likely to receive much attention from the central authorities in Manila. What it did not have was any land more than a few feet above sea level. 'You never said anything about altitude, Howard,' said Moynihan when they pointed that fact out. He was a little hurt by their ingratitude.

They landed on Fuga anyway, so that Roger could collect soil samples while Moynihan and Marks refreshed themselves at the guest house. He returned two hours later with plastic bags filled with earth, apparently satisfied by what he'd found.

Indeed, on the flight back to Manila Roger said that he might move his family to the Philippines, and asked Moynihan for recommendations on where to live. Moynihan suggested the mountain resort town of Bagio, north of Manila, where he himself had a weekend home. He had heard the schools were excellent, he said. Never mind the schools, what about the plumbing, said Roger. The plumbing? Yes, the plumbing: did it work? Ah, thought Moynihan, a typical American.

S E V E N

Robert O'Neill was going to be
the greatest football player in America, until he accepted that as
the child of a mother who was five foot one, and a father who was
just one inch taller, he was unlikely to grow up to be over six foot.
Anyway, he hated to practise almost as much as he liked to play.
So he had to fall back on his first choice of profession, which was
putting people in jail. He made the choice when he was four years
old, telling his mother he was going to build a prison on a vacant
lot near their house and lock up all the bad guys. Then he would
become a priest and redeem them.

Not many people in the Bronx would have believed it. Even
by the standards of one of New York's toughest neighbourhoods,
his reputation for fighting, both on and off the football field, was
formidable. When he first began studying law he was assigned a
book on juvenile delinquency and discovered that 'everything in
there, I had done'.

'What are you doing now, O'Neill?' said his former football
coach, years after throwing him out of a game for unnecessary
roughness.

'I'm an Assistant District Attorney for Manhattan,' said O'Neill.

'No, really, what are you doing?'

'It's true,' said O'Neill.

'God, you've changed.'

Not necessarily. In some ways the courtroom was an extension
of the football field; a place to knock the other guys down. It was

what he liked to do. He *enjoyed* it. On the football field he would always offer to help victims regain their feet, but only to make sure they knew who had knocked them down in the first place.

O'Neill – Bobby, to just about everybody – grew up in Edgewater, an extraordinary community in the east Bronx, overlooking Eastchester Bay and Long Island Sound. It consisted of a few hundred wooden houses crammed together along narrow streets in what looked like Toytown. The houses were originally built as simple summer homes by people from Manhattan to escape the heat of the city. Then Irish and German immigrants moved in, and it became a solid working-class enclave surrounded by Italian neighbourhoods in which Bobby and his friends had to learn to survive. There was nothing remotely pretentious about it, which is why O'Neill always loved the place.

Edgewater children went to the local high schools and harboured no great academic aspirations, but Bobby was much too bright for that. When he was thirteen his father told him he must take a scholarship to Regis Jesuit School in Manhattan. He did not want to go to Regis. His father said: 'OK, stay at high school and when you're finished I'll get you a job in my building and you can be a janitor like me for the rest of your life, making $13,000 a year. Or you can go to Regis and make something of yourself.'

So Bobby went to Regis, defiantly clad in his black leather jacket, determined to hate it. The broadening of his horizons began when he discovered that boys who sat with their legs crossed were not necessarily gay – a belief defiantly held in Edgewater.

Like Howard Marks, he found that learning came very easily. When he graduated from Regis he was accepted by Fordham College in New York, where he majored in political science because that is what aspiring lawyers did. In his first semester he got an average grade of B-plus without trying. After that he decided to try, and got straight As. He graduated from Fordham *magna cum laude*.

It was therefore with some confidence that he applied to Fordham Law School – only to be rejected. It was his first lesson in life that it was not what he knew but who he knew that counted. Of those accepted into Fordham Law School, 70 per cent had parents who had been there. The rest had 'connections'. O'Neill didn't, and the snub rankled. When a friend, who did have connections, offered to get him in, he said, 'No. I don't want it.'

Instead he went to New York Law School. He borrowed $15,000

in student loans, which was more money than he had ever imagined. To survive otherwise, he got a night job as an orderly in the operating room at Westchester Square Hospital, 'cleaning blood off the walls', and as a paralegal in the District Attorney's Office at the Bronx County Building, later vividly depicted as a 'fortress' of white prosecutors under siege in Tom Wolfe's *Bonfire of the Vanities*.

Bobby O'Neill, in short, had always been a fighter. He moved from the District Attorney's office in Manhattan to the US Attorney's office in Miami because Miami, as the American headquarters of Cocaine Inc., seemed to be where the action was. The fancy lawyers in the Miami office – meaning those with connections – tended to shy away from drug prosecutions, preferring the more rarefied atmosphere of fraud trials and public corruption cases offering high visibility. O'Neill, on the other hand, relished narcotics cases: not because of any crusade on his part against drugs – where he grew up 'every drug known to man' was available, and 'just about everybody' tried them – but because it gave him a shot at knocking down 'some *really* bad people'.

He had a striking resemblance to the actor Michael J. Fox (and, to his irritation, would sometimes be mistaken for him by teenage girls), and an abundant measure of Irish charm. He looked and seemed and sounded about as threatening as Peter Pan. Appearances can be wickedly deceiving.

Miami, February 1987

What Craig Lovato needed was a federal prosecutor with balls. There were none, apparently, in Los Angeles.

His putative case against Marks had languished for months in the LA office of the US Attorney while he fought other battles in the war on drugs in Miami. In September 1986, they'd said they needed a couple of months to review the file. In January, having heard nothing, Lovato called them and they said they needed another couple of months to review the file. In late February they said they would prosecute Marks – *if* Lovato did all the pre-trial work and gave them a case they could walk into court to present. That was not the way these things were supposed to work.

The investigation was now dead. Nobody – not the Los Angeles US Attorney's office, not the Spanish police, not Her Majesty's Customs in London, and certainly not Lovato's DEA managers in Miami – wanted to know. Forget about it. There were other priorities. Case closed.

Or it might have been but for Wendy Lovato and the consequences of what had seemed at the time to be an unfortunate and inconvenient assignment.

The previous August, when the Lovatos has been reunited for less than a month after Craig's two years in Spain, Wendy had been transferred by the DEA from Miami to the Fort Lauderdale office. True, Fort Lauderdale was within easy commuting distance, but her new assignment involved a lot of late nights and a good deal of foreign travel. 'Thanks, guys,' she'd said when they'd told her.

The assignment, however, turned out to be a jewel. The DEA called it Operation Man. In London it was codenamed Operation Cougar. Either way, it was the first major joint operation mounted by the DEA and New Scotland Yard and it proved to be a spectacular incursion into the complex and murky world of international money laundering.

It stemmed from the robbery of £26 million of gold bullion from the Brinks-Mat warehouse near Heathrow airport in November 1983, and the subsequent killing, during the investigation, of a Scotland Yard detective, John Fordham. It became an investigation in its own right – Operation Cougar – when Scotland Yard's hunt for the stolen gold led to Patrick Diamond, a self-styled financial consultant who ran a vast money-laundering operation from the Isle of Man.

Diamond became the unique target of a Special Operations Task Force, made up of detectives from various specialist branches of the Yard, including the fraud squad and the criminal intelligence branch. In March 1986, after months of intensive surveillance, Diamond was arrested on the Isle of Man and quickly persuaded to talk. What he told the task force led the detectives to the British Virgin Islands in the Caribbean, where in 1977 Shaun Patrick Murphy, the son of a Liverpool bookmaker, had put out his shingle. Murphy's modest office – in Road Town, the capital of Tortola, the largest of the islands – was in a wooden house above an electrical equipment store. Even so, by 1985 the *Financial Times* was able to describe it as the 'nerve centre of the islands' financial services industry'. The *Financial Times* didn't say so, but those services included laundering prodigious amounts of money for international drug syndicates and, the police suspected, organized crime.

Two British detectives, sworn in as special constables on Tortola, led the raid on Murphy's office, finding so many incriminating financial records in his files that a chartered jet was required to

165

remove them from the island. The records implicated two Miami attorneys and a number of US-based trafficking syndicates, and Scotland Yard offered to share its findings with the DEA. Murphy's records were air-lifted to the DEA office in Fort Lauderdale, where they filled an entire room. Then Murphy started talking, in return for immunity and protection. The leads he provided led Scotland Yard and the DEA into the labyrinth.

Wendy Lovato's assignment was to assist in the debriefing of Murphy, a process which took months, and to follow one particular lead he provided to a group of traffickers in Massachusetts whom the DEA dubbed 'the Boston Boys'. In the course of it she grew to appreciate the methodical tenacity of the British detectives she worked with. Perhaps they would like to have a crack at Howard Marks, she thought.

She did not approach them directly. Instead, she took a copy of *High Time* to the Fort Lauderdale office and left it on her desk, waiting for somebody to take the bait. It did not take long.

'Why are you reading that trash?' said one of the Yard men.

'Oh, Craig's working a case on him, only nobody's interested.'

'We're interested.'

'Talk to my husband.'

Except Lovato would not talk to them about the Marks investigation. Historically, the DEA's British connection was Her Majesty's Customs, not Scotland Yard. Operation Cougar/Man was a rare exception to that rule, permitted only because it was the Yard's case to begin with.

'I can't discuss it,' Lovato said when he was corralled by two of the British detectives at a party, wanting to know if he had the goods on Marks. He stubbornly refused to answer their questions, saying that a joint operation with Scotland Yard against Marks was out of the question.

But, at least in the stubborness stakes, Lovato was no match at all for Detective Chief Superintendent Tony Lundy, who led the team of British detectives in Florida. According to your point of view, Lundy was either one of the most brilliant officers Scotland Yard had ever produced, or one of the worst. Working for what used to be called the Flying Squad, he had produced spectacular results in the 1970s, earning a reputation as an extraordinary 'thief taker'. He also became mired in allegations of corruption. They stemmed mainly from his relationship with one of his informants and, in 1983, an internal Scotland Yard inquiry concluded that he was corrupt and that 'consideration should be given to removing him from duty'. Instead he was banished to one of the outposts of the London Metropolitan Police, until the urgent needs of Operation Cougar led to his recall. It was Lundy who arrested Patrick Diamond and Shaun Murphy and it was Lundy who gave Operation Cougar its drive.

One of his strengths (though it may also have contributed to his downfall) was his intolerance for red tape and disrespect for bureaucracy. Lundy said what he thought, did what he wanted and didn't care whom he upset.

Lundy's swashbuckling style earned him powerful enemies but also great admirers (including the detectives who worked for him). Ralph Saucedo, one of the deputy DEA chiefs, was among them, so, after Lovato refused to talk about Marks, Lundy went to him. Lundy didn't have the authority to say it, but what the hell: if the DEA was serious about Marks, Scotland Yard would willingly join forces in a joint operation. Indeed, Lundy said, why not just extend the scope of Operation Cougar/Man to encompass Marks?

This audacious gambit by Lundy had an electrifying effect on the DEA. Until then Lovato had hawked his tapes of Marks around the Miami office with as much success as a bible salesman at a convention of agnostics. Suddenly, he had an embarrassment of buyers.

Saucedo offered him whatever resources he needed, if he joined the Operation Cougar/Man team in Fort Lauderdale and took the Marks case with him. It was an appealing prospect for Lovato, since it meant he would be working with his wife. 'No,' said Lovato's managers in Miami when he reported the offer. 'Do it here.'

The only caveat, and it was a tough one, was that he must show 'venue': some criminal act committed in the southern district of Florida that would bring the Marks case within Miami's jurisdiction. The only thing Lovato could offer was the fact that Marks had received incriminating calls from Patrick Lane in Miami; the brother-in-law connection. It was tenuous, but it might just hold.

To test it out, Lovato went to see Bill Norris, head of major narcotics crime at the US Attorney's Office in Miami. He did not make an appointment. He just turned up, taking with him the large wall charts he had by now prepared to illustrate the Howard Marks dog and pony show.

Norris liked what he saw. He said he thought they could make a case in Miami against Marks and his friends. It would be tough but, he said, he knew just the right man for the case: Robert O'Neill, an aggressive, ambitious young prosecutor who liked a good fight. A prosecutor with balls.

Join the Justice Department and see the world!

Bobby O'Neill, who'd never been west of the Hudson river until he entered government service, found himself in San Francisco, listening to a man he'd never met describe a case he had not yet decided to take.

Bill Norris had scarcely told him about Howard Marks when Lovato called, pushing. He said he was about to address a conference of DEA agents meeting in San Francisco to exchange information on major cannabis traffickers. Why didn't O'Neill come along? He might learn something.

So O'Neill sat there in a room full of strangers, watching Lovato perform. His dog and pony now had a new conclusion: 'We're very confident,' said Lovato. 'We have an excellent US attorney working on the case.'

Oh, have you? thought O'Neill.

Back in Miami, O'Neill took home the thirty-four cassette tapes of Marks's phone conversations and listened to them on his stereo system. 'What you've got, Lovato,' he said to himself, 'is shit.'

There was nothing there – or at least nothing he could take to a jury. The conversations were heavy with innuendo but when you got right down to it, when you analysed what Marks had said word by word, he was nothing like as reckless as he seemed. He had clearly conspired to do *something* illegal but that didn't prove he'd shipped tons of dope into Los Angeles. Lacking the dope and *sans* the money, the best the government had was a case based on what Lovato *thought* the conversations meant. It wasn't enough. O'Neill didn't doubt that Lovato was right in his conjecture but it remained just that: guesswork.

That was approximately what O'Neill told Lovato when they met for their first formal discussion on the case. He said they had to go back to the beginning and support every allegation with a document or a piece of testimony: the paper trail. But, more important, they had to press on with a proactive investigation: they had to assume that Marks was still shipping dope, and they had to catch him.

'Fine,' said Lovato. 'Welcome aboard.'

Lovato calculated that a proactive investigation into the Howard Marks organization would cost $87,000. That might have been mere petty cash to any self-respecting drug dealer, but it was vastly more than the DEA's regular budget could stand.

Lovato and O'Neill were therefore required to go before a special committee to seek the necessary funding. Called OCDETF – the Organized Crime Drug Enforcement Task Force – it existed under presidential authority to approve, or not, multi-agency investigations. The ground rules were simple: if at least two federal agencies believed an investigation was worthwhile, OCDETF would normally approve the funding.

It went very smoothly. Lovato repeated his dog and pony show and O'Neill expressed great confidence that the case could be prosecuted. Both of them predicted fulsome international cooperation. These things are decided in advance, of course, and the DEA's OCDETF liaison man had already lobbied his counterpart from the Internal Revenue Service. Thus, the IRS expressed its full support for the investigation, and OCDETF applied its rubber stamp.

Lovato was designated case agent and therefore given the right to select the operation's codename. He chose 'Operation Eclectic', which was apt, given the diversity and global reach of Marks's activities, but also unfortunate since few of those who would become involved in the investigation around the world had any understanding of what eclectic meant.

Having gained his prosecutor, his operation and his funding, Lovato went to Charlie Lutz, the head of the DEA enforcement division in Miami, to seek office accommodation.

'That's not my problem,' said Lutz. 'I've told you you can have it. Go find it.' When Lovato returned in search of a staff, Lutz said: 'Christ, Craig, do you want me to do *everything* for you?'

Manila, 3 March 1987

For seventeen years Lord Moynihan's only contact with the Filipino press had been the occasional restaurant column he wrote, under a pseudonym, for one of Manila's business newspapers. With Marcos gone, however, it was, perhaps, only a matter of time.

His Philippine newspaper début was splashed across five columns of the front page of the *Daily Inquirer:*

FUGITIVE LORD TAKES OVER 'FAT CAT'S' BUSINESS
A fugitive English lord has taken over the multi-million-dollar drug smuggling operations of jailed drug trafficker Dennis 'FatCat' Smith.

The aristocrat, who is known in the Manila under-world as Lord M, has been in the country since 1970. He is now in his early 50s.

Earlier reported as the frontman of several cronies of deposed President Marcos, the Englishman is being investigated by at least four government agencies including the military's anti-narcotics unit and the Commission of Immigration and Deportation . . .

The main, extremely shaky, plank of the allegations was the fact that, seven years before, an Australian Royal Commission had identified Moynihan as 'a shadowy figure [who] is an associate of a number of Australian drug traffickers'. The commission's report had attempted to untangle, without much success, some complex financial dealings between Moynihan and an Australian named Robert Rolla Evans, who was suspected of dealing in heroin, though he was not charged. The commission never interviewed Moynihan or even approached him, but was still able to conclude that he 'is, or was, in some way involved in, or assisting, the importation of heroin from Manila'. Moynihan vehemently denied the allegation, but that did not prevent it from being reported in newspapers around the world. Except in the Philippines. Until now.

He did not as a rule read the *Daily Inquirer* – he preferred the *International Herald Tribune* – but he soon heard about it from friends. He called the newspaper to protest his innocence.

He said they had the wrong Smith. His Australian friend was called Joe, not Dennis – and certainly not Fat Cat. He said the Australian Royal Commission report was very old news and, what's more, bunkum. He admitted 'certain difficulties' in England in the past – the *Inquirer* had reported that he was wanted on fraud charges – but that was all behind him. He said he had been a 'good immigrant' to the Philippines, employing hundreds of Filipinos over the years. 'Are you going to write more about me tomorrow?' he asked.

The answer appeared in the *Inquirer* the next day, again on the front page:

FUGITIVE LORD TRAVELS ON FALSE PAPERS

This allegation at least had the virtue of truth. Moynihan had for years travelled on a fake British passport in the name of William Kerr, to avoid any difficulty that might be caused by the fact that Interpol continued to circulate his name as a fugitive.

However, the *Inquirer* went on to say that Moynihan was wanted for two robberies committed in London in 1967, including the theft of a painting, worth £1,000, from the Preston Art Gallery in King Street. It was true that Moynihan had been arrested for art theft after the gallery owner had seen his picture in a newspaper and said he *looked* like the thief. What the *Inquirer* did not say, or perhaps know, was that he was released after proving he was out of the country on the day of the theft. ('Milord, where were you that afternoon?' said the police. 'How the bloody hell do I know?' said Lord Moynihan. 'Ring me secretary and tell her to look in me bloody diary.')

But art theft was nothing compared to the revelation the *Inquirer* had in store for day three of what was clearly going to be a long and sensational series:

LORD M'S FEUD WITH SLAIN BRITISH
BUSINESSMAN PROBED

The *Inquirer* said that Moynihan was a main suspect in the murder of Robert Walden, who had been found shot in the head in a nightclub in Manila in November 1986. Though the newspaper didn't mention it, Walden was the husband of Moynihan's former Filipino wife, Luthgarda. Police had regarded it as a professional hit. Lord M, said the *Inquirer*, 'was alleged to have ordered the killing'.

And so it went on. Day four:

LORD M TAGGED IN FRAUD CASES

Fugitive English peer Lord M is believed to be behind a series of fraud cases in the past seven years, costing four banks and three other firms 2.027 million pesos . . .

Then:

LORD M LINKED TO SEX TRADE

A manpower placement agency owned and operated by fugitive English peer, Lord M, has exported nearly 2,500 Filipino women to brothels in Australia and Japan . . .

Heroin trafficking; murder; the sex-slave trade; what next? Eager correspondents from British newspapers began appearing on Lord Moynihan's doorstep. He decided he had better do something.

*   *   *

171

In the midst of the storm Roger, the agronomist, returned to Manila. He travelled on a Brazilian passport issued to Roger Odom, but his real name was William Roger Reaves. Whether or not he knew anything about cultivating cannabis, he certainly knew about trafficking in drugs.

Until 1982, when he was arrested in Los Angeles and convicted of running a Continuing Criminal Enterprise, Reaves was the pre-eminent American pilot for Colombia's Medellín cartel, suspected of flying tons of cocaine into the United States. After serving two years in prison, he was released on twenty-five years' probation but fled the US with his family, moving first to Brazil and then to the South of France. Indicted again in 1985, this time in Miami for cocaine trafficking, he remained near the top of the DEA's most-wanted list. Until he saw the headlines in the *Daily Inquirer*, he thought the Philippines might be a suitable place to hide.

Moynihan, knowing nothing about Roger's background, sought to reassure him when they met for dinner in Manila. He said the *Inquirer* was a 'cheap rag' and that the storm would eventually blow over. There was no need for Roger to abandon his plans.

The next morning, Roger left the Philippines without saying goodbye. Moynihan never saw or heard from him again.

London, May 1987

Detective Chief Superintendent Tony Lundy sat in his office at Scotland Yard surveying British newspaper accounts of Lord Moynihan's troubles. *Today* reported:

> DRUG PEER, LORD MOYNIHAN,
> TO BE KICKED OUT
>
> A British peer accused of drug-dealing, fraud and prosti-tution is expected to be thrown out of the Philippines.
> Lord Moynihan, 51, half-brother of Tory MP Colin Moynihan, has been called before immigration officials and is likely to be deported in a week. There was no information last night where he might be sent . . .

Lundy had obtained a copy of Lovato's DEA 6, summarizing the fruits of his investigation in Spain, so he knew Moynihan was part of the Marks mob, as he called it. He sent a message to the police in Manila, via Interpol, asking 'the current situation regarding your ongoing investigation of Lord Moynihan'.

The reply was disconcerting: 'What ongoing investigation?'

He tried again, setting out what the newspapers had said. This time there was no reply from Manila.

He was still pondering what to do next when he received a call from an Australian businessman who said he was on holiday with his wife in England. 'I'm ringing on behalf of Tony Moynihan,' he said. 'Can I come and see you?'

'Tony is interested in talking to you,' he said when he arrived at Scotland Yard with his wife. Lundy attempted to question him about Moynihan but he would not be drawn. 'Shall I give Tony a message?' he said. It was Lundy's turn to be noncommittal.

Two days later, Moynihan tried the direct approach. He called Lundy from Manila, saying he'd seen his two messages sent via Interpol. He proposed that Lundy come to Manila to talk to him. Lundy said he would like to but couldn't travel abroad without authorization. 'Don't worry, old boy, I'll get you permission,' said Moynihan.

Now there's a worried man, thought Lundy. He knew that what Operation Eclectic badly needed, and what Lovato was looking for, was somebody on the inside of the Marks mob, an informant.

He called Craig in Miami: 'Moynihan's your man.'

Manila, May 1987

Lord Moynihan's first inclination had been to ignore the *Daily Inquirer*'s attack. But when the immigration department told him he had been placed on the 'stop list', unable to leave the country, pending 'investigations', he knew he had to do something. He went to see 'Robbo'. Had the *Inquirer* known, it might have been shaken to its editorial foundations.

John Robinson was the drug liaison officer for the Australian Federal Police (AFP) in Manila. He and Moynihan were occasional golfing partners and friends. Unlike the royal commission, and the *Inquirer*, Robinson did not believe that Moynihan was any kind of drug trafficker. Moynihan did come across some pretty exotic people in the course of his business deals, however, some of whom were of interest to the AFP. So they had reached an informal arrangement whereby Moynihan checked out any suspicious associates with Robinson – 'Just to make sure I don't end up in any more of your bloody royal commission reports.' Robinson would sometimes look at the latest name on Moynihan's list, shake his head, and tell him to 'get a new partner'.

Moynihan told Robinson he was going to sue the *Inquirer*. He knew he wouldn't win – nobody won libel suits in the Philippines – but at least he could register his indignation, protest his innocence. He needed witnesses who would say he was *not* regarded as Fat Cat's successor. He needed Robbo.

'No problem there,' said Robinson. 'I'll be there on that one.' He said he just needed to check with head office to get clearance.

'Well, be a good guy and go get it,' said Moynihan.

A few days later Robinson called back. 'Listen, I've got somebody who wants to meet you.'

'Who's that?'

'Somebody from the DEA.'

'What's that?'

'The Yanks.'

'What have they got to do with this? How did they get in the act?'

'They're a bit worried. This clearance you wanted me to get, they don't seem to think you're as clean as I do.'

'Well, what are they talking about? I really don't understand.'

'Listen, you'd better come and meet this bloke, all right?'

It never had been in Art Scalzo's nature to delay coming to the point.

He could, when he wanted to, soften his air of brooding impatience with rollicking good humour, but that usually happened off-duty. Above all else, Scalzo had the manners and mannerisms of a thoroughly irritated enforcer for the Mob, which is what he pretended to be for the first six years of his career with the DEA. He was not physically large; Moynihan was heavier and several inches taller. Nevertheless, there was something inherently threatening about him. In New York his colleagues nicknamed him 'Street Warrior'. He played the part of a 'wiseguy' so convincingly, the Mob eventually got fed up with him and sent a real enforcer round to his house. Thus, his transfer to the Philippines.

In John Robinson's office at the Australian Embassy, where Lord Moynihan went, as he thought, to 'clear up any difficulties', Art Scalzo met him as though he had just kicked down the door. Even Robinson, who had recommended that Scalzo employ his tough-guy act, was taken aback.

Scalzo didn't actually read him his Miranda rights but he might as well have done. Moynihan should not underestimate the trouble he was in, said Scalzo. The DEA had evidence of Moynihan's involvement in a conspiracy to import tons of hashish into the

United States. It was enough to get him indicted, enough to get him extradited, and enough to put him away for twenty years. He was going away, no doubt about it. His only chance – chance, mind you, no guarantees – was to co-operate with the DEA, to tell everything he knew, *now.*

Moynihan – when he later recalled the moment, acting it out as though it were a scene from a play – underwent a transformation. The jovial *bon vivant,* the 'call me Tony' egalitarian, the man who said he rejected inherited titles and privilege, vanished. In his place sat the 3rd Baron, his eyes bulging, his dignity rampant; a man who, had his father not squandered away his inheritance, would have known exactly how to deal with recalcitrant retainers; an outraged former officer of Her Majesty's Coldstream Guards, the finest regiment there is; no argument.

'Now, just a minute, you get one thing in your mind,' said the 3rd Baron. 'I am *not* an American citizen. We are *not* in the United States of America. And if the United States of America sinks tomorrow I don't give a fuck. I am an English lord. You do not necessarily have to call me Milord, but' – his voice rising now, every word a distinct separate volley – 'that might be A GOOD FUCKING START.'

Robinson suggested they start the meeting over again. Just pretend it had never happened. Christ, calm down!

It was therefore on a much calmer level that Scalzo re-described Moynihan's predicament. He told him, with just a touch of exaggeration, that Assistant US Attorney Bobby O'Neill was ready to go before a grand jury to seek an indictment against Marks and various members of his organization, 'including you'. Scalzo said the charges would be brought under the RICO statute (Racketeer Influenced Corrupt Organizations), which was about as serious as it gets.

Moynihan was incredulous: 'But dear boy,' he said, 'I haven't been to America for years, and I don't care if I never go there again.'

It didn't matter, Scalzo told him. Any act furthering a conspiracy to smuggle drugs into the United States, carried out anywhere, by anybody, of any nationality, was an offence under American law – and made that person a legitimate target of the DEA.

'Who *are* you people?' said Moynihan.

How you doing, Tony? How's it going, Tony? Thought any more about it, Tony? Tony, you've got to do the right thing.

175

Moynihan had gone away to 'think things over'. He said he would get back in touch, but Scalzo didn't leave it to chance. He called him at home. He bumped into him at places he knew he would be – because the Armed Forces Narcotics Command (NARCOM) were tapping his phone. How you doing, Tony? Made a decision, Tony?

He kept on and on about drugs. Marijuana was harmless, right Tony? Wrong, Tony. Scalzo arranged for him to visit a drug rehabilitation camp run by NARCOM and badgered him until he went.

The visit touched a raw nerve. Ten years before, his first child, Mandy – the daughter of his marriage to Shirin Berry, the exotic dancer – had been prosecuted in England for possession of cannabis. Her lawyer described her as 'part of the wreckage' left behind when Moynihan quit Britain.

'I understand her father's great interest is dog-breeding, and this seems more important to him than his own offspring,' said the lawyer.

'BONGO BARON TREATED DAUGHTER WORSE THAN HIS DOG,' said the *Sun*.

Howard's clients today, Tony, said Scalzo. Junkies tomorrow.

Eventually Moynihan said he would co-operate with the DEA. He insisted, however, that he was not concerned about any threat of American charges against him. His concern, what he wanted in return, was the British fraud charges dropped. He wanted to go home.

No promises, said Scalzo. See what you can do, said Moynihan. You've got to do the right thing, Tony, said Scalzo.

'I would have done it in the first place, if you'd just asked me nicely.'

Moynihan was almost where the DEA wanted him. Almost.

He called Marks, who happened to be in London. 'I need to see you right away,' Moynihan said. 'Something very heavy is going down.'

Howard did not want to go to the Philippines at that moment, so he sent Tom Sunde, who had become his 'intelligence consultant' virtually full-time.

They met by appointment in a parking lot in Manila. Moynihan told Sunde that the DEA were out to get Howard and that he was under considerable pressure to help them. He said that because of his precarious position in the Philippines, he was obliged to

176

co-operate – or at least to pretend to. That's what he wanted Howard to know: he would *pretend* to co-operate.

You're doing the right thing, said Sunde.

In June the most persistent of the British newspaper correspondents in Manila, Kathleen Barnes of *Today*, finally secured an interview with the fugitive peer. Lounging by the pool in his Philippines retreat, as she put it, they discussed the *Inquirer*'s allegations against him of mayhem and murder. 'Does one look like a killer, dear girl?' he asked.

London, June 1987

Dodge Galanos and Phil Corbett were both renaissance men; both painfully aware that Howard Marks could run rings around them because law enforcement had failed to get its act together. Most illegal drugs were produced in poor countries and sold in rich ones so, by definition, drug traffickers operated internationally. Cops, by and large, did not. The DEA was the exception, but with 3,000 agents scattered in sixty-three offices in forty-three countries – and with an annual budget of less than the Pentagon spent on an average day, before lunch – it was spread desperately thin. In the United Kingdom, with its fifty-two separate police forces, there wasn't even a national approach, save for that provided by Her Majesty's Customs – which had just 600 officers in its Investigation Division. 'DO WE HAVE TO BE THE DRUG TRAFFICKERS' BEST FRIENDS?' was the plaintive title of an article Commander Corbett wrote for *Police Journal*.

So Dodge Galanos (whose real first name was Diogenes, but nobody outside of Greece could pronounce it), as SAC of the DEA Miami field division, and Corbett, as head of the Criminal Intelligence branch at Scotland Yard, were disciples of a new order: one in which a co-ordinated response from specialized forces would make international borders as irrelevant to law enforcement as they were to the traffickers. Operation Cougar/Man was, for both of them, a model of what could be achieved.

Corbett therefore strongly supported Tony Lundy's desire to join forces with the DEA again, and go after Marks. He raised it with Galanos while on a visit to Miami. Galanos said he, too, thought it was a good idea.

Galanos still thought it was a good idea when he visited England to give a speech to the Association of Chief Police Officers.

Then, suddenly, he thought it was a very bad idea; indeed, impossible. He sent a stiff note to London saying the DEA could not – *would not* – co-operate with Scotland Yard in the Marks investigation. So much for the new order.

Ironically, the original opposition came from within the DEA. Mike Campbell, the DEA country attaché in London, and the man responsible for liaising with the British authorities, dealt almost exclusively with Her Majesty's Customs. As far as he was concerned, Customs did major drug investigations in Britain. The police, with whom he had little contact, dealt with the petty stuff – street dealers and users.

Campbell's view was shared by Her Majesty's Customs. It was one of Britain's oldest institutions (there were references to it in the Magna Carta) and it had always regarded smuggling as its exclusive territory, which it guarded jealously. The antipathy between Her Majesty's Customs and Scotland Yard, in particular, was very real, especially when it came to guarding their turfs against each other. There was co-operation between them, but it usually resulted from the common sense of individual officers down the line.

It was easy for Campbell, therefore, to imagine the likely reaction of Customs to a compact between the DEA and Scotland Yard. You can't allow it, he told Galanos.

But the genie was out of the bottle. Thanks to Lovato's DEA 6 on the Marks organization, Scotland Yard was now fully aware of crimes committed in Britain; crimes that, so far as the Yard could see, were not being actively investigated by Her Majesty's Customs. The response to Galanos's stiff note was diplomatically phrased but it still amounted to 'Fuck you'. Like it or not, and with or without the DEA, the Yard was going ahead with its own investigation.

When Her Majesty's Customs found out, the eruption was every bit as calamitous as Campbell had expected. Customs claimed it was already investigating members of the Marks organization, and that it was unnecessary and disruptive for the Yard to come barging into the case.

Worse, Customs accused Lovato of 'bad faith' for giving a copy of his DEA 6 to Scotland Yard. He'd breached an understanding which said that information developed in joint investigations would not be given to third parties, including – and, perhaps, especially – the British police.

It wasn't *him* who'd given it to the Yard, Lovato said in his own defence. And, anyway, the report hadn't contained any information derived from Customs; it was all the DEA's own work. Sure, said

Her Majesty's Customs. There was serious talk in London that co-operation between Her Majesty's Customs and the DEA might cease, permanently.

There were those at the Yard, Tony Lundy among them, who said 'So what?' They regarded most Customs men as civil servants, searchers of baggage and revenue collectors who were out of their depth when it came to serious drug investigations. Once a consignment of drugs got into Britain – because Customs *failed* to stop it getting in – it became a police matter, surely. There were also those at the Yard who had little time for Mike Campbell. He'd shown almost no interest in Operation Cougar/Man, presumably to avoid offending Her Majesty's Customs.

Lovato didn't care much about Customs' sensitivities either. Long-term relations with the British were a meaningless concept if they didn't bring him the help he needed to get Marks. He also had little time for the protocol that insisted the DEA contacts with Her Majesty's Customs were never direct, agent to agent, but were always supposed to be conducted through the country attaché. He thought that British institutions were hopelessly bureaucratic.

But for the DEA, the prospect of its relationship with Her Majesty's Customs coming to an end was appalling. Whatever its shortcomings, Customs was a single agency with one central hierarchy operating nationally. How could the DEA liaise successfully with a police force split into fifty-two separate constabularies?

At Campbell's urging, Dodge Galanos decided he must do what he could to repair relations with Her Majesty's Customs. He ordered Charlie Lutz, who was one of his deputies, and Lovato to London to 'sort out the mess'. They were to attend a summit meeting of senior officials from Customs and the Yard, arranged by Campbell and held at the American embassy in London.

The atmosphere was sufficiently tense to make Lovato grateful that, for the most part, British law enforcement officers do not go armed.

Tony Lundy and the Operation Cougar detectives were ordered by their superiors at the Yard not to see Lovato while he was in London, in case Her Majesty's Customs accused them of using personal friendships to influence the DEA. For Lundy, the order perfectly expressed how childish the whole affair had become.

Customs officers were under no such restraint and, before the meeting, one of then gave Lovato the front page of a tabloid newspaper. It heralded more accusations that Lundy was corrupt, and it was handed over with a smirk – as if to say: 'There you are, look at the kind of people you're dealing with.' Lovato thought it a sleazy trick. (Lundy was convinced the story had been leaked by Customs to influence the DEA.)

The purpose of the London summit, apparently, was to weigh the rival claims of Customs and the Yard that Marks was 'their case', though much of the time was spent trading mutual recriminations.

Customs – represented by John Cooney, an assistant chief investigating officer, and one of the most vigorous defenders of Customs' turf – argued they had prior claim to Marks.

He had, they said, staked that claim in the computers of the National Drugs Intelligence Unit. NDIU, based at Scotland Yard, had been set up to collate and distribute intelligence on drug traffickers, and to resolve territorial disputes between police and Customs, and between different police forces. Under NDIU rules, once Customs or a police force 'flagged' the name of a suspected trafficker in the computer, they held exclusive rights. Marks was undoubtedly 'flagged' to Her Majesty's Customs. He was, therefore, their man, Cooney said. End of argument.

But Scotland Yard's representatives, including Commander Corbett, argued that flagging a name in the computer didn't mean a thing unless it signified an active investigation. Customs hadn't done anything about Marks for months, they said. And some of Marks's associates – John Denbigh, for example – hadn't even been flagged.

We'll get around to it, said Her Majesty's Customs.

Too late, said Scotland Yard.

And on and on it went, two rival regiments squabbling over spoils that had yet to be won.

It was Lovato's boss, Charlie Lutz, who came up with the only possible compromise. Why did they keep going over old ground? he said, finally becoming impatient. What they needed to do now was decide how to move forward. He proposed that since both Her Majesty's Customs and Scotland Yard wanted the case, both of them should work on it. Customs, he suggested, should take the historic part of the investigation – the Los Angeles load – since they had already worked on it. The Yard should take the British end of the proactive investigation.

It was an elegant solution because its logic was difficult to argue against, and it won the immediate support of the two senior officers representing NDIU. Eventually the Customs men agreed to the

Lutz plan, though only with transparent reluctance. They had been outmanoeuvred by the Yard, and they knew it.

Lovato left London relieved at the outcome of the summit but also uncomfortably aware that he'd left behind some very bruised egos. Diplomacy, he decided, was not his forte. Later on, when Mike Campbell ended his stint as the country attaché in London, Wendy suggested Craig should apply for the job. 'Are you crazy?' he said. 'The Brits will have me locked up in the Tower in a week.'

London, 16 July 1987

Any satisfaction that Tony Lundy felt at the outcome of the London summit evaporated like rain in the desert. He was hoping to go to Manila to join in the interrogation of Lord Moynihan when he was abruptly placed in limbo. Scotland Yard issued a taciturn statement: 'A detective superintendent of the Serious Crimes Squad has been suspended from police duty. This follows an internal investigation conducted by the director of the Complaints Investigation Branch into allegations of a recent breach of discipline.'

Lundy's colleagues were told the matter was 'minor' and that he was being sent home on sick leave because of stress, but they knew better. They were told not to associate with him, but some of the Operation Cougar detectives said 'The hell with it,' and met him for a drink anyway. They knew, as did he, that his career was effectively over. Seventeen months later, still suspended and facing a disciplinary tribunal, Lundy would be allowed to take early retirement on medical grounds. Nothing was ever proved against him. 'BENT OR BRILLIANT?' the *News of the World* inquired of its readers. The question is unlikely to be resolved.

Lundy's abrupt departure took the heart out of the Operation Cougar team and, at first, it gravely damaged the British end of the Marks investigation.

Scotland Yard sent two other detectives to Manila to see Moynihan, neither of whom knew anything about the Marks case. They were on their way to Australia on another inquiry and were diverted to the Philippines en route. The decision made budgetary sense, but not much else.

The burden of the Marks inquiry in Britain now fell on Terry Burke, who had been a surveyor until he joined the Metropolitan Police in 1974. He'd become a specialist in international fraud and therefore an expert in difficult multi-jurisdictional cases, which is

one of the reasons he was recruited for Operation Cougar. He'd
spent the best part of a year in the US and the Caribbean working
on Cougar, and he shared the enthusiasm for the new order. He
was quieter than Lundy and, as a detective sergeant, he didn't
have Lundy's clout. What he did have was determination every
bit as stubborn as that of Craig Lovato.

Manila, 20 July 1987

'Lord Moynihan, you have the right to remain silent. You have the
right to an attorney. If you cannot pay for an attorney, one will be
provided for you . . .' Craig Lovato did read Lord Moynihan his
Miranda rights, and watched his face for a reaction. He thought
Moynihan looked distinctly nervous. Moynihan thought Lovato
was bluffing.

'I am not concerned at all about America, or Americans, or
America's threats,' he said, once again assuming the imperious
posture of the 3rd Baron. 'I haven't done anything in America.'

Lovato was expecting this. In all his conversations with Art
Scalzo, and even in agreeing to this meeting at the DEA's Manila
office, Moynihan had never conceded doing anything wrong. He'd
had a couple of conversations with Marks, sure, but that was the
extent of it. It was all nonsense, he said. Marks had been an
unimportant footnote in his life. Sorry, can't help you.

Lovato pressed on. Lord Moynihan should understand American
law on conspiracy. If he'd agreed to take any part in an operation
intended to smuggle marijuana into the United States, that counted
as conspiracy to commit an illegal act which carried a penalty of
between one and fifteen years in prison.

'Well, I haven't, *dear boy*,' said Moynihan.

'I believe you have,' said Lovato.

'Well, just remember who you're talking to,' said Moynihan.

It was not going well. They had nothing on Moynihan other
than the recording of his phone conversation with Marks in which
he'd talked of 'samples of a considerable size'. Samples of what?
Dope, undoubtedly, but how to prove it, and how to prove it was
destined for America? Moynihan was right: Lovato was playing
with an empty hand. All he had was the instincts of Art Scalzo and
Tony Lundy that said Moynihan wanted to do a deal. He wasn't
behaving like it. He was the 3rd Baron Moynihan, rampant with
righteous indignation.

They – Lovato, Scalzo and the two detectives from Scotland

Yard – agreed to take a break to let tempers cool, and Moynihan was left alone with George Pasenelli.

Taking him along on the trip to Manila had been an inspired decision by Lovato. Pasenelli was a DEA analyst, and DEA analysts are supposed to sit in offices and collate intelligence from the reports of agents in the field. They are civilians, without badges or guns, and Lovato did not always have great respect for their product: 'Intelligence', he said, 'is what you wipe your ass on.' Pasenelli, however, was not a typical intelligence analyst.

He'd been a cop in Illinois for thirty years, most of them in Waukeegan, on the shore of Lake Michigan, the last six as chief of police of McHenry. It was a nice little town of 14,000 people, where nothing ever happened – until the coroner of McHenry County found arsenic in the body of Michael Albanese. Old Mike owned a company that made sports trophies, and since arsenic was used in the plating process, the coroner's finding wasn't necessarily suspicious. But Pasenelli didn't like it. He dug around and discovered that Mike's company sub-contracted the plating work and hadn't used arsenic for years. He also discovered that one of Mike's sons was in a wheelchair, suffering, they said, from a nervous disorder. Pasenelli had some tests done on the boy and found traces of arsenic. He got court orders to exhume the bodies of three other members of the Albanese family, and found they'd all died from acute arsenic poisoning. On the first anniversary of Mike Albanese's death, Pasenelli arrested his eldest son, Charlie, and eventually sent him to Death Row. He was, in short, an old-fashioned investigator by training and instinct; somebody Lovato could readily relate to.

He had retired at the age of fifty-four because his second wife, Burdena DeWaard, a high-flying FBI agent, was promoted to Washington, DC. They moved to Alexandria, Virginia, where he got a call from the DEA inviting him to apply for a job as an analyst. He couldn't even spell the word, and had little idea of what the job entailed, but he took it. He moved into a tiny office on the tenth floor of DEA headquarters in Washington in January 1986, just as Lovato was sitting down for the first time in the Palma listening room. He was assigned to the marijuana unit of Operational Intelligence and in February he was told to monitor the Marks case. He began by digging into the DEA's unfamiliar filing system where, he discovered, there was 'an awful lot of paper'. For six or seven months he sifted and collated a vast array of apparently unrelated facts on Marks and his associates,

183

then he went to see his boss, the head of the marijuana desk, and said, 'I don't know what the hell I'm doing.' His boss told him to call Lovato.

They hit it off immediately, one old-fashioned cop talking to another. Pasenelli received the benefit of an early version of the Craig Lovato dog and pony show, and from that point on he lived and breathed the Marks case. When his wife received another promotion from the FBI and they moved to San Diego, California, he told the San Diego office: 'I'll do anything you want, but please let me keep Marks.' He said the same thing when she was promoted again (to become the first woman assistant director of an FBI bureau) and they moved to Houston, Texas.

Pasenelli became Lovato's human database, the repository of every detail, known and conjectured, about Marks and his associates. He was also Lovato's sounding board, adviser and, sometimes, critic. They argued over detail: for example, whether Dick Sharpe, another British trafficker, was part of the Marks organization or analogous to it. Pasenelli thought he was part and parcel, Lovato insisted he was not. 'OK, Craig, it's your case – but you're wrong,' Pasenelli would say. There was rarely a day they didn't talk to each other. In the dark days, when nobody else wanted to know about Howard Marks, Pasenelli was Lovato's one constant ally, refusing to accept that the case would not go forward.

Lovato took him along on a trip to Manila because, if Moynihan agreed to co-operate, Pasenelli would be indispensable to the debriefing. He also took him along because he was a canny, seasoned interrogator, and it was always likely that getting Moynihan 'on side' would require artful persuasion.

Left alone with the still-bristling 3rd Baron, Pasenelli addressed the unspoken issue that was on everybody's mind: what could they do for Lord Moynihan? Whether or not he was intimidated by American threats, Moynihan had always made it clear that his primary concern was the British fraud charges. If he was going to co-operate with DEA, he wanted them dropped.

The problem was, the British police do not make deals – or, at least, that is the well-maintained myth. Plea bargaining, without which the American justice system would collapse, is an alien – and, indeed, unlawful – concept in Britain. Nobody from Scotland Yard, nobody in his right mind, would openly tell a villain: 'You do this for us, and we'll do that for you.' When deals are made, they are sealed with nods and winks; implicit and secret understandings that are never committed to paper.

Pasenelli could make no worthwhile promises on behalf of the British, of course. What he could do was persuade Moynihan how vital his co-operation was. He was in a unique position to deliver the fatal blow to the Marks organization. In return, the Americans would give him complete immunity from prosecution, here and now, no problem. As for the British, well . . . The men from Scotland Yard couldn't and wouldn't make any promises, but just the fact that they had come all the way to Manila indicated how seriously the British took the case. If Moynihan agreed to help – and he was the only one who could – Pasenelli was sure, he said, that the British would show their gratitude. Somehow, it would be worked out. Trust me.

Moynihan went home to think about it overnight. He returned to the DEA office the following morning, bringing with him his diaries for 1985 and 1986, and a new amenable attitude. For three hours he talked into a tape recorder about the details of his relationship with Marks.

For Lovato, his revelations were something of a disappointment. Most of his dealings with Marks, it turned out, had been entirely legitimate: Howard had sought the concession for his Hong Kong travel agency to be the main agents for Philippines Airlines in London, and Moynihan had attempted to help him. Aside from the fanciful 'back-up project', he knew little about Marks's trafficking activities; nothing about the Los Angeles or future loads.

But he was still in contact with Marks and had a standing invitation to visit him in Palma.

'All right,' said Moynihan when he had finished telling his story, 'what do I have to do?'

'Go and see Howard,' said Lovato. 'And wear a wire.'

EIGHT

The nerve centre of Operation Eclectic – this multi-national investigation authorized and financed by the president's Organized Crime Drug Enforcement Task Force, no less – was a storage closet. True, it was fairly large as closets go: a windowless room in the headquarters of the DEA Miami field division where the training department normally kept its files and equipment. The only furniture was an old conference table on which sat hastily installed telephones, their wires trailing from the ceiling. It was the best accommodation Lovato could find; temporary, he hoped. The steadily-growing mountains of paper that represented the product of the historic part of the investigation were stacked on the table and, when that was full, the floor. There were no cabinets in which to file them and, even if there had been, nobody to do the work. Operation Eclectic's secretary came in two afternoons a week.

The operation did have its own computer, albeit a clone of the most basic IBM PC available from the local rental store. A DEA technician installed a simple database program in which, in theory, each piece of documentary evidence and the essential details of each potential witness were to be logged. Unfortunately, the technician's own computer skills were only exceeded by his inability to pass that knowledge on to anybody else. Lovato briefly grappled with the mysteries of the program, and then gave up. If Marks was going to be caught, high-tech would have little to do with it.

Indeed, the success or failure of Operation Eclectic now depended

186

on the stamina and stubbornness of six men: Lovato, sometimes helped by other Miami DEA agents, though it was difficult to persuade them that sitting in a glorified closet, sorting through mountains of paper, had anything to do with drug enforcement; George Pasenelli, who worked absurd hours co-ordinating every scrap of intelligence that crossed his desk, trying to predict when and where the next Marks load would arrive; Bobby O'Neill at the US Attorney's office, who continued to insist with reckless optimism that the case could be prosecuted in Miami; Art Scalzo in Manila, who babysat Lord Moynihan, preparing him for the all-important visit to Marks in Palma; an IRS agent named Brad Whites from the Criminal Investigation Department of International Operations in Washington DC, who was used to working with documents and who brought some order to the chaos; Terry Burke in London, who may not have been the last surviving disciple of the new order at Scotland Yard but who sometimes must have felt like it. They were all frustrated by the lack of resources and the inertia of their own bureaucracies, knowing that if Operation Eclectic was half as grand as it sounded Marks would already be in jail.

Burke's path in London was particularly lonely. Commander Corbett, who'd argued so strongly for the Marks investigation, was on the point of retiring from the police force to become head of security at the Bank of England, leaving Burke without a major sponsor. His superiors at the Special Operations Task Force allowed him to continue working on the case but, in the absence of any obvious breakthrough, their enthusiasm for what they saw as 'an American job' was limited. Lovato knew the feeling well.

But Burke, like Lovato, is most intractable when the odds are stacked against him. Lacking resources and manpower, he compensated by working sixteen-hour days. His pager would go off a dozen times a day, as often as not signalling yet another call from Lovato. Even so, he always responded when Lovato (forgetful or uncaring of the time difference) would call again at three in the morning. He worked weekends and endlessly delayed his holiday. Burke's colleagues, and his wife, accused him of being obsessed by the case. They were probably right. 'Cases are not supposed to get to you,' he would remind himself, but this one did.

Lovato bombarded Burke with requests. At first, as dictated by protocol, he sent them through his DEA supervisor, Charlie Lutz, to Mike Campbell, the DEA country attaché in London, who in turn passed them on to Scotland Yard, which in turn sent them down the line to Burke, based at the Special Operations Task Force headquarters in London's Tottenham Court Road. Burke sent his replies to Lovato back along the same circuitous route.

But after a brief demonstration of Lovato's insatiable appetite for information, and Burke's willingness to feed it, all the intermediaries threw up their hands. 'Deal direct,' they said – which had been Lovato's objective all along. No longer restrained by protocol, Lovato and Burke developed a loyalty to each other that gave the investigation a special and powerful impetus: as much as anything else, it was driven by their mutual determination not to let each other down.

Burke was critical to Lovato because he represented the best – perhaps the only – chance to catch Marks in the act. All of the members of the Eclectic team were pinning their main hopes on Lord Moynihan's forthcoming visit to Palma, but none of them knew if he would be willing and able to pull it off. And even if he did wear a wire, and trapped Marks into saying something incriminating, it was unlikely that it would be the details of Howard's *next* load. Why would Marks tell him what he was planning? The best they could reasonably hope for was taped indiscretions about the past. To put 'powder on the table' – which is what Bobby O'Neill was insisting on – they needed somebody to lead them to the spot, and by far the best candidate was in London.

As a last-minute substitute for Peter Combs, John Denbigh had acquitted himself extraordinarily well in Los Angeles. Gerry Wills had praised 'the Vicar' lavishly to Marks ('He can have a job with me any time'), and Marks had made his own gratitude clear. It was, therefore, a reasonable working assumption that whenever and wherever the next load came in, Denbigh would be there, taking care of Marks's interests. Follow Denbigh, and find the load. Perhaps.

So Terry Burke pounded the pavement, tapping all his contacts and informants to discover what he could about Denbigh. His first major revelation was about one of Denbigh's friends, and it was startling.

Denbigh, along with Marks, was a founding director of a British company called Drinkbridge Ltd. It had been set up shortly after Marks's Old Bailey trial with the apparently legitimate intention of importing truckloads of French wine into Britain, but it had since acquired a Hong Kong subsidiary and an account at the State Street Bank and Trust in Boston, Massachusetts. The bank account records, secured by a grand jury subpoena, showed that in the summer of 1986, $30,000 worth of money orders had been paid into the account by one 'J. Francis', with an address in Yonkers, New York.

The name, and Yonkers, rang a bell in Lovato's memory. From the paper debris on his desk he extracted the report filed by the DEA's New York office more than a year before of its all-too-brief surveillance of Denbigh. There it was: John Edward Francis of Yonkers, New York; the owner of a gold-coloured Mercedes; the man with striking red hair whom Denbigh had met in Clarke's bar.

George Pasenelli quickly established that Francis had a NADDIS number, meaning he was listed in the computer as a suspected drug trafficker, and that he was Irish by birth with British associations. Over to you, Terry, said Lovato.

Before joining the Fraud Squad, Burke had worked as a detective in the East End of London, targeting professional villains, and though the crimes he dealt with now were generally more rarefied, he'd never neglected his informants from the old days. From them he learned that the fifty-year-old Francis was 'a face': somebody well established in London's criminal milieu. Though he'd lived in New York for many years, he visited Britain regularly. He could often be seen in drinking clubs in Fulham with all the 'right people' – or, more accurately, the wrong people, the élite of the criminal underworld. He had a fearsome reputation as a cold and calculating operator. He was, Burke was told, Mob-connected: a one-time bodyguard of Russell Bufalino and still an associate of Jerry Langella, a *capo* in the New York Colombo family. He was into everything from arms trafficking to drugs.

Francis was not listed in the computers of the National Drugs Intelligence Unit at Scotland Yard, but Burke received a tip that he might be involved in a drug investigation being conducted by Dave Young of the Number 4 Regional Crime Squad based in Stoke-on-Trent, Staffordshire.

Young, it turned out, was another obsessive. In his investigation he had accumulated a mountain of paper to rival that of Lovato's. Francis was not Young's target but he had walked 'into the frame' while Young's team was keeping a hotel under surveillance. Young told Burke that he had also trailed Francis to a branch of the Allied Irish Bank in Hammersmith, London, where he maintained an account in the name of John O'Keefe.

Burke got a court order to obtain the records of the account from the bank. He used persuasion to get the rest of the story. A little over a year before, in July 1986, Francis had walked into

189

the bank with a suitcase containing $300,000 in cash. On 11 August 1986 he had wire-transferred $190,000 to account number 10000002207780 at the Crédit Suisse Bank in Hong Kong; Howard Marks's account.

Burke was understandably pleased with himself. On 24 August 1987 he gave Lovato a summary of what he'd found out. It was exceptionally good news: the fact that Marks and Denbigh had used a Mob-connected gangster to launder money was spice guaranteed to stimulate the interest of even the most jaded supervisor.

But it was Burke's second call to Miami that day that electrified Lovato. He said he'd learned from a 'confidential source' – a euphemism that can disguise anything from a highly placed inform-ant to a telephone tap – that Denbigh had returned to the United States. His telephone number, Burke said, was 604-683-7373.

Sometimes you just get lucky, thought Lovato. Burke was wrong: 604 was not an American area code but Canadian, assigned to British Columbia. Lovato knew that because he had just returned from a brief trip to Vancouver, where he'd done a favour for the drugs squad of the Royal Canadian Mounted Police, helping them with a case.

'Do me a favour,' he said, asking the Mounties in Vancouver to check on the subscriber of the telephone number. It turned out to be the Granville Island Hotel in the eastern outskirts of the city. Denbigh, the Mounties said, had stayed there off and on since the middle of August.

'Do me another favour,' said Lovato, and two detectives went to the Granville to see what Denbigh was doing. They arrived just in time to see him checking out. They photographed him as he waited for a taxi, then followed him to the Nelson Place Hotel in downtown Vancouver.

'He's met somebody,' the Mounties told Lovato later that same day. 'Name of Phillip Sparrowhawk.'

'Christ!' said Lovato.

Then they called back again and said Denbigh had met a second man, named Gerald Wills.

'Jesus Christ!' said Lovato. 'There's a load coming in. There's got to be.'

As persuasively as he knew how, Lovato urged Ken Ross of the Vancouver drugs squad to place Denbigh, Sparrowhawk and Wills under immediate constant surveillance. The timing was not good, since Vancouver was preparing for the Commonwealth Conference and the Mounties were at full stretch providing security for the leaders and delegations of forty-seven nations. Ross, however, didn't hesitate, assigning two of his best men – Murry Dauk and Stan Brooks – to the case.

Sometimes you just get lucky.

Barcelona, Spain, 9 September 1987

'I'll meet you at the Hotel Manila, seven o'clock,' Art Scalzo had said. The name of the hotel was a nice coincidence, a good omen perhaps. Even so, Scalzo was not convinced that Lord Moynihan would be there.

It was Moynihan's habit to take a long summer holiday with his wife each year, visiting old haunts and friends in the Middle East and Europe (though, obviously, not Britain), and the fact that he was about to become an undercover agent for the DEA did not deter him. So it was several weeks since Scalzo had seen him, and he made the long journey from the Philippines to Barcelona fully prepared for the possibility that Moynihan would fail to show.

But the 3rd Baron was there, in the bar, right on time. Scalzo and Terry Burke were waiting for him and it was immediately clear to them that something was wrong. As Scalzo says, Moynihan is not a person who hides his emotions. It took a couple of Scotches to calm him down and get him to describe what had happened the night before.

'I'm in Barcelona,' Moynihan had said, calling Marks at home in Majorca as arranged to announce his own imminent arrival in Palma.

'Great, I'll be in Barcelona tomorrow,' said Marks. 'Why don't we get together?'

They'd met for coffee at the Hotel Manila the next morning and Moynihan asked Marks if he was free for dinner. Marks said he already had a dinner date, with James McCann. 'You'll remember the name because it features very heavily in *High Time*,' said Marks.

'I'd love to meet him,' said Moynihan.

'Well, Jim's strange about meeting people, but I'll sound him out.'

Time had done nothing to temper the outrageous boasts of James McCann, Marks's former partner in the 1970s. At dinner that night McCann told Moynihan that he was a leader of the Provisional IRA and, indeed, the organization's main supplier of guns. He bragged that he also still ran drugs through Ireland. When Marks excused himself to go to the bathroom, McCann said that he was the real boss of the organization; Howard merely worked for him. Though he had only just met Moynihan, he did not hesitate to proposition him: would Moynihan be prepared to live in Madrid and 'front up' some unspecified but obviously illegal project?

But what had truly alarmed Moynihan, and sent him to the Hotel Manila in need of Scotch, was an incident before dinner, when McCann had collected Moynihan from his hotel. McCann had arrived in a beige-coloured Mercedes driven by an enormous Dutchman named Dac. Before allowing Moynihan into the car, Dac had opened the boot to demonstrate that his duties included more than driving.

'He had a machine-gun in there, Art,' said Moynihan. 'A bloody Uzi.'

Scalzo did his best to reassure Moynihan that there was nothing to worry about; that the task he was about to undertake in Palma was not really dangerous.

'I'll be there with you, watching your back,' said Scalzo. 'Nothing's going to happen.'

Scalzo hoped that he sounded much more confident than he felt.

Vancouver, British Columbia, 10 September 1987

The list kept growing. Denbigh, Sparrowhawk, Wills . . . then Ronald Allen walked into the frame.

'Wills's partner,' said Lovato when the Mounties reported their latest sighting at the Nelson Place Hotel.

Next came Michael Goulbourne.

'Younger brother of Kevin, Sparrowhawk's sidekick,' said Lovato.

The five men didn't do much. They played golf on a pitch and putt course. They visited the Pacific National Exhibition. They met other men, unknown to Lovato, in parks and bars and restaurants.

Allen had a woman with him and he and she and Wills and Denbigh went to a make-your-own-video establishment where they pretended to be the Rolling Stones, miming to 'Let's Spend the Night Together', Denbigh giving a very fair impression of Mick Jagger.

'They're waiting for the load,' said Lovato.

Palma, 11 September 1987

The DEA has electronic transmitters the size of shirt buttons. They can hide them in pens or the rim of a baseball cap. In the absence of sophisticated anti-bugging equipment, these tiny microphones are almost impossible to detect.

The problem is the recorders that go with them. They are much smaller than they used to be, but taped to the body of some inexperienced CI they assume huge proportions – in the CI's mind. There is something about wearing a 'wire' that makes most people sweat.

Scalzo was not sure Lord Moynihan could cope with the psychological pressure. Better to go the low-tech route, he thought. So the 'wire' with which he equipped Moynihan was nothing more sophisticated than a Panasonic mini-cassette recorder of the type used by businessmen to dictate notes to themselves. It was simple to operate and it fitted comfortably in the top pocket of the safari suits which Moynihan liked to wear while on holiday.

'But what happens when it gets to the end of the tape?' Moynihan asked.

'It turns itself off,' said Scalzo. With a distinct click.

That click assumed huge proportions in Moynihan's mind. He imagined luring Howard into some amazing piece of self-incrimination and . . . CLUNK. 'What's that?' Howard would say. 'Are you recording me?'

Moynihan wasn't afraid of Howard. He didn't think for one moment that Howard would become violent. It was the sight of Dac's Uzi that flashed before his eyes every time he thought of the CLUNK.

He devised his own strategy to forestall any such emergency. Moynihan and his wife, Editha, were staying in Palma as Howard's guests, not at his house in La Vileta but at a small apartment Marks maintained in Palma Nova. Moynihan decided that he would record his conversations with Howard only when they were in the apartment together, and then only for twenty-nine minutes – one minute less than each side of the tapes lasted. Then he would make an excuse to go into the bedroom ('I'll just check if Editha's still asleep' – something like that), turn off the recorder and hide the damn thing in the room.

The only problem was how to deceive Editha as well as Howard. Moynihan was insistent that she must not know what he was up to. He did not think she would approve.

'Good morning,' said Lord Moynihan.
  'How are you, Tony?' said Marks. 'How's Editha?'
  'Good. She's still asleep. She's not going to come with us.'
  'OK. You sleep all right?'
  'Beautifully.'
  'You sound like it.'
  'Listen, sit down. Um, let me . . . If you can give me five . . . Do you mind giving me five minutes?'

The most important thing, Tony, is don't talk too much, Scalzo had said. First, Tony, because you like to talk, and, second, because most CIs try to hide their nervousness by talking too much. Some of them talk more than the target. So, don't be long-winded. Let Howard do the talking. OK, Tony?
  Scalzo had also given him a list of priorities.
  Get Howard to talk about his activities as a doper. Get him to talk about the 'back-up project' in the Philippines and, if possible, get him to put up some seed money because that would be exemplary evidence.
  But, first and foremost, get him to talk about money laundering.
  Above all else, the Eclectic team wanted Marks to talk about his brother-in-law, Patrick Lane, for the simple reason that Lane lived in Miami. If they could get solid evidence of Lane doing something illegal for Marks in southern Florida, the thorny problem of venue would evaporate.

'OK, the first thing, Howard, is this,' said Moynihan, reading from a list of things he'd written down. 'I am desperately going to need to make some money fairly soon. Now, I've got a fellow in the United States and he has in excess of a million dollars – it might be 2 or 3 million dollars – that he wants to get out of the United States.'
  'Yeah?'
  'I mean a money washing operation is what we're talking about, right? Do you know anybody who can do this?'
  'Oh, I'm doing it all the time, obviously. Is it in cash form?'
  'It could be in any form you want, but I imagine cash form is easier for him.'

'Right. Well, the chances vary, OK? They vary depending on whether you just want to sort of physically lift the cash into another country or whether you want it laundered into an account so that it looks like payment from business – commission, or a client fee or something.'

'That's what I would imagine,' said Moynihan.

'Whether you just want a straightforward transference of cash or laundering as well . . .'

'I think it's the laundering as well he's after.'

'Well, then it's up to about 10 per cent. Straightforward is about 5 to 7½ per cent.'

They talked about percentages for a while, and speculated on whether the charges might come down if more than a million dollars was involved, to allow Moynihan to take his own cut of, say, 2½ per cent. Very likely, said Marks.

'Right, what do I do? What do I tell him?' said Moynihan, talking of his imaginary American.

'You tell him you can certainly do it,' said Marks, assuring Moynihan that he didn't want a cut for himself. 'I don't need to make anything else, believe me.'

'No, I know. I understand. You're not small-time, Howard, I know that.'

Marks was at pains to describe how easy it was: 'They get money in all sorts of forms. They're usually small bills. I give someone a suitcase full of small bills. I pay the 10 per cent and I get a nice little cheque in Hong Kong.'

'I've obviously got to guarantee him, Howard. I mean, it's a lot of money. I mean, for me it's a lot of money.'

'No, it is a hell of a lot of money. Yes, of course we would have to guarantee it.'

'Yes,' said Moynihan.

'I guarantee it,' said Marks.

'Oh, very good,' said Moynihan, meaning it. 'Now, the second thing is . . . I made some notes here so I could ask you about these things. Talk to me for a moment about McCann.'

'Jim is a very, very serious person, very dear to me,' said Marks. 'Jim and I have always been on the best of terms but use this sort of public pact that we are enemies. I mean, very, very few people actually know we're as friendly as we are.'

'Is he just into running guns or is he . . . ?'

'No, he hardly ever runs guns,' said Marks.

'Does he do grass with you?'

'Yes, he does grass with me.'

Ticking off the items on his list one by one, Moynihan led Marks deeper and deeper into the pit of self-incrimination. Then, exactly twenty-nine minutes after the conversation began, Moynihan said: 'That's really all I wanted to straighten out. I'll just go and see if Editha's awake.'

The tape ended with the sound of the bedroom door being closed.

'Art, I've done it, I've done it, wait until you hear.'

They met at the Ramada Inn in Palma, the first of a series of rendezvous points Scalzo had nominated. Moynihan arrived bursting with excitement. He insisted on describing his coup to Scalzo in detail.

As soon as he decently could, Scalzo took the tape and returned to his own hotel to transcribe it, but Moynihan wouldn't leave him alone. He kept calling up: Art, is it OK? Art, what do you think?

Scalzo thought it wasn't half bad. Moynihan had been a little pushy at times, and he talked too much, but overall it was a very impressive first effort. Scalzo finished the transcription and took it to the American consulate in Palma to be telexed to Madrid.

Then he could relax. Marks had told Moynihan on the tape that he was going to London for a few days to take care of some business, so there was nothing to do but wait for his return.

Scalzo thought he would use the time to get to know Moynihan a little better. He was growing rather fond of him. Funny old world, he thought. Here he was, posing as Tony DiAngelo, a New York Italian 'businessman' – in case anyone should ask – with an English lord for a CI, hanging around a sun-soaked Mediterranean island, waiting for a Welshman to talk himself right into an American jail.

Well, it could be worse. The women in Palma were pretty, and he'd remembered to pack his swimming trunks.

Vancouver, 13 September 1987

It was getting beyond a joke. There were now so many people to keep under surveillance, the Mounties would have been stretched even without the demands of the Commonwealth Conference.

Still, they stuck to it – to Lovato's enormous relief. Waiting in Miami, he was never more than a few feet from a telephone.

It was a Sunday, but drug traffickers generally do not break for weekends. Indeed, they prefer them, since most law enforcement agencies, constrained by budgets, cannot usually afford to pay the overtime that Sunday work requires and manning levels are at their lowest. But not this Sunday, not in Vancouver.

They knew something was about to happen. The exhaustive surveillance on Denbigh, Sparrowhawk, Wills, Allen and Goulbourne had led the Mounties to other men, who in turn had led them to others, until about a dozen people were in the frame.

At 6.30 p.m. one of that dozen led them to Delta, across the Fraser River from Vancouver, to the yard of S&M Products, where the man went aboard a small fishing boat, the *Supreme I*, moored on the river. By 10.00 p.m. there were seven or eight men there, and three Chevy trucks.

As the Mounties watched from their hidden vantage point, large and obviously heavy bales were hauled from the hold of the boat and sent ashore by conveyor belt, where they were loaded into the trucks.

The trucks left the yard one by one at twenty-minute intervals, and were stopped one by one a few blocks away by police reinforcements. The trucks contained a total of $6^{1}/2$ tons of Thai marijuana.

In the early hours of Monday morning, Denbigh, Wills and Allen were arrested in their hotel rooms. In Allen's room, and in the trunk of his car, the Mounties found 1.7 million Canadian dollars.

Sparrowhawk and Mike Goulbourne were nowhere to be found. Sparrowhawk, it seemed, had been tipped off. In the rented apartment he had shared with Goulbourne, the Mounties found a handwritten note from him:

HELLO MIKE,

MIKE, AS SOON AS YOU RETURN MAKE IMMEDIATE PLANS TO RETURN TO THE UK. PACK EVERYTHING WITH YOU. WE WILL NOT BE RETURNING TO THIS APARTMENT. PACK THE ANSWER PHONE, BOOKS, EVERYTHING. THE *VERY* WORST HAS HAPPENED SO BE VERY CAREFUL. TRY AND GET SOME DEPOSIT BACK, IF YOU CAN'T THEN FORGET IT. WHEN YOU GET BACK TO THE UK CONTACT DAVE. IF YOU DON'T HAVE A NUMBER OR ADDRESS YOUR SISTER WILL HAVE A CONTACT.

MIKE, BE CAREFUL.

REGARDS, PHIL

But though Sparrowhawk had escaped, there was apparently potent evidence that he was the supplier of the load.

Each of the bales of marijuana unloaded from the *Supreme I* had carried a sticker, approximately three inches square, printed in red and blue ink, with the words 'PASSED INSPECTION' and a hand-made drawing of a rampant bird with crossed swords held in its talons.

It was an odd-looking creature, though obviously some kind of bird of prey. In some ways it resembled the eagle of the DEA's crest.

'It's not an eagle,' said Lovato. 'It's a sparrowhawk.'

London, 14 September 1987

Howard Marks received the news by telephone from his wife, Judy. She had heard it from Gerry Wills's latest girlfriend.

The details were sketchy. All Judy knew was that Wills, Allen and Denbigh had been arrested in Vancouver, and some dope and some money had been seized.

The load belonged to Wills, not Howard. Even so, since Marks had arranged for Sparrowhawk to supply it, he was due to receive a middleman's commission of 5 per cent of what it was sold for in Vancouver. It had arrived in Canada in June, brought from Thailand on board the *Axel D* and stashed sixty miles north of Vancouver. The dope was not of the highest quality and had sold slowly. Marks had so far received 260,000 Canadian dollars as his share of the profits. He had been hoping for a great deal more.

Shit! It was not just the loss of money that bothered him. With Denbigh under arrest, there were going to be lawyer's bills to pay and money required for Denbigh's family.

Howard sent somebody to the Canadian embassy in London, to photocopy the latest editions of the *Vancouver Sun*, in the hope of learning more about what had happened. The only new facts he learned were estimates of how much money and dope had been seized.

As much as 8 tons, which was what the newspaper said, and $1.7 million wasn't all of it, but it was bad enough. Shit!

After three more days in London, Howard pocketed the newspaper report of his misfortune and headed for home, worried and distracted.

Palma, 18 September 1987

If it hadn't been for the Vancouver bust, if Marks had been thinking more clearly, perhaps he would have been alarmed by Moynihan's persistent questions. Certainly he should have been. Later, when Lovato listened to the tapes, he told Moynihan: 'Jesus! I wouldn't interrogate a guy like that if he was on the stand and I was the prosecutor. It was like you were grilling him under a spotlight with a rubber hose.'

'How many major deals have you put through in twenty years?' Moynihan said to Marks once the tape was running. 'One a year, two a year, three a year?'

'I really have no idea,' said Marks.

'Very many or . . . ?'

'Yeah.'

'How many?'

'Many, many.'

'More than two or three a year?' said Moynihan, still not satisfied.

'Yeah, maybe. Maybe two or three a year,' Marks admitted.

Marks had told Moynihan about the Vancouver bust and, getting even bolder now, Moynihan questioned him about it: 'So, Gerry was not in charge of shipping, he was in charge of off-loading, right?'

'He was in charge of transportation,' said Marks.

'Of transportation?'

'Yes, not the off-load particularly . . .'

'But how was Gerry picked up?'

'Probably through certain conversations and things in hotels, you know.'

'And they got all the stuff?'

'They got 8 tons, I believe.'

'Out of how much?'

'I don't know. I mean, there will be some they didn't get for sure.'

Marks said that because of the bust, the back-up project in the Philippines would have to wait. He said he had other things to worry about: 'Looking after wives and kids and other people.'

'Yes, it's a drag,' said Moynihan.

'Has to be done, you know,' said Marks.

But meanwhile, Moynihan said, he was going to New York to proceed with what he called 'the money transfer business'.

'I believe the money will be available to me in cash, in 100-dollar bills,' he said.

'Sounds good to me.'

'Now, are your telephones safe? Can I talk to you about it on the telephone?'

'No,' said Marks. 'No.'

They agreed on a safe way to communicate, and discussed the way in which the (mythical) $1 million would be laundered. Moynihan, on Scalzo's instructions, asked if a trial run, with $50–100,000, would be possible.

'Sure, sure, I would do the same,' said Marks. 'That's OK, as many trial runs as they like . . . I'm certainly happy to do it in small lots if they're nervous. Totally understandable.'

'I think you probably know this is drug money,' said Moynihan. 'I mean there is no doubt about the fact that it is.'

'Yeah,' said Marks. 'It usually is.'

After twenty-nine minutes, Moynihan made his stock excuse to go to the bedroom and turned off the tape.

Later that day he turned up at the rendezvous to meet Scalzo, understandably excited. But Scalzo wasn't there. He wasn't at the second, fall-back rendezvous, either, nor at the third, nor at his hotel. He'd vanished.

In a state of growing alarm, Moynihan called the American consulate. Scalzo had told him to do that only in an emergency. Well, it was growing late on Friday, the consulate was about to close for the weekend and this, surely, was an emergency.

Moynihan told the telephone operator at the consulate that he was working undercover for the DEA and that his back-up agent had disappeared.

'He's in hospital,' said the operator. Why, she wouldn't say. Dac's Uzi loomed ever larger in Moynihan's mind.

Killing time on Friday morning, waiting for his rendezvous with Moynihan, Art Scalzo had put on his swimming trunks and prepared to go to the beach. He was standing in front of the mirror in his hotel room when he experienced a stab of pain unlike anything he had ever felt.

At the clinic where he went they told him he had a rectal cyst. It could burst at any moment and poison his blood system, even kill him, they said. He needed an immediate operation. There was no time, and no way, to tell Moynihan.

It was Sunday before Scalzo was released from the hospital and returned to the hotel. Moynihan was waiting for him, anxious and petulant.

Scalzo, still in great pain, told Moynihan he was in no mood for

200

'your fucking histrionics'. Embarrassed about the precise nature of his operation, he would only give Moynihan the barest of details.

'Haemorrhoids!' said Moynihan. 'I thought you'd been shot!'

'It wasn't fucking haemorrhoids, Tony. Shut up and give me the tape.'

There was one last meeting between Marks and Moynihan, one last chance to get Marks to seal his own fate. Get him to talk some more about the Vancouver bust, said Scalzo. Get him to talk about his brother-in-law.

So, on Tuesday evening, Moynihan waited for Marks at the apartment, turning on the tape as soon as he heard Howard's knock on the door. He was getting good at this undercover work, he'd decided. Nothing to it.

'Sorry,' said Marks. 'We have to leave immediately. I'm late for an appointment.'

There was no opportunity for Moynihan to get rid of the recorder or turn off the tape. 'Where are we going?' he said, as he climbed into Howard's car.

'Palma. I have an appointment to meet Mike. Remember Mike? You met him in the Philippines. I've installed him in Majorca. He can relate directly to the authorities, you know, so I'm just keeping him with me from now on.'

Moynihan didn't know that Mike's real name was Thomas Sunde, or that he was known to the DEA as RW. He did know that Mike 'related directly to the authorities'. In Manila, when they'd met in a parking lot and Moynihan had reported his first, turbulent meeting with Art Scalzo, Mike had claimed that he worked for the CIA. Stuck in traffic in the crowded, narrow streets of Palma Nova, Moynihan thought about what he was going to do if the journey lasted more than twenty-nine minutes – when CLUNK would announce the end of the tape. He also wondered if CIA agents were able to tell if somebody was carrying a concealed tape recorder. Still, he pressed on with his mission.

'What's the news of Gerry?' Moynihan asked.

'Well, he's in jail,' said Marks. He gave Moynihan the latest clipping from the *Vancouver Sun*. Moynihan said he couldn't read it without his glasses.

'It just says this is the result of a very long investigation, a matter of months,' said Marks. 'They nailed twelve people, they nailed them on a boat coming in. They think there's a mother ship out there which they are looking for. They also got $3 million cash.'

'Three million cash? Was that your cash or Gerry's cash?'

'Well, it wasn't anyone's yet. Gerry's really. I mean, he would find it difficult saying it's not his.'

'But I mean, will he not pay you because it's gone? Is it his fault that it's gone, or what?'

'We never think of things like that,' said Marks. 'It's basically all our faults for not doing it right. And I hope no one points a finger because that always leads to trouble. I don't think it's anyone's fault. It's the combined stupidity of the outfit.'

'How much will you personally have lost out of this? Is this a big problem for you or not?'

'It's only a problem in that certain friends of mine, who are known to be friends of mine, are in jail.'

'No, I was speaking financially. I mean, from a financial point of view, how much have you lost? Have you lost a fortune?'

'Well, you never know until it's over with. I never make that kind of projection. Honestly, I'm not being evasive. I just really never think like that.'

'You must have lost at least a huge potential amount of profits.'

'Yeah, but I haven't lost any investment . . .'

'I say, you're taking it awfully well. You're not crying into your whisky.'

'No, I only worry about security. I really don't want any more money. I give a fuck about money when I'm doing it, but this time I don't really mind. It's all the same to me.'

That should do nicely, thought Moynihan. Now, the brother-in-law: 'I did get on the telephone again today, to this fellow in America, which is my number one priority at the moment.'

'Right, I'm sure,' said Marks.

'And the only problem is that the money, physically, is not in New York. It is in Miami.'

'That's OK.'

'Now, is there anybody that we can have there or do we have to move it? I don't want to move it to New York.'

'At the moment, I do have a friend in Miami who is capable of doing that sort of thing. That's my brother-in-law. The only problem with that is that if he gets stopped on the way, that's a bit close to home. But I've used him in the past. He is obviously 100 per cent honest and reliable . . .'

They reached the Valparaiso Hotel in Palma, where Sunde was staying, just in time. Moynihan turned off the tape while Marks parked the car. Then, while Marks went up to Sunde's room for 'a private chat before dinner', Moynihan waited in the hotel bar and found a sofa cushion under which to hide the tape recorder. He could retrieve it later. He was in the clear, he thought.

'Art, they're on to us!' said Moynihan.

It was two o'clock in the morning. Moynihan was shaking and close to tears. Scalzo was none too calm either. This time they both needed Scotch.

In Scalzo's hotel room, Moynihan described his alarming confrontation with 'Mike' over dinner. 'He's CIA,' said Moynihan. 'He mentioned your name. He accused me of working for the DEA. He said you'd probably sent me wired up to record the conversation. You don't know how my heart stopped at that moment. God!'

'Anybody follow you here?' said Scalzo.

'No, I took a circuitous route.'

'Let's get out of here, anyway.'

They abandoned the room for the comparative safety of Scalzo's rented car, taking with them what was left of his bottle of Johnny Walker Black Label. For the next three hours, Scalzo drove furiously around the back roads of Majorca until he was absolutely sure that nobody was following them.

Returning to the hotel, he took the three tapes of the Moynihan/ Marks conversations and hid them in his car. Then he wrote a detailed report of what Moynihan had told him and described where the tapes were hidden, and gave it to the night desk clerk. 'Put it in my box,' Scalzo said. He figured if anything happened to him, the police would find it.

He did not breathe easily until Moynihan and his wife left Palma for Paris later that morning. Scalzo had originally intended to go with them to France but he was in too much pain. He told Moynihan he would see him in Miami. Meanwhile, he was going to New York, to see a proper doctor.

'Hope your haemorrhoids get better,' said Moynihan.

'Tony, it isn't fucking haemorrhoids,' said Scalzo.

Miami, 29 September 1987

The Vancouver bust and Moynihan's sterling undercover work in Palma were sufficient to send Bobby O'Neill before a Miami grand jury. He wasn't quite ready to ask for an indictment yet, but he thought it prudent to let the members of the grand jury know what was going on; get them involved.

For, when the time came, O'Neill wanted the grand jury to hit Howard Marks, and as many members of the organization as they could rope in, with the most comprehensive and serious set of charges he could devise. Marks wasn't going to walk away from this one. O'Neill intended to prosecute him under the draconian RICO statute: the Racketeering Influenced Corrupt Organizations law originally enacted by Congress to attack the Mob, but now increasingly used by the government against drug traffickers. To make the charges even more serious. O'Neill intended to prove a conspiracy going back almost twenty years.

To bolster the case, the DEA summoned to Miami many of those who had participated in the hunt for Marks, and who would play roles in the final act of the drama.

Harlan Bowe of the DEA flew in from Karachi to testify to the grand jury about his exhaustive investigation into the Las Vegas seizure in 1973. Though it had happened so long before, O'Neill believed that part of the case was immaculate. In documenting the loads imported inside sound speakers, Bowe had provided the cornerstone of the RICO charges.

Julie Desm flew in from Los Angeles to testify about her arrest of Peter Combs. The Spanish police sent an inspector, the Mounties sent Stan Brooks to talk about the Vancouver bust, and Terry Burke of Scotland Yard flew in from London. And Art Scalzo, reassured about his medical condition though still in pain, arrived from New York.

Scalzo told the grand jury of his recent adventures in Palma. Then O'Neill asked him about the immediate future: 'You have stated you are to meet Lord Tony Moynihan on the first of October, here in Miami?'

'Yes, sir,' said Scalzo.

'After he arrives, does the DEA intend to try to run an operation [in] which Lord Tony Moynihan will be tendering a sum of US currency to Patrick Lane?'

'Yes, sir.'

For the best part of a year, Patrick Lane had lived fish. They were 25lb monster salmon with razor-sharp teeth, and Lane learned to cut, gut, brine, fillet and smoke them. His wife, Jude, did most of the selling. They worked up to eighteen hours a day supplying gourmet food shops, restaurants and hotels from Miami to Palm Beach, and, through the contacts of their employer, Raoul del Cristo, the best eating clubs on Wall Street. (Lane made weekly runs to Eastern

Airlines with sealed crates which were airfreighted to New York and then rushed to Wall Street by special delivery. Later, Lane wondered what Craig Lovato would have made of that?) It was all to no avail.

By March 1987 the declining del Cristo empire could no longer afford to subsidize European Smoked Fish, and del Cristo pulled the plug. Patrick and Jude attempted to continue the business on their own, but it failed. By the summer of 1987, Lane, no longer the executive on his way up and with no definable, marketable skills, was searching in vain for a job while the family lived on unemployment cheques of $350 a week. He was ill, with a bad back and epididimitis – both conditions ascribed by the doctor he could not afford to the working conditions at the fish factory. Then the unemployment cheques ran out.

By September 1987 he was borrowed to the hilt, unable to make the payments on his house or his car. He became obsessed with every penny and lay awake at night wondering how the family would survive. A couple of miles or so away from their home in Coral Gables was a black ghetto, infamous as a twenty-four-hour open drug market. In bed, his youngest daughter, Bridie, asked him: 'Are we going to have to live in a shack with the black people?'

Then Howard called.

Marks said that a friend of his was in Miami, and could he put him in touch with Lane?

'Sure. What's the problem?' said Patrick.

'Oh, I don't know. He's English, he's in Miami, and he contacted me to ask if I knew anyone who could advise him about money or international finance or whatever. So, naturally, I thought of you.'

'OK. Who is he?'

'You've probably heard of him. Lord Moynihan, yeah? He's an old friend of mine. Well, the family, really. He's Golly's godfather.'

'Yes, I remember. The lord from the Philippines. Marcos's chum.'

'That's the one, yeah. I don't know what he's on about, some nonsense, yeah? But you should be able to get a meal and a few laughs out of it anyway, yeah? Listen, I don't know what name he's travelling on. I mean, I don't know if he's over there as a lord or not, so just wait till he introduces himself, OK?'

'OK.'

'And I didn't know if you wanted him to know your name or not, yeah? That's up to you after you meet him, yeah? So I told him Mr Street.'

'Oh, OK.'

'So is it OK if I give him your phone number, yeah?'

'Sure . . .'

Lord Moynihan and Lane met in the bar at the Biltmore Hotel in Coral Gables on 2 October 1987. Lane arrived, as he had said he would, wearing a light-coloured jacket and carrying a copy of *Newsweek*. He didn't notice the DEA agent in the parking lot who took his photograph. Nor did he notice the only two other men in the bar: Lovato and Stan Brooks of the Mounties, who pretended, quite convincingly, that their only interest in being there was to flirt with the woman behind the bar.

'I am a friend of Howard Marks and I believe you are expecting me,' Moynihan said to Lane. Then he excused himself to go to the bathroom, where Brooks gave him a tape recorder which Moynihan concealed in the pocket of his safari suit – 'my Third World tuxedo', as he called it.

Thus equipped, Moynihan joined Lane on the Biltmore's patio where they could talk without being overheard. Moynihan's pitch, scripted by the DEA, was that 'these friends of mine' had $3 million in drug profits in Miami that they wanted to hide from the IRS. Moynihan and Lane haggled about commissions and percentages, and where the money would be delivered and the denominations of the bills. The bottom line was, Lane agreed to do it for a commission of 10 per cent. He said he wanted $5,000 'up front' as a 'good faith' payment.

Moynihan gave him the money (supplied by the DEA) in a manila envelope the next day. They met in the bar of the Sofitel hotel, where Moynihan was staying, and he tossed the envelope on to the table. 'There's your money,' said Moynihan. 'You can take me out to dinner.'

Socializing with his target was the same disarming technique he had used on Marks. In Palma he had become so close to Howard and Judy's children they'd called him 'Uncle Tony', and he was appointed godfather to Francesca – 'Golly', as everybody called her – their youngest daughter. Similarly, in Miami, he made a great fuss of the Lanes' two daughters, drawing up elaborate plans for Peggy, the eldest, to spend a vacation in the Philippines. He went out with the Lanes to dinner and brunch, he ate at their house, he had cocktails with their neighbours, and he went jet-skiing with their children. In one of his several unrecorded conversations with Patrick, he confided that his wife was unable to conceive a child and that they were going to California to see a specialist. Such intimacies put him beyond suspicion in Lane's mind.

On 5 October Moynihan told Lane he was going to New York. He said he would return in two weeks' time with 'my friend' to negotiate the final details.

'Sure,' said Lane. With 5,000 desperately needed dollars in his pocket – or what was left of it after entertaining Moynihan – he would have agreed to almost anything.

Miami, 10 October 1987

As Moynihan was rapidly learning, DEA CIs work hard for their keep. (The per diems and expenses eventually paid to Moynihan amounted to $21,700.) When he wasn't bugging Lane, or socializing with Lane's family, he was required to submit to interminable debriefings. Lovato and Terry Burke of Scotland Yard questioned him over and over about every detail of his relationship with Marks and Howard's associates.

From photographs he was able to identify: John Denbigh, who had been released on bail in Vancouver, on condition that he remain in Canada; Phillip Sparrowhawk, who had escaped from Vancouver and returned to Bangkok (Moynihan knew him as Brian Meehan, his partner in the Panache massage parlour); Kevin Goulbourne, Sparrowhawk's sidekick; Jim Hobbs, who, having been released from jail in Lisbon, was now living in Palma, where Moynihan had met him; Gerry Wills, who had also been released on bail in Vancouver and allowed to return to Los Angeles, on condition he report to a probation officer every week; and Roger Reaves, who Moynihan knew as Roger the agronomist.

That left 'Mike', putative agent of the CIA, whom Moynihan had met in both Manila and Palma. Of all the characters in the drama, he was the one the Operation Eclectic team was most anxious to identify, because of Marks's claim that 'Mike' had a hot-line to 'the authorities'. Who was he?

It was Julie Desm who provided the answer. At Lovato's request, she had brought with her to Miami the extra Polaroid photographs of Rex and RW secretly taken by her partner, Neil Van Horn, when they had asked for fake Oregon driver's licences.

Moynihan took one look at the picture of RW and said, 'That's him. That's Mike.'

'Shit,' said Lovato. It confirmed his worst suspicions. Ever since Rex and RW had appeared on the scene, highly recommended by US Customs; ever since Julie Desm had said, 'God, Craig, they know everything'; ever since Rex had turned up in Australia while they were putting the sat-track on the *Axel D* – and then the signal had gone dead; ever since RW had turned up at the US Customs conference in New Orleans, looking for all the world like he was part of the team, Lovato had worried about these people. As he said to Julie right at the beginning, 'Who *are* they?' Now he was sure he knew: 'They're fucking doubles. They work for Howard.'

As fast as they could, the Eclectic team assembled every fact they knew about Rex and RW. The results didn't amount to much.

REX JOHNSON

Real name: **Reiner JACOBI.**
Born: **West Germany, 24 June 1942.**
Aliases: **Rolf Gerhard Koenig.**
    Reinhardt Koenig.
Description: **Height 5ft 9in. Weight 172lb. Blue eyes, salt and pepper hair. Keeps himself very fit.**
Occupation: **Exporter. Also claims to be an agent of the US Central Intelligence Agency.**
Location: **Last known US address: 31220 La Baya Drive, Westlake Village, California. Owns two apartments in Queensland, Australia. Frequents Hilton Hotel, Düsseldorf. Last heard of in Hong Kong.**
Marital status: **Divorced. Former wife and children live in Portland, Oregon.**
Passport: **Has at least two: Australian passport number N314062, issued in San Francisco, 11 November 1982; Canadian passport number K773292.**

RW

Real name: **Thomas Jay SUNDE.**
Born: **California, 19 March 1948.**
Aliases: **Major Ross Woods.**
    Werner M. Graebe.
Description: **Height 5ft 10in. Weight 185lb. Brown eyes, balding, brown moustache. Keeps himself very fit. Sometimes uses the fake birthdate of 6 September 1945.**

Occupation: **Former 'gofer' for Ernest 'Peter' Combs. Claims to be an agent of the Central Intelligence Agency.**
Location: **Last known US address: 8015 J Street, Sacramento, California. Last heard of in Palma, Majorca. Believed to have a home in Osaka, Japan.**
Marital status: **Married. Wife's name, Satchyo.**
Passport: **US passport number A225792.**

To which could be added, in the case of both of them: trusted Confidential Informants for US Customs – and agents for Howard Marks. It was an alarming scenario.

Three days later, on 13 October, with the consent of his supervisor, Lovato called Larry Ladage, SAC of US Customs in New Orleans and the main mentor of Jacobi and Sunde, to warn him that Sunde 'certainly', and Jacobi 'in all probability', were working for the other side.

Ladage would not believe him. He was not alarmed that Sunde was with Marks in Palma, supposedly working for him as his 'security consultant': How else was he supposed to get information about the Marks organization? So far as Jacobi was concerned, Ladage had the utmost faith in him. Since Jacobi had approached US Customs in 1984 or early 1985, offering his services as an informant, he'd provided valuable information – information that had checked out – on arms shipments to European terrorists and illegal high-technology exports from the United States. Jacobi had also given Customs information on drug deals, nothing to do with Marks, that had led to at least one major seizure. And, so far as the Marks organization went, whatever Jacobi and Sunde had told the DEA, they'd given Customs good, solid information – not recycled garbage taken from *High Time*.

'If they've done anything wrong, indict them,' Ladage told Lovato. Until then, he said, Customs would continue to use them. The only concession he would make to Lovato is that they would be 'cut out of the loop' on the Marks investigation; they would learn nothing more about it from Customs.

Later, after things got worse, Ladage said he could not remember his conversation with Lovato.

Miami, 19 October 1987

Gil Charette laundered money for the Medellín cartel. He ran a company called Euro-Mex Incorporated which took some of the

US profits of Colombia's most successful, and most violent, cocaine trafficking organization and sent them overseas, minus a small percentage. The Medellín cartel did not suspect that Charette was, in reality, a DEA agent, working undercover on 'Operation Pisces', one of the more elaborate DEA stings. He'd fooled the Colombians for years and he easily fooled Patrick Lane: Patrick had never met anybody more terrifying in his life.

They – Lane, Charette and Lord Moynihan – were sitting on the patio of the Biltmore Hotel where Lane attempted to explain to this large, brooding man a money-laundering system that might justify a commission of 10 per cent – a commission which Charette had already said he thought 'quite steep'. Lane was very aware that he had already received, and mostly spent, $5,000 of this man's money. Until now he had thought of it as 'a jape – a bit of fun with Lord Tony'. After one look at Charette, he no longer thought that. He made it up as he went along, talking about 'finder's fees' for non-existent real estate deals in Europe, and bank accounts in Togo. There was not a chance that Lane would have noticed Wendy Lovato, sitting at a table eight feet away, recording the whole thing on videotape with a concealed camera.

Lane boasted and bluffed his way through it, claiming that 'my people in New York' could handle $50–100,000 a week. He and Charette agreed that Moynihan would get a commission of 2¹/₂ per cent on the first $3 million Lane laundered. Lane's commission would be 'negotiable'.

They agreed on a 'trial run' of $50,000. The money must be in $100 bills, Lane insisted, wondering what on earth he was going to do with it.

'OK,' said Charette, wondering where on earth he was going to get it.

It was going sufficiently well that the next day Bobby O'Neill took Lord Moynihan before the members of the grand jury.

It is doubtful that they had ever seen an English lord before, certainly not one in the middle of an undercover operation for the DEA, and they were intrigued by him. Wasn't his life in danger? one of them asked.

'I think it might be,' said Moynihan. 'I don't have any physical protection at all. My only protection is that the major people involved in this case have absolutely no idea whatsoever as to what I'm doing. They believe that I am one of them. So long as they believe that, they're not going to hurt me, are they? I sincerely

Craig Lovato: Sheriff's deputy, Las Vegas, 1968

Craig Lovato: With his step-mother Beth, younger brother Brent, father Lee and sister Marcia; with his three sons, Thor, Grant and Gregory; *(opposite page)* on assignment in Bolivia during Operation Titicaca; undercover, as Johnny Luna; fingerprinting former Panamanian leader, General Manuel Noriega

Circumstantial evidence: The bird of prey logo, found on the load seized from the *Supreme I* in Vancouver, September 1987

Key players: Charlie Pasenelli, 'The Computer'; *(opposite page)* Randy Waddell of NIS; Bobby O'Neill, a prosecutor with balls; Tom Cash, SAC of the DEA, Miami

International lineup: Some of the Operation Eclectic team. *(Back row, left to right)* Randy Waddell, NIS; Mike Gough Cooper, Her Majesty's Customs; Ed Wezain, DEA; Terry Burke, Scotland Yard; Craig Lovato; Brad Whites, IRS; Dale Laverty, DEA. *(Front row)* Pepe Villar, Spanish National Police; Harlan Bowe, DEA; Bobby O'Neill, US Attorney's office; Murray Dauk, Royal Canadian Mounted Police

Lord and Lady Moynihan:
The 3rd Baron Moynihan,
and his fourth wife, Editha

Check mate: Craig Lovato, Miami, 1990

hope that the DEA will see that they are all arrested before they do know.'

Trust us, Tony.

Lovato couldn't get the money. DEA headquarters in Washington said 'No.' They wouldn't give Patrick Lane $50,000. What if he just walked off with it?

'Try Pisces,' said Gil Charette.

So Lovato went, cap in hand, to the group supervisor of Operation Pisces and asked for the money, 'in large bills, please'.

The Pisces supervisor was used to taking risks – and, anyway, it wasn't the government's cash. He gave Lovato $50,000 of the Medellín cartel's money.

'Sorry, I've only got 10,000 in hundreds,' he said. 'The rest will have to be in twenties.'

Patrick Lane would not take it. When Charette tried to give it to him at the Biltmore Hotel the next day he balked. He wanted 100-dollar bills or nothing, he said. He did not tell Charette the reason, but uppermost in his mind was the memory of the last time he'd walked through an airport with a suitcase full of cash.

'He's not only a greedy bastard, he's a lazy bastard,' said Lovato when he learned what had happened. 'Why doesn't he go and change it?'

'I don't know,' said Charette. 'Let's go to the bank.'

It was not until Thursday 22 October that Lane sealed his own fate by finally accepting 500 $100 bills from Charette in the men's room at the Sofitel hotel. Late that night he took the last flight from Miami to New York and then a taxi to Raoul del Cristo's home in Sutton Place – followed every mile of the way by DEA agents.

Moynihan also left Miami that day, his job done at least for now. He and Editha flew to California to see the specialist they hoped could overcome her problems in conceiving a child, so that she could give Moynihan the one thing in the world he wanted: a son, an heir to the title.

Miami, 23 October 1987

Lovato was on his way to the office when his car phone rang. It was Charlie Lutz, his boss, calling to say that the Mounties had no choice but to meet Jacobi and talk about the Vancouver bust. Lovato better get his ass on a plane.

It was unbelievable, Lovato thought. Despite his warning to Larry Ladage just ten days before, despite the fact that Ladage had agreed that Jacobi and Sunde would be 'cut out of the loop', here was US Customs pushing the Mounties to talk to Jacobi. They said he had 'valuable information' on the bust. Sure. On Lovato's advice, Ken Ross of the Vancouver drugs squad had declined to meet Jacobi, but now he was getting pressure from RCMP headquarters in Toronto.

'I've got to talk to him, Craig,' said Ross when Lovato called him from Miami international airport.

'I'm on my way,' said Lovato.

They agreed they wouldn't tell Jacobi who Lovato was. Let him assume he was Canadian – 'the only Mexican Mountie', as Lovato put it. Lovato and Ross also agreed that the Mounties would 'play dumb', pretending they had no idea as to who was behind the load they had seized. 'Remember who he works for,' said Lovato. 'He's trying to find out what we know.'

So when they met Jacobi in Vancouver, on Monday 26 October, Ross did not tell him that the Mounties had already prepared and circulated a chart which showed the members of the organization they believed responsible for the Vancouver load, with Howard Marks at the head. It didn't matter. Jacobi already knew.

He said the Mounties were wrong in believing it was Howard's load. Marks had had nothing to do with it.

We never said he did, said Ross.

Yes you did, said Jacobi, you prepared a chart.

What chart? said Ross.

Jacobi asked to use the phone. He called US Customs in New Orleans. He asked to speak to a Customs intelligence analyst named Holland. He told Holland to go to a particular office – a 'secure' office, one with highly restricted access – and retrieve a chart: 'It's in the third drawer on the right,' he said.

A few minutes later, Holland called back. At Jacobi's prompting, he confirmed that the chart carried the imprimatur of the Royal Canadian Mounted Police, and that it placed Howard Marks at the head of the organization.

'Jesus,' said Lovato, after Jacobi had made his point and left in a state of high dudgeon, saying he was not going to waste his time talking to people who lied to him.

Back in Miami, Lovato wrote a report on this disturbing incident. It went to Washington, to the Office of Professional Responsibility at the Justice Department, and it caused an unholy row between the DEA and Customs.

Larry Ladage continued to defend his two informants, saying if they had done anything wrong, he would be the first to arrest them – but where was the evidence against them?

Bobby O'Neill told Customs he wanted Jacobi and Sunde to appear before the grand jury in Miami to answer some very tough questions. Customs said Jacobi and Sunde were out of the country at the moment. They would pass on the message to them as soon as they could.

Miami, 30 October 1987

Patrick Lane came jogging into view, wearing shorts, a T-shirt and running shoes. It wasn't exactly how Gil Charette – waiting for him in a truck in the parking lot of the Holiday Inn – had expected him to arrive. There were a couple of other surprises in store for Charette.

Lane gave him a cheque, drawn on the Florida National Bank and made out to Euro-Mex Incorporated. A cheque!

'If I'd wanted a cheque I could have gone to the bank and gotten it myself,' said Charette. This was not how money laundering was supposed to work. The idea was to 'wash' drug money through any number of phony businesses and bank accounts – *overseas* bank accounts – until it was 'clean', meaning untraceable. A cheque!

'Sorry,' said Lane. Euro-Mex had a New York bank account and, Lane explained, 'my associate' was not willing to launder money directly into an American account; it was too risky. Euro-Mex would have to set up an overseas account into which money could be laundered.

There was another problem. The cheque was for only $48,750. What had happened to the other $1,250? Charette wanted to know.

'Moynihan's commission.' said Lane.

'Listen, in future I'll pay Moynihan's commission,' said Charette. 'You give me *all* the money.'

Charette left the parking lot looking distinctly unhappy, saying that he was going to make damn sure Moynihan had been paid. 'I'll be in touch,' he told Lane, ominously.

Their ambition had been considerably greater. They believed that

213

Patrick Lane laundered money for Howard Marks and, by tracing back the route the $50,000 had taken, they'd hoped to discover the method and the accounts Lane used. With luck, he might have led them to Howard's hidden fortune.

As it was, he led them practically nowhere. With the aid of a subpoena, the Eclectic team quickly discovered how amateur Lane's 'system' was.

He had simply given the DEA's cash to Raoul del Cristo, his former employer, in New York. ('Help me,' Lane had said to del Cristo, who still felt guilty about pulling the plug on the fish factory. 'You owe me one.') In return, del Cristo had given Lane a cheque drawn on the account of his American International Financial Group.

The cheque had been made out not to Lane but to Barry John Doyle, the alias Lane used in all his dealings with Charette. Lane had cashed the cheque at the Florida National Bank, and then bought another for the same amount to give to Charette. It barely qualified as money laundering, and it certainly told the DEA nothing about Marks.

They decided to try again, by giving Lane more money to launder, this time insisting he do it properly. But where to get the cash? Moynihan insisted to Lovato that Lane had not given him the missing $1,250. Lane, on the other hand, insisted to Charette that he had. It was, in the scheme of things, a trifling amount of money, but so long as it remained unaccounted for, even Operation Pisces was unwilling to stump up any more cash. Brad Whites, the case agent from the Internal Revenue Service, said he would get his agency to put up $100,000 – but he'd not reckoned on the intractable bureaucracy of the IRS.

For the remainder of 1987, the sting against Lane stalled, with Lane complaining to Charette that he was 'losing credibility with my people' because of the delays, and Charette bitching to Lane about the missing $1,250, using it as an excuse, becoming ever more threatening in his manner.

Then Bobby O'Neill said, 'Enough.' He decided that even without a more positive demonstration of Lane's money-laundering skills, Lane had done enough to give them venue in Miami. O'Neill was ready to take the field against the Howard Marks organization.

The evidence the Eclectic team had gathered was, in O'Neill's opinion, more than sufficient to prove a racketeering conspiracy going back almost twenty years. He ticked off the counts of the indictment he was planning to ask the grand jury to return.

On the 1973 load into Las Vegas they were solid, thanks to the immaculate detective work of Harlan Bowe.

There was then an embarrassingly long gap of more than ten years, with no specific charges, but they had found former associates of Peter Combs who were willing to testify about his partnership with Howard Marks. The jury would be left in no doubt that these two had worked together for a very long time.

In 1984 they had the Alameda load. They had a witness who would testify that Combs had invested in the hash found on the naval base. And they now had solid evidence of Marks's involvement in the Alameda load, thanks to a new member of the Eclectic team named Ed Wezain. He'd been a DEA rookie agent in Miami for only a couple of months when he was recruited by Craig Lovato in much the same way that Howard had seduced women at Balliol: 'Come here,' said Lovato, 'see if you can make sense of these documents.' The documents happened to be about what the Naval Investigative Service had called 'The Dead Fred Affair'. By extraordinary coincidence, Wezain had joined the DEA from NIS. 'I know somebody who knows all about this,' said Wezain. 'Call him,' said Lovato. Thus, Randy Waddell – the NIS agent who had identified the mysterious 'Mr Dennis' in Karachi as Howard Marks – arrived in Miami, bringing with him his Dead Fred file. He and Wezain had spent an entire night in Eclectic's glorified closet, sifting the piles of paper until they could compose a coherent account of what had happened at Alameda. So that one now was solid, too.

For the 1986 Los Angeles load, they had neither the dope, nor any real idea of what happened to the money, but they did have Craig Lovato's cassette tapes of Howard's telephone conversations. They would rely on them.

Then they had the 1987 Vancouver load. Vancouver wasn't the United States, of course, so the bust there was of limited value. But Eclectic now had evidence that the 6½ tons of marijuana seized in Vancouver was only part of the load – and that the rest of it had been destined for the United States. Part of the evidence came from Marks's own mouth: his taped admission to Moynihan that 'there will be some they didn't get for sure'. More important, a load of 500lb of marijuana subsequently seized in San Jose, California, had carried an identical 'PASSED INSPECTION' label with the bird of prey logo. And in Reno, Nevada, one of the men identified by the Mounties during their surveillance in Vancouver had been arrested by the FBI, attempting to launder $7.5 million through Nevada casinos. That should be sufficient to prove an American connection, O'Neill decided.

He knew there were parts of the case where the fabric was stretched extremely thin, where challenges from clever defence attorneys might threaten the admissibility of some of the evidence. But O'Neill was at his best in a courtroom, on his feet, and, as with football, he couldn't wait for the game to begin. With 'Lord Tony' as their star witness, he knew they would win.

By the beginning of 1988, the morale of the Eclectic team had never been higher. They had identified more than 100 people associated in one way or another with the Marks organization, scattered around the world. And while that was far too many to extradite to America, and far too many to prosecute under one indictment, it gave other countries a chance to have a crack at some of 'the bodies'.

The excitement was contagious. Back in London, Terry Burke no longer felt he was working on his own. The prospect of Marks being almost 'in the bag' exhilarated Scotland Yard and even Her Majesty's Customs, now providing yeoman service on the historic aspects of the case.

And in Miami, a new SAC arrived at the DEA in January 1988, bringing with him unbridled enthusiasm for multi-national investigations. Tom Cash had spent most of his own DEA career working overseas and he believed that Operation Eclectic was precisely the kind of inquiry the agency should be leading. It was he who dubbed Marks 'Marco Polo'. He thought it an excellent thing that they were about to put an end to his world travels.

But Cash, who is fond of using aphorisms, warned Lovato not to relax until Marks was arrested, extradited, convicted, sentenced and locked away: 'The opera ain't over till the fat lady sings,' said Cash.

Which is approximately when they learned of the contract on the life of their star witness.

Manila, February 1988

'Howard's trying to have me killed!' said Lord Moynihan in absolute astonishment.

'We don't know that it's Howard,' said Scalzo. 'We just know there is a contract out on you.'

The tip had come from a DEA informant and, in the nature of these things, it was impossible to verify. But it couldn't be ignored.

'Art, how serious is this?' said Moynihan.

'Tony, in the dope business you always have to take threats seriously.'

'So what do you want me to do?'

'Go to Miami,' said Scalzo.

'When?'

'Now.'

'And what do I tell Editha?'

Good question. Moynihan had never told his wife about his undercover work, either in Palma or Miami, or since their return to the Philippines. She'd met the Marks family and the Lane family, totally unaware that her husband was in the process of helping to put Howard and Patrick in jail. In Miami she had also met Art Scalzo, though she thought he was a New York Italian businessman named DiAngelo.

Scalzo went to Moynihan's home to confess to her who he really was, and what her husband had done. Moynihan sat there sheepishly, looking to Scalzo like a naughty boy who'd been found out. She was not angry at him for becoming a DEA informant. She was, however, far from pleased she had not been told.

With her consent Moynihan flew to Miami, where he placed himself under the protection of the DEA. The protection did not amount to much: he was installed under a false name at the Radisson Hotel and spent most of his evenings at Craig and Wendy Lovato's house, playing Trivial Pursuit.

He soon became thoroughly bored. 'Craig, how long is this going to go on for?' he said.

'Till the fat lady sings,' said Lovato.

ACT THREE
The Endgame

The popular notion persists that chess is an epic battle when masters get together. Far into the night the wrangle goes on, with the adversaries ascribing to each other subtle and profound nuances in every play. This is a somewhat coloured version. Many a time, on the contrary, a game is over before one of the contestants can say 'discovered check'.

I.A. Horowitz, *All About Chess*

NINE

'**W**hy won't you stop?' It had been Judy Marks's refrain for months. Indeed, she'd been unhappy and scared about the dope business for a long time. When she'd first met Howard, and joined him in his life as a jet-setting international fugitive, the danger had been part of the attraction. She'd found it glamorous and fun – and she'd certainly enjoyed the profits. But life on the run had palled after a while and his trial at the Old Bailey had badly frightened her, his acquittal notwithstanding.

In Palma she lived in constant terror that his addiction to dope would lead to the house being raided by the Spanish police. Whenever he went away on one of his long trips, she would search the house for his hidden caches of hash and flush them down the toilet. He'd come home and find them gone and say to their eldest daughter, Amber, 'Oh, Mummy's been house cleaning again.'

Judy helped him with his enterprises, of course, though she reconciled that by saying she did no more than answer the phone in her own home. And, of course, they lived off the proceeds. But she disliked many of the people he worked with (she wouldn't have some of them in the house), she hated his long absences and she lived in dread of the DEA. She was tired of it. She was devoted to her children and she wanted them to have a normal life. 'Why won't you stop?' she said, over and over.

Well, he'd tried. Over the years he'd come up with any number of money-making schemes, some of them more legitimate than others.

221

There had been the lucrative racket of finding Englishmen –
usually gay Englishmen, friends of Jim Hobbs – willing to marry
Chinese women from Hong Kong, in order to provide them with
British citizenship. There'd been a scheme to sell bottled Welsh
water to Saudi Arabia, and a plan to build rest-stops with cafés
along the great highway linking China to Pakistan. He was
genuinely a working director of Hong Kong Travel in London,
and they'd come within an inch of securing the right to become
the main agents for Philippine Airlines in Britain. Moynihan had
provided the right connections in Manila and they would probably
have clinched the deal if the Marcos regime hadn't fallen. Marks
had plans to get the Arabs to invest in Disneyland-type projects
in Majorca, and for the Taiwanese to build factories in Wales. But
nothing had quite clicked.

'Just a couple more years,' he'd told Judy. His intention, he said,
was to back out of the dope business gradually by acting only as
a middleman, bringing together suppliers and distributors. They
would pay him a commission at first, but after a couple of deals
they wouldn't need him any more and he'd be cut out – whatever the
promises they made. It was his way of making himself redundant,
eventually.

His promise to retire had been provoked by the arrest of Peter
Combs in Los Angeles in 1986, and the realization that he himself was a target of the DEA. Marks thought the Los Angeles
investigation had run out of steam but it still left him uneasy.
He was disturbed by the American government's increasing use
of the RICO statute against drug traffickers, and alarmed by
the New Sentencing Guidelines which effectively did away with
parole in the United States. The new guidelines, contained in the
Sentencing Reform Act, said that anyone convicted of a serious
offence committed after November 1987 would have to serve a
minimum of 85 per cent of their sentence, instead of one third.
Suddenly and dramatically, the US dope market lost much of its
appeal.

So Marks had vowed to concentrate on the markets in Canada
and Britain, where the consequences of selling dope were not yet
the risk of life imprisonment, and where there was no Craig Lovato
to worry about. 'Just a couple more years,' he promised Judy.

Then he discovered it was already too late.

Their Christmas had been ruined by Tom Sunde. Marks was
spending the holiday in London with his family when Sunde

called to say the worst had happened: Howard was going to be indicted in Miami, and extradited to the United States. The DEA were making a big, big thing of this case, said Sunde. Edwin Meese, the Attorney General, was going to appear on television to announce it.

It came as a stunning shock. The last time Marks had talked to Sunde about the DEA was in Palma, a few weeks after Moynihan's visit. They'd discussed the Vancouver bust and Sunde had said Howard was in the clear: Jacobi had spoken to the Mounties and they didn't suspect the load had anything to do with Howard.

So what had changed?

There's this prosecutor called O'Neill, said Sunde, who was determined to prosecute Howard for the 1986 Los Angeles load.

What could be done? said Marks.

Well, they could stall it, said Sunde. They couldn't make it go away, but Jacobi's contacts, and Howard's money, could delay the indictment indefinitely.

How much money? said Marks.

Well, they would need $50–100,000 immediately, said Sunde, and further payments down the road. Marks said he couldn't possibly afford it. Well, pay what you can, said Sunde. He promised that the very least he and Jacobi would do was warn Howard when he was about to be arrested. Sunde said that if ever he called and began the conversation by saying, 'How are things?' Howard would know that the DEA was about to move against him.

Marks didn't know what to think. Half of him said it was a scam by Jacobi to extract money. The other half of him said it was real. He spent Christmas in a state of paranoia, trying in vain to hide it from the children.

'What's wrong, Daddy?' said Amber.

'The Americans are going to arrest me – I think.'

It wasn't until the family returned home to Palma in early January that he knew for sure. Judy took the first two calls from a man with an American accent who gave his name as 'Top Cat'. He said: 'Is your husband there, Judith? It's important I talk to him.' She thought it strange: hardly anybody called her 'Judith'.

Finally Top Cat called when Howard was at home. He said he had information about 'rival travel agents. Are you interested?' Then he said a grand jury in Miami was about to indict Howard for 'CCE' – running a Continuing Criminal Enterprise, the most serious racketeering charge there is. Top Cat said Howard's phone in London was already being tapped, and his phone in Palma soon would be. And, within a couple of months, Howard would be arrested and so would Gerry Wills, John Denbigh and Phillip Sparrowhawk. 'Don't underestimate the DEA's reach,' he said, adding (correctly) that they had just seized the *Axel D* in Peru.

Howard pressed him for more detail but Top Cat said he was in the business of selling information, not giving it away. He said he wanted $250,000.

Marks said: 'How do I know you're not just pulling a line? You could be anybody.'

'Well, I know that your brother-in-law's alias is Doyle,' said Top Cat.

Now Marks knew he was serious. The Barry John Doyle alias was one that he had manufactured for Patrick while awaiting trial at the Old Bailey in 1981. He'd wanted Patrick to disappear, and so he had arranged for a fake British passport to be issued in that name. As far as he knew, Patrick had never used the passport or the name. He thought that nobody else in the world knew about Barry John Doyle – until now. Whoever Top Cat was, he clearly had very good sources.

Marks asked Top Cat if he was able to stop the indictment.

No, said Top Cat, it would be 'less than honest' for him to claim that. But he could provide Howard with a copy of the DEA's entire file, including the grand jury testimony, 'so you'll know what's coming in a couple of months'.

Howard declined. He said he didn't have $250,000.

'Well, I wish you the best of luck,' said Top Cat, and rang off.

Who knew about Doyle? Marks called Patrick Lane in Miami to ask if he had ever used the alias. Who else knew about it?

Only Tony Moynihan and Tony's friend, said Lane.

Marks called Moynihan in Manila: 'You know your friend that you introduced to my brother-in-law? Is he OK? Because Pat seems a little worried that something's got back and he wanted me to check with you that your friend was, you know, OK.'

'As far as I know, dear boy,' said Moynihan.

But there was something about the conversation, something about Moynihan's tone, that left Marks unsettled. He'd wanted Moynihan to allay his suspicions but he hadn't done so. He'd been too glib.

From that point on, Marks *knew*: Tony was working for the other side.

Michael Katz was American but he operated his law practice out of

London. He was much less expensive than other American lawyers Howard had approached, who wanted at least $10,000 down and $150 an hour. He was also willing to fly to the United States more or less immediately, and 'find out what's going on'.

While Katz headed west, Marks flew east, to Taipei, the capital of Taiwan. He had legitimate business there. Hong Kong Travel had become the top seller of tickets for China Airlines in London and there was a prospect of opening a branch office in Taiwan to cement the business further. But Taiwan had other attractions for Marks: it had extradition treaties with nobody. There wasn't even a US Embassy there. 'What a wonderful place,' said Marks.

He liked it even more after he'd run into a group of men in a bar. He knocked a glass of water over them and was apologizing profusely when one of them said, 'Where are you from?' Wales, said Howard, and the man started talking to him in Welsh. He was, it turned out, a New Zealand government official who had spent his childhood in the same valleys as Howard. They became bosom pals overnight, and business associates. The New Zealand government was recruiting immigrant workers from Taiwan, and Howard, through Hong Kong Travel, could supply the workers with airline tickets cheaper than anybody else. The next morning he found himself part of the New Zealand delegation, meeting with Taiwan government ministers in the Grand Palace Hotel, treating them to his unique rendering of the Welsh national anthem. They appeared to enjoy it.

He thought it was an omen. 'What a wonderful place,' said Howard. 'I should stay here.'

Miami, March and April 1988

Craig Lovato was convinced there was a leak. He couldn't be sure that Marks, or any of his friends, were responsible for the contract on Moynihan's life, but he had no doubt they knew the DEA was getting close. Things had gone awfully quiet. The Spanish police had reinstalled the tap on Howard's phone but they were picking up hardly anything. He either wasn't in Palma or he wasn't talking to anybody. It was very unlike Howard, very strange.

To confirm his worst suspicions, Lovato asked Moynihan, still killing time in Miami, to call a London solicitor named James Newton. He was an old school chum of Moynihan's – they'd been at Stowe together – and, later on, Newton had been associated with some of Moynihan's business deals in England. When

Moynihan had quit the country and his seat in the House of Lords to avoid the fraud charges, Newton had been one of those left behind to face the music. He was arrested and charged with providing false references for Moynihan and, though acquitted, had abandoned practising law. Newton now made part of his living by providing false passports for, among others, Lord Moynihan and Howard Marks.

Moynihan called him in London from Miami with the excuse that he needed a new fake passport in order to return to the Philippines. He urged Newton not to discuss the matter with anyone. 'I mean nobody,' said Moynihan. 'Phillip, or the Welshman, or anyone.' Then, following Lovato's script, Moynihan said: 'Have you done any more business with the Welshman or with the others?'

'No, none,' said Newton. 'As a matter of fact, they are all lying very low and keeping very quiet at the moment. I understand that they are not doing any business at all right now. I think it's a very bad time.'

'They know,' said Lovato to Bobby O'Neill – who, soon afterwards, obtained his own, definitive proof of a leak.

He was out of the office when Michael Katz dropped by. Katz spoke to another Assistant US attorney, saying he represented Howard Marks, who understood the government was preparing an indictment against him. Katz said he wanted to talk to O'Neill about it but couldn't wait because he had a plane to catch. He left his phone number in London with a message asking O'Neill to call him.

'What did he look like?' said O'Neill when he returned to his office later that afternoon. Given a vague description – 'English, tallish, longish hair' – O'Neill immediately jumped to the wrong conclusion. He called Lovato at the DEA and said: 'I think Howard's just been in my office, pretending to be a lawyer.' They both raced to the airport from their separate offices and searched the departure terminals, looking for Howard Marks. The fact that they did not find him only confirmed their suspicions that Marks was playing games with them, sending them a message: he knew.

'We've got to close it down and plug the leak,' said O'Neill. He and Lovato convinced themselves that if Marks discovered the indictment was imminent he would flee. So would his associates, most of whom were overseas and highly mobile. Somehow, they had to be convinced they were safe.

O'Neill called US Customs in New Orleans and spoke to one of the intelligence analysts he'd been badgering for weeks to produce Jacobi and Sunde to testify before the grand jury. Customs had continued to insist the two informants were unavailable, out of the country. Now O'Neill said: 'You can tell them to forget it. This case is going nowhere. I'm closing down the investigation.'

Within a week O'Neill's spurious claim had crossed the Atlantic. Terry Burke of Scotland Yard received a call from a West German colleague, commiserating with him on the 'failure' of the Marks investigation. 'What the hell's going on?' said Burke when he called Lovato to report the conversation.

Operation Eclectic went underground. Only a handful of people knew that the investigation was still very much alive, and all of them became secretive to the point of paranoia. They didn't trust anybody. Burke in London stopped producing written reports of his inquiries. In Miami, Lovato and Ed Wezain – now his *de facto* partner – took to going into the DEA office at the dead of night to do their work, when there was nobody else around. The additional pressure had bizarre results. For example, Lovato once called O'Neill at home at 3.00 a.m. to tell him to expect a call from Terry Burke in half an hour. Five minutes later Lovato called back.

'What time is it?' he asked.

'Three in the morning,' said O'Neill.

'Christ! I thought it was afternoon. Terry's calling you at three thirty this afternoon.'

Their case was now all but complete. O'Neill was almost ready to ask the grand jury to hand down a 'true bill'. Almost.

Taipei, Taiwan, 25 April 1988

Marks and Michael Katz were supposed to meet in London, where the lawyer was to report on the inquiries he had made in the United States. Then Howard though better of it: Taiwan seemed the safest place to be until he knew the score. He persuaded Katz to fly to Taipei. The news the lawyer brought with him was not entirely encouraging.

Katz's researches had been most productive in Los Angeles, where he'd examined the court records generated by Julie Desm's arrest of Ernest 'Peter' Combs in 1986. Katz had discovered something Marks did not know: when Julie had abandoned the charges against Combs, the hearing had been held in camera, and the record of that hearing sealed.

227

To Marks that could mean only one thing: 'Ernie's done a deal,' he said. 'He's talking.' Given that their partnership went back so far, and had been so intimate, the implications for Marks were appalling.

But Katz, who knew only Howard's highly edited version of the truth, was not so pessimistic. Nor was Tom Sunde, who had also been summoned to Taiwan by Howard. Katz believed what Howard had told him: that the Marks–Combs partnership had ended years before and, if Combs was saying otherwise to the government, he was lying. Sunde, who knew better, said Combs would never talk.

Katz proposed that they tackle the matter head on, by talking to Bob O'Neill. 'I'll call him,' said Katz. 'Let's do it from Hong Kong,' said Marks, who was not anxious for the American government to know precisely where he was. 'I'll tape it,' said Sunde, for reasons that were not entirely clear.

So the next day the three of them flew to Hong Kong, from where Katz called O'Neill in Miami, and Sunde taped the call. O'Neill was not expecting it. Thinking fast on his feet, however, is one of the things he is exceptionally good at.

Katz gave O'Neill a garbled version of Marks's relationship with Combs, adding that his client was worried that Combs had told the government something 'that might have implicated him for some reason. It's as if his whole past is coming back to him. He's extremely worried. And I've said to him: "Look, you've got nothing to worry about because you haven't done anything." I mean, whatever [Combs] has said, there has to be more than just somebody saying it. You have to have some other evidence from other sources.'

'Oh, absolutely,' said O'Neill. 'Especially if you say Combs was also a drug dealer. As you know, it is very difficult for us to make a case on the word of a drug dealer.'

But what about the conspiracy laws? Katz asked. 'I mean, from my point of view, I could say to my client that in theory all you need to have a conspiracy is an agreement between two people, and if one of them says that, then that is evidence that could in theory be used.'

Well, if it was all in the long-distant past there was nothing to worry about, said O'Neill. 'You understand there's a five-year cut-off in the Statute of Limitation laws?'

'Exactly, but what he's worried about is that if Combs said to someone that they were involved in a conspiracy since five years ago. I mean, he really doesn't know what's happened to Combs, but he thinks it's the only possible connection that could have anything to do with him.'

'Yeah, but I can state unequivocally to you that in Miami there's no way we would prosecute any individual on the uncorroborated word of a drug smuggler. You know what I mean?'

'Yeah, sure,' said Katz.

'If Combs is a drug smuggler, like you said originally, unless there is other evidence it's impossible because no jury in America would believe him.'

'Exactly what you've said is what I've told him: that there wouldn't be a prosecution based on uncorroborated evidence of someone who is heavily involved in drugs dealing,' said Katz.

'Exactly,' said O'Neill.

Later, when he heard about the call, Lovato said: 'I bet they taped it.'

'I *hope* they did,' said O'Neill.

Partially reassured by Katz's conversation with O'Neill, and by Sunde's insistence that 'everything's OK', Marks flew home to Palma. He was still there on 15 June, when the Spanish police announced the dramatic arrest of Roger Reaves – Roger the agronomist. Ironically, Marks regarded it as a most encouraging development.

Reaves had moved to Palma, with Howard's help, after his inclination to settle in the Philippines had been killed stone dead by the *Daily Inquirer*'s series of attacks on Lord Moynihan. Encouraged by the fact that Howard continued to live an uneventful life on the island, he thought he would also be safe. But in early 1988, Scotland Yard and the West German police had uncovered a plot to ship tons of Moroccan hashish into England, aboard a West German freighter named *Telmo* – an enterprise masterminded by a stocky, balding American in his fifties, who spoke with a pronounced southern accent and who lived in Majorca. When Terry Burke had passed on that description to Lovato, he'd identified him immediately: 'It's Roger,' he said. 'The description fits him like a glove.' Once they had positively established that Reaves was in Majorca, the West Germans said they wanted him arrested. 'Why not?' said Lovato. 'One less for us to worry about.' He also believed that, when the time came, the West Germans would agree to 'hand over the body'.

Reaves had not gone quietly. When the Palma police had stopped his Mercedes in the middle of town, he'd abandoned the car and escaped on foot. Eventually captured, and taken to court in handcuffs, he'd jumped through a second-floor window. It was his sheer bad luck that the car he landed on belonged to the police, and that the startled occupants were able to grab him.

Marks went to visit Reaves in jail and was enormously relieved to discover that the warrant for his arrest had been issued by the West German police. Marks thought the DEA was virtually omnipotent and could not believe that the Americans would tolerate West German interference if they themselves were about to move against what they called the Marks organization. It did cross his mind that the West Germans might also be looking for him, since he had been involved with Reaves in the scheme to ship Moroccan hash to England. Still, on balance, it was far better to be a West German target, rather than an American one. He left Reaves in jail, feeling a little more confident about his own continued freedom.

Yet he was still uneasy. It no longer required the sight of an international frontier to provoke an acute attack of the flutterings. He'd be feeling fine, then dark doubts would creep up on him like an ominous cloud, overwhelming him with despair.

'Why don't we all move to Taiwan,' he said to Judy one day when the cloud was particularly oppressive, 'you, me and the kids. It's a fantastic place.'

Judy would not hear of it. She wanted to move, but to England, where she believed that the children would get a better education than in Palma. Taiwan, however fantastic, was not her idea of a suitable place to raise children. Nor would she submit them to a life on the run.

But she understood, she said, if Howard felt safer in Taiwan. If he thought there was less chance of the DEA being able to arrest him there, then that is where he should go. She said it would not be the end of their marriage as far as she was concerned. They would get back together, sooner or later.

Feeling a mixture of relief and guilt, the latter-day Marco Polo resumed his travels.

Miami, June and July 1988

On 28 June and again on 12 July, Craig Lovato appeared before the grand jury, armed with his charts and his cassette tapes, to summarize the entire case against the Howard Marks organization. His dog and pony show was by now so familiar to him that he could recite it with his eyes closed, but its favourable reception had never been more important. Grand juries rarely refuse a prosecutor's request for an indictment. Rarely, but sometimes. Lovato was intensely aware that two-and-a-half years' work by a lot of people would go down the drain if the grand jury balked.

It did not. On 13 July the grand jury issued a 'true bill' which, though ponderous in its language, was every bit as formidable as O'Neill had hoped. It began:

> From on or about an unknown date, at least as early as April, 1970, and continuously thereafter, up to and including December 22, 1987, an Enterprise existed within the meaning of Title 18, United States Code, Section 1961 (4), that is, it was a group of individuals and entities, foreign and domestic, associated in fact for the purpose of importing and distributing marijuana and hashish, laundering the proceeds and profits, and investing monies derived from marijuana and hashish importation and distribution through the use of foreign and domestic corporations, financial institutions, and business entities utilized to conceal the true owners of the acquired assets and the true source of the finances for the acquisition of these assets.

The same day the US federal court for the Southern District of Florida issued arrest warrants for the twenty-two people named in the indictment. As a routine precaution, the indictment was sealed by the court. Nobody was to know about it until the arrests had been made – which in this case would be anything but routine. Half of the suspects were scattered in seven foreign countries, all of which required the presentation of 'arrest packages' by the United States government before they would move. Getting the arrest packages issued was an exquisitely elaborate exercise, requiring, in each case: certified copies of the indictment and arrest warrant sent to the Office of International Affairs at the Justice Department in Washington; which sent a Provisional Warrant of Arrest to the State Department; which sent it to the Attorney General's office for his signature; which sent it back to the Department of State, which authenticated the Attorney General's signature and sent it on to the embassy of the country concerned; which authenticated the State Department's authentification, and sent it back to State; which sent it to Interpol, the international police clearing-house; which sent it to the local police force.

And while all this was done, the Eclectic team could only hope that no word of the indictment would leak, that none of the suspects – and particularly Marks – would learn they were about to be arrested. It was, of course, a vain hope.

Taipei, 18 July 1988

'Are you absolutely sure?' said Marks.

'No, I'm not sure,' said Gerry Wills, calling from California. 'It's what he said.'

'He' was Wills's man inside the DEA – or at least, that's what Wills claimed. In Howard's experience, almost every American trafficker in the business claimed to have somebody inside the DEA, tipping them off. It was impossible to tell if these were idle boasts. But wherever Wills had got his information from, it was truly alarming.

'It's going to happen to you on the island very soon, Howard,' Wills had said.

'When?'

'I don't know. Soon. That's all he said.'

The news came at a psychologically devastating moment. After less than three weeks in Taiwan, Marks had decided he didn't want to live there – not without Judy and the children. His eighth wedding anniversary was coming up in a few days and he wanted to go home. Indeed, he'd made up his mind to go; he'd told Judy he was coming. Then this.

Marks called Sunde: 'Any problems?' he asked.

'No, you're all right at the moment,' said Sunde.

Marks went for a walk around the campus of Taipei University, melancholy and more than a little bit frightened. It was sunset and the tranquillity of the place reminded him of Balliol and more carefree days.

'Nostalgic rubbish,' he said, pulling himself together. In a brighter mood he headed for Buffalo Town, a raucous discothèque popular with foreigners, in search of his New Zealand friends. He had made his decision. He was going home.

But before he did he took two last precautions.

The first was to call a chief inspector of police in Palma, who was in charge of security at the airport, and whom Marks had befriended. From time to time he would bring the chief inspector small gifts – usually electronic gadgets – from Tokyo or Hong Kong. Marks called him to ask if there was anything he wanted brought back from Taiwan. He listened very carefully to the tone of his voice, convinced that if there was a plan to arrest him in Palma, the chief inspector would know.

There was nothing about the conversation to unnerve Marks. The chief inspector was as friendly as ever. Yes, he said, he would like a small television set; one of those equipped with an alarm.

Howard's second, impromptu precaution was to make his offering of gold leaf and prayer at the Temple of the Dog. Then he flew home, to whatever fate awaited him.

Palma, 21-24 July 1988

The watchers missed him at the airport because Marks was met by the chief inspector, who greeted him with a huge smile on the other side of Customs. He accepted his television set and offered Marks a ride home, taking him out of the airport terminal through a side door. By the time the watchers gave up, mystified as to what had happened, Marks was with his wife and children, watching them unwrap the gifts he had brought.

The next day, Friday, was the Marks' wedding anniversary. Howard spent most of the day in bed, sleeping off his jetlag, then in the evening he and Judy went out for a celebration dinner at Tristans, a fashionable and extremely expensive restaurant at Portals Nous. Over dinner they talked about the future, deciding that they would move back to England within the next two months. Judy had already put the La Vileta house on the market and their two daughters had been accepted in English schools. Howard said he was going to work nine to five at Hong Kong Travel, developing the new opportunities he'd discovered in Taiwan. This was it: he was going straight.

On Saturday – the day Craig Lovato arrived in Palma, bringing with him George Pasenelli's silver handcuffs – Marks spent the day with his children, adorning the house with stickers he had bought in Taiwan. They were in hopelessly ungrammatical English and Howard thought them hysterically funny. The one he posted on the outside of the iron gates leading to the courtyard said: 'NO IN WITHOUT VISIT.'

'That should keep them out,' he said, laughing.

The only vantage point that Craig Lovato could find was the upstairs bedroom of an adjacent house. By opening the heavy wooden shutters he could glimpse the upper storey of Howard's house, and the entrance to the alley where Howard's car was parked, and from which he would eventually have to emerge if, please God, he was at home. With the shutters open, Lovato could hear much better than he could see, and he strained to listen to the voices of the people splashing in the pool. Was Howard's among them? Was he there? Lovato couldn't tell. The shutters made air-conditioning unnecessary, but only if they were kept closed. Opening them defeated their purpose. For twelve hours of that sultry Sunday he endured the stifling heat of the upstairs bedroom, contemplating the awful possibility that Marks had fled.

Lovato shared his vigil with a Spanish policeman named Nico. As the afternoon and then the evening passed, they would take it in turns to slip out of the house and walk down the street to the village *plaza*. It was not designed to accommodate the posse of Spanish cops and American observers who monopolized the Bar Luis, waiting for the raid to begin, trying unsuccessfully to be inconspicuous. Lovato or Nico, whoever's turn it was to take a break, would report developments – or rather the lack of any – to the waiting posse and collect refreshments: beer for Nico, bottled water for Lovato.

They could have raided the house at any moment, but Lovato was determined to wait. If Howard was not there, if, for some reason, he was staying somewhere else on the island, Lovato feared he would get word of any raid and vanish – just as he'd vanished in 1974, evading capture for almost seven years. And if he was in the house, playing with his children by the pool, a direct assault by the police would allow him time to destroy evidence. The iron gates leading to the courtyard, controlled by an electronic lock, looked much more formidable than they really were. Lovato imagined the Spanish police battering them down with sledgehammers, while Howard calmly erased the databases on which, Lovato was convinced, he kept the details of his organization. They had come too far, and were now too close, to be driven by impatience. Adolfo Rodríguez, the commissioner of police, had agreed: they would wait until they were sure Howard was there and then they'd trick their way through the gates, surprising him. Lovato and Nico were content to wait all night if necessary. At least it was cooler now.

Then their vigil was called off. At 9.00 p.m. Dave Herrera, the DEA country attaché from Madrid, recommended they call it quits. He said they'd tasked the Spanish police long enough for one day. They could resume the surveillance in the morning.

Lovato didn't want to quit. From the days when he had stalked Marks, getting to know his habits and movements, he knew that Howard liked to eat dinner late. It was not uncommon for him to go out to a restaurant at ten o'clock at night or even later. Just one more hour, Lovato said. Herrera would not be persuaded. The posse had also been hanging around in the heat for twelve hours. It was time to let them go home.

They'd only just got back to police headquarters in Palma when Adolfo Rodríguez received a call from one of the villagers – one of the few people in La Vileta who knew what was going on: Marks's grey Ford Sierra had been driven away from the house. Whether Marks was in it, the villager could not say. But the car had gone, only moments after the police had withdrawn.

Had Howard known all along? Had he known they were there all day, and waited for them to leave to make his escape?

Lovato, and every member of the posse still around, raced to the airport, ignoring the speed limit. Almost every driver in Palma habitually ignores the speed limit, but rarely so excessively as the police did that night.

There was no sign of Marks at any of the terminals and he was not booked on any flight – at least, not in his own name. For the next three hours they searched the western coast of Majorca, looking for the grey Sierra, led by Lovato to every one of Howard's known haunts. Neither he nor the car were anywhere to be found.

When it came right down to it, forget fancy food in expensive restaurants. What Howard liked more than anything – except, perhaps, Welsh rarebit – was the prawn vindaloo served by the Taj Mahal in Magaluf. An added attraction of the Taj Mahal was its immediate proximity to Taffy's Bar, run by another expatriate Welshman. Howard would go back and forth between the two places, eating his prawns in the restaurant, washing them down with pints of beer in the bar. The Taj Mahal was also a favourite of the children, because its owner indulged them, allowing Amber to play at being a waitress.

Unaware of the panic he was creating, Howard and Judy and their three children spent three happy hours at the Taj Mahal. They thought it was one of the last times they would be able to enjoy it, because they were moving back to England.

It was not until they were on their way home that one of the children, Amber, became irritable. She asked her father to please

235

drive slowly because she was scared. He said he wasn't driving fast. She said she was still scared, anyway.

'What of?'

'I don't know.'

At police headquarters they said there was nothing more to be done until daylight. It was too late to eat. Nico said to Lovato, 'What about a drink at Victoria's?'

'Let's take one more look,' said Lovato.

So Nico borrowed a police car and they drove to La Vileta, slowly cruising its now deserted streets. As they passed Marks's house, they caught a glimpse of the grey Sierra parked in the alley.

'He's home,' said Nico.

'Let's hope,' said Lovato.

Palma, 25 July 1988

They were back at their vantage point in La Vileta by 9.00 a.m., under ever-increasing pressure to do something. Around the world other arrest teams were ready to move, yet restrained by the admonition to wait – 'until Howard is in the bag'. In London the arrest team had been assembled since 4.00 a.m. Terry Burke called the house to say he couldn't hold them much longer.

'Terry, you've got to,' said Lovato.

'I don't know how, but I'll try,' said Burke.

The most pressing issue remained to establish if Marks was at home. They knew they could call his house just across the road and hope that if Marks was there he would pick up the phone. But whoever called had to be able to recognize Howard's voice, and they must not alarm him otherwise he might begin destroying evidence.

Lovato called his wife in Miami, where it was still the middle of the night. He asked Wendy to rouse Moynihan, asleep in his hotel, and get him to call Howard. He certainly knew Howard's voice, and Howard would not be alarmed by a call from Moynihan; surprised, perhaps, but not alarmed.

Moynihan did as he was told. In fact, he called Howard twice, once on each of his numbers. Each time it was Howard who answered the phone.

'What did he say?' said Lovato when Moynihan called him to report.

'Nothing. I just hung up.'

Christ! Two hang-ups in succession were enough to alert any-body. Lovato grabbed the phone and dialled Marks's number. As soon as Howard answered, Lovato handed the phone to a Spanish policeman who spoke unintelligibly to him in Majorcan dialect. 'You've got the wrong number,' shouted Marks, and this time it was he who hung up.

So he was definitely there. That left the problem of how to get through the iron gates. The solution proposed itself when two people turned up and disappeared into Marks's courtyard: one a blonde woman Lovato had never seen before; the other David Embley, who Lovato recognized as Howard's tennis partner. Adolfo Rodríguez ordered his men to drive their cars into the alley. Whenever the gates opened again, to let anyone in or out of the courtyard, the arrest team would rush in.

But it happened too soon. The police and Lovato had only just arrived in the alley when the gates opened to permit Embley to leave – and slammed shut before anybody could move.

Embley found himself confronted by a group of men in plain clothes, one of whom – Rodríguez – was thrusting a badge in his face, asking him questions. Though he spoke fairly fluent Spanish, Embley pretended not to understand, protesting loudly that he spoke only English. Lovato was certain that Howard would hear the commotion. He was wondering what to do when a quick-thinking Spanish cop named Ramón simply pressed the doorbell on the side of the iron gates.

They opened. Ramón and Lovato slipped inside, then heard the gates close behind them before the others could follow.

Across the courtyard they saw Howard Marks walking towards them, a broad congenial smile on his face.

Marks had got up early, his normal routine. He'd spoken on the phone to Tom Sunde, who was in Hong Kong.

'Everything OK?' he'd asked.

'There are no problems where you are at the moment,' said Sunde.

He'd gone for a swim in the pool and then fixed breakfast for Golly – Francesca, his youngest daughter. Judy, Amber and Patrick, the baby, were all still asleep.

David Embley had dropped by to fix up a tennis game for later that day. Then Roger Reaves's wife, Maarie, had arrived to talk about her husband, still in jail in Palma, resisting extradition to Germany. The phone rang a couple of times. There was nobody

237

there. A tiny alarm bell rang in Marks's mind but he ignored it. Then another call, this one from some Spaniard, a wrong number. Wrong numbers were a fact of life in Palma.

David left. 'See you later,' said Marks. Then the doorbell rang. There was an intercom on the wall by the iron gates, connected to a phone in the kitchen. Marks picked up the phone to ask who was there but all he heard was Spanish voices he didn't understand. He pressed the switch to open the gate. He thought it was probably somebody wanting him to move his car.

He walked from the kitchen into the courtyard to see men – he thought there were three of them – staring up at the palm trees. He thought they had come to ask for work, pruning the leaves. As they walked towards him, Marks noticed that one of them was carrying a small purse. He pulled a gun from it, and pressed the barrel into Marks's stomach.

Marks put his hands above his head. The man said something in Spanish. Marks said, '*Tranquillo*, I won't do anything.' He knew they were police. The thought that flashed through his mind was, 'I'm going to spend the next twenty years in jail.' Behind him he could hear Francesca screaming.

He was turned around and handcuffed, then pushed into the kitchen and told to sit down. There were more men in the house now, moving through it, some of them going upstairs. He heard Judy scream. Then she began shouting: 'Howard, Howard . . .'

Lovato watched as Ramón handcuffed Marks, and felt a small stab of satisfaction. Those were George Pasenelli's handcuffs. He'd told Adolfo Rodríguez that, if at all possible, he wanted them used on Howard, but it was sheer luck that Ramón had been chosen to carry them.

Ramón was still very much on top of things. He ducked into the kitchen and pressed the switch to open the iron gates, allowing the remainder of the arrest team to swarm into the courtyard. Lovato wondered how on earth he knew where the switch was. 'If it had been up to me,' he told Rodríguez later, 'you'd all still be waiting outside.'

Lovato went into the house and up the stairs. Judy was there in her nightgown with Amber. A Spanish policeman was trying to explain to Judy that she was under arrest, but she couldn't understand what he was saying. Amber did understand the words but nothing else. 'Why are you under arrest?' she kept asking her mother. Both of them were crying.

When Lovato identified himself, the fear turned to anger. 'Who do you fucking Americans think you are?' said Judy. 'World policemen?'

He told her he was there to help interpret so that she would understand exactly what was going on. He also told her he had international Provisional Warrants of Arrest for both her and Howard on drug charges. They would both be extradited to the United States.

They let Howard put on a pair of shoes and then they led him away to the alley, where a gaggle of curious neighbours and a marked police car waited. As he was led through the courtyard, Marks looked up at the bedroom window, hoping to catch sight of Judy. Instead he saw a man watching him. Somehow he knew it was Craig Lovato.

It took a long time to search the house. They kept Judy there while they did it, so that she could witness what was taken away: Howard's passports, the real one and the fakes; hollowed-out toothpaste tubes which Marks used to smuggle his personal supplies of dope; stacks of business cards and address books; several hand-held computers which, they hoped, contained the secrets of the Marks organization; a radio scanner which allowed Marks to monitor police radios and which, had it been turned on that morning, would have told him the net was closing in.

While the search went on, Lovato played with baby Patrick, hoping to calm the atmosphere a little. Patrick was only twenty months old, far too young to realize he was about to lose his mother. The police called Judy's youngest sister, Masha, who lived in Palma, to ask if she could come and take care of the children.

Then Lovato got an urgent call from police headquarters: 'The handcuffs, the handcuffs you gave us for Marks. Where are the keys?'

At police headquarters they kept him in a holding cell with a Peruvian awaiting deportation and a Spanish drunk who hadn't yet woken up. Some time in the afternoon, they let him out to go to the toilet. As he came out of the bathroom he looked into the cell immediately opposite and saw Judy's face at the bars. He tried to pretend to himself it was somebody else, somebody who looked like her, but it was not a delusion he could sustain.

'What are you doing here?' he said.

'They're extraditing me.'

'What!' He had never imagined it could happen.

The guards said he must not talk to other prisoners. 'That's my wife,' he said, but it didn't make any difference. They took him back to his cell where he waited, long into the evening, for his first meeting with Craig Lovato.

I was in the office and Adolfo Rodríguez came out and said: 'Craig, Marks has asked me, "Is Craig Lovato here?" And of course I didn't know if you wanted him to know if you were here or not, so I said, "Who's Craig Lovato?" And he said, "Craig Lovato is the man who has harried me throughout the world, and if he's here, I'd appreciate very much being afforded the opportunity to speak to him." If you want to talk to him, he has requested to speak to you.' And I said, 'Well certainly, I'll talk to him.'

So I walked into Adolfo's office and Howard was sitting there, and I said, 'Hello, Howard, how are you?' And he stood up and shook my hand and he says – I forget his exact terminology, but it was something like – 'Well, we finally get the opportunity to meet face to face,' and I say, 'Yes.'

He says, 'I been wanting to talk to you,' and I say, 'I suspect so. What is it that you wish to know?' And he says, 'Well, obviously, I'm concerned about my situation, and I want to know how serious it is.' And I say, 'Well, it's quite serious at this stage.'

He says, 'What about my wife?' I tell him, 'Well, the charges against her are serious as well.' And he says, 'Is there some way for me to work this out?' I say, 'Conceivably, there might be. Plea-bargaining . . .' A lot of Europeans aren't familiar with plea-bargaining, while here in the United States, it's a method that is employed on a daily basis, quite popular. I said, 'Plea-bargaining is available in the United States, but you will have to be in the United States to partake of it.' And he says, 'How quickly could that occur?' I say, 'Well, if you're willing to waive extradition, I suspect we could leave this week.'

And he says, 'Well, is there any chance of my wife being let free?' I said, 'Absolutely not. I can't see any circumstances under which you or your wife would be released without any criminal liability whatsoever.' He says, 'Well, is there any way of her not being arrested?' And I said, 'No, Howard, she's already been arrested, and what you have to understand is two things. One, plea-bargaining doesn't exist in Spain and your arrest on this extradition is carved in stone. It is non-negotiable because the Spanish don't recognize plea-bargaining. And, two, the United States government will not request your or Judith's extradition and then withdraw that. If it's serious enough for us to ask another country to extradite someone, it's serious enough that we would not recall that request. Now, if you wish to waive the extradition and go to the United States, you or your wife, once you're physically in the United States, you can sit down and submit yourself to plea-bargaining, and you are afforded an opportunity to have a hearing for bail.' And then I said, 'I would suspect quite strongly that with you being in custody, and your wife having children, that she would be afforded some type of bail. I don't think that a judge would set a bail for you – I'd be very surprised if he did. Or it would be some astronomical figure because you have already demonstrated in the past your propensity not to show up for court dates. But,' I said, 'once you were there, if there is something that you know, that you felt you could bargain with the government in regards to your charges, or Judith's, we'd certainly listen to it.'

And he said, 'Well, I think you know that I do know things that would be very beneficial to you and your agency.' I said, 'I certainly suspect that.' And he says, 'You know that I know about certain things, and I can tell you how they came about.' And I said, 'Well, I would want to know those things.'

He said, 'Is there anything else that might influence you?' And I said, 'Only in the United States would I be influenced, Howard, but I would certainly like to know what your assets are.' And he says, 'Yeah, I guess you would.' I said, 'I suspect the details might be in those little microchip computers you have.' And he says, 'We can certainly discuss that. I think that would be a negotiable item. When could we speak on this in earnest?'

And I told him, 'I don't feel comfortable speaking to you without an attorney, without you being represented by an attorney. If you did waive extradition, it would have to be a formal, legal situation. So,' I said, 'do you have an attorney?' And he said, 'Well, I have one, but I haven't been able to contact him because he's out of the country.' I said, 'Well, let me contact him and then we'll come and see you together, and if it is your decision to waive extradition, we'll do it and get it over with.' He said, 'All right,' and he gave me his attorney's telephone number, and he said, 'When would you come to see me?' I said, 'Well, I'll come and see you tomorrow.'

At some point in the evening, I was brought up from the cells to a room where the police were, including the one who'd stuck the gun in my stomach. Judy was there in tears. She was in a terrible state, crying bitterly. She'd already been shown a piece of paper saying she'd smuggled 100 million dollars'-worth of dope into the US. She said, 'Look what they're saying!' And I said, 'Fucking Nazis! What the fuck's going on?' Then she was taken away and I was shown the same piece of paper but with my name on it.

Then the police started being very aggressive. They said, 'This is your lawyer,' and I said, 'Well, that's not the lawyer I requested.' They said, 'Today's fiesta, we can't get the lawyer you requested.' I said, 'OK, don't *worry about it,' but they said I had to have a lawyer because I'd already been in custody for more than eight hours. And I'm asked if I'd sign various things and waive extradition, and I say, 'No.'*

Then one of the guys who'd been aggressive started smiling and said, 'You're very famous, there's been a book written about you.' And I said, 'Yeah, I'll give you a signed copy if you let me go.' Then he asks me the same question, would I go voluntarily to the United States? He's trying to be jokey, you know. I say I can't go because I haven't got a visa, and that makes him laugh. Then I said something about them being pawns in the American game – something like 'Still doing the Yanks' bidding, then?' And then I mentioned Craig's name to him. I just said, 'You working for Craig Lovato?' or something like that. He seemed surprised. Then I was taken back down to the cells.

Later on they brought me up to the room again and I forget what they wanted – to sign some other form, I think. Anyway, Craig came in. I had pictured him with a moustache but for some reason I thought he would be slimmer and I expected him to have glasses. Somehow I had the idea that he'd look like an American college student.

He came into the room where I was sitting and he said, 'Hello, Howard,' and then he turned his back to me. This ass appeared in front of my face because he had to squeeze himself between the desk and the chair. He wasn't being rude or anything, it was just cramped and he had to squeeze himself in like that. He said, 'I'm Craig Lovato,' and I got up to shake hands with him. I said, 'Well, it's good to meet you at last.'

He says, 'Yeah, I gather you knew this was coming, and obviously that's something I'm annoyed about.' I assume he's referring to Sunde and Jacobi. He doesn't mention their names, but I assume that's who he's referring to. And I say something like, 'Oh yeah, they're information and money junkies.'

Then he said he wanted to establish a relationship with me. I didn't give him any of the obvious snide replies. He said he wanted me to voluntarily extradite myself, and I said, 'Well, I'm very, very upset about my wife being here, and if there's any way you could see to releasing her today, then I would very probably come to the United States voluntarily.' Which I meant, I was being sincere then. And he seemed to pick up at that, and he mentioned O'Neill's name. He said he would get Bob O'Neill to come over the next day and sort that out. That was certainly my understanding. He must have said something very like that.

Then he said, 'Well, you know what's going on, you've been through the mill before.' He said there were fourteen charges against me, and one against Judy. He said that I might get off on a technicality, beat the extradition or beat the case, but that he was born and bred in Las Vegas, a betting man, and he bet he would get me. I thought he actually did have me at that point, so I didn't take the bet.

242

He said he wanted me to give him the code for breaking into my databanks. I didn't say anything, and he said, 'Well, we can get Washington to do it,' and I said, 'Yeah, I should think you'd find it pretty easy.' Then I asked him how Tony Moynihan was. I was just being devilish, just letting him know that I knew Moynihan was a witness – you know, trying to gain some points. He said, 'Tony's going to come out of this smelling like a rose.' And then he said, 'By the way, he thinks you've got a contract out on him.' And I said, 'He can't possibly think that, and neither can anyone else.' Craig said, 'Well, somebody has,' and I said, 'Well, it's probably the Australians.' He said, 'Why is that?' And I said, 'Probably because he ripped them off in some hotel business.'

And then he said I'd got beautiful children, and I asked him could he please talk to my wife to let her know there was a possibility of this deal, of her being released. He said he didn't want to because he didn't like talking to people when they were distraught. I think I made some sort of quip like, 'That must limit your conversations.'

And he said, 'Anyway, I'll be seeing you tomorrow. I want to let these Spanish people get back to their families.' They always say something like that. It's supposed to make them seem human.

The meeting the next day did not take place. By the time Lovato was able to contact Marks's lawyer on the island, Howard was gone: transferred from Palma to the Alcala Meco high-security prison near Madrid on the grounds there was a risk he might escape.

It was not until four months later, in November 1988, that they met again, after Marks had sent Lovato a letter saying, 'I am prepared to see you any time at your convenience.' Lovato and O'Neill flew from Miami to Madrid, where they became convinced that Marks was not interested in doing a deal. By then he was determined to fight extradition tooth and nail.

Afterwards, Lovato said he could never understand how Howard could allow his wife to become involved in the dope business and then refuse to save her, depriving the children of their mother. Marks said he could never understand how Craig could use Judy as a lever against him, and then refuse to allow her to go free.

Both said they would never forgive the other for 'using Judy'. In doing so they perfectly expressed the dichotomy between them.

With Howard in the bag, the other arrest teams were unleashed. Some fared better than others.

In Palma, Spanish police arrested Geoffrey Kenion, 'the Sewage

243

Engineer', who had twice couriered money from the United States for Marks. He also vowed to resist extradition. Roger Reaves, already in jail, was arrested again. He now faced competing extradition requests from both West Germany and the United States. It didn't seem to matter which one won.

In London, Scotland Yard arrested Chi Chuen Lo, better known as Balendo Lo, the manager of Hong Kong Travel, and seized the company's records. They also arrested James Newton, old friend of Moynihan, former solicitor turned purveyor of false passports. Since he refused to answer the door of his house, they knocked it down. He was standing behind it at the time and suffered a bloody nose.

In Bangkok, Thai police arrested Phillip Sparrowhawk, Marks's principal supplier of marijuana, at his home.

In Amsterdam, the Dutch arrested James Hobbs, the former operator of Marks's 'communications centre', his pal from Brixton jail, and the man who'd once said he'd trade a year in jail for the pleasure of one month of Howard's company. He just about got his wish.

The Dutch also netted another Englishman, William Ronald Robb, a comparative pawn in the game, who had arranged for the *Axel D* to receive repairs in the Philippines in 1986. His capture was almost too easy to count. Robb had been in the Philippines on the day of the big bust. He was travelling on a false passport so, at the DEA's request, he was deported and put on a plane to Amsterdam. In Bangkok, where the plane stopped, Robb disembarked and tried to get through immigration, but was turned back. In Dubai, the second stop, Harlan Bowe of the DEA, who happened to be there, got a friendly police captain to take him on to the tarmac. They boarded the plane before anybody could get off and told Robb, 'Don't even bother getting up.' He was arrested on arrival in Amsterdam.

In Vancouver, the Mounties picked up John Denbigh, 'the Vicar', who had scrupulously obeyed the conditions of his bond and remained in the city. He did not respond to this sudden decline in his fortunes. He said to the Mounties what he'd always said: precisely nothing.

In Los Angeles, Julie Desm was allowed the pleasure of arresting Ernest 'Peter' Combs and his common-law wife, Patti Hayes. Combs was very displeased on two grounds. First, he had not long been released from jail after serving his time for the Las Vegas sound-speaker load. Second, and more important, he thought he had immunity. In December 1987, at the insistence of the FBI, he had testified to a grand jury in San Francisco about a number of matters, including his involvement in the Alameda and Los Angeles loads. He had been given 'use immunity' by the FBI, meaning that his testimony could not be used against him. The DEA insisted that all of its evidence against Combs had been gathered independently, but that didn't sit well with Peter. 'Hey, Julie, what's going on?' he said as he was led away in handcuffs. 'I have immunity.'

In Los Angeles the DEA also arrested Rick Brown, another comparatively minor player, accused of delivering a bag full of money to Combs. They also got Wyvona Meyer, the former wife of Gerald Wills, who had carried money, hidden under her skirt, from Los Angeles to Marks in London. But they missed Wills who, having reported to his probation officer – a condition of his bond in Vancouver – abruptly left town. They also missed Wills's partner, Ronald Allen, and Bradley Weller, who had helped Wills buy the *Axel D* and who had carried money to Marks's bank account in Hong Kong to pay for the Los Angeles load.

In New York they got John Francis, the Mob-connected money launderer. And in Karachi they eventually got Saleem Malik, the supplier of the hashish that went to Los Angeles, though they believed there wasn't a chance in hell of getting him extradited. Pakistan had never before sent a wanted drug dealer to the United States.

They did not arrest George Lane, Judy Lane's younger brother, because they didn't know where he was. He and his wife, Assumpta, had abandoned the International Language Centre in Karachi after an almighty row with Marks over money. George had not only run the school for Howard, providing him with a useful front, he'd also acted as a courier, flying to Hong Kong to collect money to pay Saleem Malik for the Los Angeles load. He believed Howard owed him $20,000. Marks said he did not. After a confrontation in London, George flew to Bangkok, determined to start a new life, vowing that he would never speak to Howard again. The DEA knew he was in Thailand, but that was all, and he remained a fugitive. (In truth, he wasn't that hard to find. We interviewed George in Bangkok in January 1990. His wife had returned to England and he was living, in very reduced circumstances, with a prostitute whose name he didn't know. He called her Twinkle. He was drinking heavily and was obviously ill. He remained very bitter towards Marks, blaming him for his condition.)

In Miami the DEA arrested Teresita Caballero, an employee of

Raoul del Cristo, who had helped Patrick Lane 'launder' the DEA's money during the sting operation against him – or so the DEA alleged. All she had done was write a letter to the Florida National Bank, authorizing 'Barry John Doyle' to pick up a cheque. Perhaps because her role was so minimal, she had not been properly identified by the DEA. They first arrested the wrong woman: another female employee of del Cristo's. The mess wasn't sorted out until Caballero walked into the office and said, '*I'm* Teresita.'

That left Patrick Lane.

His fortunes had improved a little in the six months since the sting operation ended. The previous year, he'd borrowed $22,000 from the bank and, in an all-or-nothing gamble, started his own desktop publishing business called Mr Write. With his wife's help, he researched, wrote and produced reports, brochures and slides. Gradually the business had built, gaining major clients, including an international bank. When the DEA arrived, Patrick and Jude had spent the previous several weeks working virtually nonstop, producing brochures for a company which sold sophisticated weapons overseas. His first thought when armed men, wearing raid jackets, burst into the house was, 'Oh, shit! This is all illegal. You're not allowed to be dealing in arms.'

It was not until he was in handcuffs, being taken away from his house, that Lane realized he was considered a leading member of the Howard Marks organization. Brad Whites of the IRS, who led the arrest team, assured him of a life behind bars – unless he told them everything he knew about Marks and Peter Combs. He was still in a state of shock when he replied, 'No deal.'

The arrest of Marks and the others received extraordinary media coverage in Britain. The competition in hyperbole has rarely been more intense. The *Daily Mirror* called him 'the evil genius behind the world's biggest marijuana and hashish racket'. *The Times* said he was 'one of the top four drugs barons in the world'. *Today* said he ran 'the world's biggest hashish ring' with an estimated turnover of £200 million. The *Daily Mail*, as imaginative as any, said: 'The gang graduated from using hired boats to owning a fleet of ships and planes. Undersea hollows and hideaways were used as hiding places off Florida and Spain and the drugs were later recovered at night by divers.'

Lord Moynihan found himself elevated to almost heroic status: 'the Ermine Pimpernel', according to the *Daily Express*; 'Lord Supergrass', said the *People*, 'the terrified man the world is hunting.'

Only Marks added a sour note, calling him 'the nastiest little shit of the worst kind'.

In Miami, Dexter Lehtinen, the US Attorney, was quoted as telling reporters that the Marks gang had 'moved thousands of tons and even bought their own ship'. *Newsweek*, latching on to the words of Tom Cash, labelled him 'the Marco Polo of drug trafficking'. Later on, ABC Television's *Prime Time Live* called him 'the King of Cannabis'.

It was mostly nonsense – or as Marks described it, with justification, from his jail cell, 'a senseless Hollywood comedy'.

The truth was that, in terms of his productivity, Marks barely ranked as major international trafficker. In almost twenty years – and assuming every allegation against him was true – he'd smuggled less than 100 tons of dope. Based on the amount of cannabis available in the United States each year, that was enough to keep America going for less than one day.

But it wasn't the statistics that interested the media so much as the myth: the myth Marks was largely responsible for creating. If he wasn't the biggest drug dealer the DEA busted that year, he was almost certainly the most audacious. In almost everyone's view, he had it coming to him. As Jack Hook, then the DEA spokesman in Miami, said: 'After Marks was acquitted at the Old Bailey he is quoted as saying he was too smart, too sophiscated for any law enforcement agency to catch him. We are very pleased to have had the chance to make him eat his words.'

Well, perhaps. In Britain, a new paperback edition of *High Time*, now re-titled *Howard Marks: His Life and High Times*, was rushed to the printers with a hastily-written epilogue which concluded:

> But all the DEA had was a sporadic pattern of meetings, phone calls and contacts across the globe. As a stool-pigeon, Moynihan did not exactly have a reputation for stainless honesty that would easily convince a jury. Howard Marks was far too skilled after eighteen years in the dope trade to leave his fingerprints on a single lump of hashish. So the charming self-made millionaire from the Welsh valleys may not have been completely out for the count.
>
> Is the story of the biggest dope smuggler in the world over yet?

Or as Tom Cash would continue to remind Lovato: 'The fat lady ain't sung yet, Craig.'

247

T E N

Michael Katz, Marks's London lawyer, flew to Palma and attempted to counter the media ballyhoo with some remarkable claims of his own: 'The charges are emphatically denied,' Katz said. 'My client was involved [in drugs] fifteen years ago and he pleaded guilty to it . . . The judge in England accepted that from 1973 onwards Howard has led an honest and industrious life . . . He works very hard and spends a lot of time trying to develop his business.' But Marks knew it would take more than rhetoric to deny Lovato his victory. He also hired Gustavo Muñoz, a Madrid attorney with impeccable credentials, an excellent grasp of English, and some interesting ideas on how to thwart what he saw as American judicial imperialism. After he'd taken the case, Muñoz told another lawyer that he might not win the battle over extradition but, of all the defendants in the case, Marks would be the last to arrive in Miami. He was proved wrong, though not through any lack of effort on his part.

Muñoz thought it extraordinary that Marks was going to be tried in America when most of the acts he was accused of had been committed or planned in Spain. If the allegations were true, Marks had certainly broken Spanish law. Therefore, Muñoz said, he should be charged and tried in Spain. Marks wholeheartedly agreed. In America, he now knew – having received a copy of the New Sentencing Guidelines from Muñoz – he faced three consecutives life sentences, without the prospect of parole. In Spain, the very worst he faced, on essentially the same charges, was twelve years, of which he would have to serve a little over two before becoming eligible for *permissos*. It is, by most countries' standards, a rather liberal concept which allows prisoners to spend one week at home every month. Marks knew precisely what he would do the first time he was granted *permissos*: vanish.

'I'm guilty of breaking Spanish law,' he said. 'I should pay the penalty.'

The trouble was, the Spanish authorities studiously ignored Marks's attempts to confess his guilt, even when he made them very public. During an interview with *Panorama*, one of Madrid's leading news magazines, Marks drew an elaborate map which showed his supposed drug smuggling routes, from the Far East to Mozambique *to Spain*. To support his confession, he solemnly showed the reporter from *Panorama* the transcripts of Craig Lovato's telephone taps. 'See,' he said, '"Champagne in Mozambique"; "champagne" was code for marijuana and it came here via Mozambique.' The magazine printed his 'confession', map and all. Unfortunately for Howard, the Spanish authorities, unlike *Panorama*, didn't buy it.

So Gustavo Muñoz arranged for a private prosecution to be brought against his client. Spanish law allows for an *acción popular* to be mounted by outraged citizens against any criminal the authorities have failed to deal with. Muñoz went to the College of Lawyers to get the necessary thirty signatures on the petition. The lawyers who signed said: 'How disgusted we, the Spanish, should be that we welcome these foreigners to our country and they come in here and set up drug empires and we, the Spanish, ought to take care of these problems . . .'

Nice try. The lower court rejected the petition, without saying why, and the high court rejected Muñoz's appeal. He was, however, nowhere near being defeated.

Muñoz bombarded the courts with motions. He said that Marks could not be extradited to America for crimes that did not exist in Spain: racketeering, conspiracy and money laundering. He said Marks could not be extradited on the 1973 Las Vegas charge, because he had already been prosecuted for that in England, and it would amount to double jeopardy. He argued that, anyway, Spain's Statute of Limitations rendered the 1973 charge obsolete.

None of it worked. At the end of March 1989, Marks and his wife Judy, whom Muñoz also represented, were informed that the US requests for their extradition had been granted. Still Muñoz did not give up. He appealed to the Supreme Court on the grounds that since Spanish nationals could not be extradited, and since Spain was now a member of the European Community, citizens of other EC countries living in Spain were entitled to the same protection. Meanwhile, Howard and Judy launched an *antiquício*, a private lawsuit, against the judges who had ordered their extradition, claiming that they were not impartial. That gave Muñoz grounds to appeal to Spain's constitutional court, arguing that the decision the judges had made could not be enforced until the *antiquício* had been resolved.

It was a gala performance and probably worth the $50,000 Marks paid – though, afterwards, he said he didn't think so. The most important consequence was that Marks and Judy remained in Spain, in separate prisons, for well over a year. They therefore missed the main event, the seminal act of the drama: the Trial.

West Palm Beach, Florida, April through July 1989

To Patrick Lane, to Peter Combs and his wife, Patti, and to the other three available defendants, it felt as if they were up against a powerful, well-oiled machine.

It didn't feel like that in the prosecutor's room. The case was heard in West Palm Beach, not Miami, because that is where the judge assigned to it, James Paine, happened to sit. West Palm Beach is too far from Miami comfortably to allow a daily commute, so the prosecution moved, lock, stock and barrel, to the Comfort Suites Hotel, taking over ten rooms. They operated out of what had been used as a storage closet in the courthouse – frantically.

They intended to present more than 100 witnesses, some of them flying great distances, some of them appearing with great reluctance, if at all. For a case of this magnitude, O'Neill should have been supplied with an assistant, but he wasn't. Nor was he relieved of his case load. More than anything else, the success of the prosecution depended on his ability to think on his feet. That, and the efforts of the hard core of Operation Eclectic: Terry Burke of Scotland Yard, Peter Nelson of Her Majesty's Customs, Brad Whites of the IRS, Randy Waddell of the Naval Investigative Service, and Ed Wezain, George Pasenelli, Harlan Bow and Art Scalzo of the DEA – who prepared witnesses for testimony, collected them from and delivered them to the airport, quibbled over their expenses, and briefed O'Neill, sometimes at the very last minute, on the questions he should ask.

The trial was, in one sense, Hamlet without the Prince. With Marks still in Spain – and with Denbigh, Sparrowhawk, Malik, Wills and Allen, among others, also missing from the stage – it was a sideshow, except for those involved in it.

In Howard's absence, his brother-in-law became the principal defendant. The case was entitled *United States of America* vs. *Patrick Alexander Lane, et al.* The government saw and portrayed Lane as the long-time professional money launderer for the Marks cartel, somebody who had personally made $29 million out of other people's misery. Lane saw himself as a middle-aged man who, through his own stupidity and the government's grinding determination to 'get Howard Marks', had been plunged into a surreal nightmare. For the nine months leading up to the trial, he was held in Miami's Metropolitan Correction Center (MCC), in lieu of bond of $1 million – while his wife and daughters wondered how to feed themselves. He could not – or, in the government's view, would not – spend any of his supposed hidden fortune on a defence lawyer, so he was given a court-appointed attorney, an overworked public defender who admitted he was not at his best in the courtroom. Lane therefore prepared much of his own defence, closeted in the prison library. He was convinced that, under the Fourth Amendment of the Constitution, the Spanish wiretaps of Marks's phone, on which the case hinged, were inadmissible. They failed, by a very long way, to meet the standards laid down for a lawful telephone tap (known as a Title III) in the United States. For example: the original tapes had been erased and only Craig Lovato's cassette copies existed; Lovato had arbitrarily decided which conservations to preserve, and which to junk; the recording process had not been continually and constantly monitored – and so on, and so on. Lane studied every aspect of the Fourth Amendment, which promises protection against unreasonable search and seizure, and absorbed every case on record concerning judicial restraints on Title III investigations. He – along with most if not all of the defendants' lawyers – was convinced that the tapes would be suppressed and that, without them, the RICO charges would fail. He really did believe that the case was held together by the spit and wishful thinking of Lovato and Bob O'Neill and that, denied their tapes, there would be – could be – no trial.

But then, his whole new life was one of continuing disbelief. Every night as he went to sleep in his cell he said: 'This can't be happening to me. This can't be real.'

* * *

251

On days when inmates are to appear in court they are woken at 3.00 a.m., briefly fed, and put in a large holding cell. There is not usually time to shave or shower. Thus the day begins with forty violent and bad-tempered men crammed together into a single cell with a toilet in the middle of the room. Court clothes are handed in, and the inmates change from their normal prison uniforms into suits and ties or whatever they usually wear in the outside world. It is often an extraordinary transformation. Before your startled gaze some foul-mouthed, low-life scumsucker, just by combing his hair and changing his clothes, suddenly looks like the president of a savings and loan. Then you discover he is the president of a savings and loan.

But it is still only 4.30 a.m. or 5.00 a.m., and you are still crammed together in a hot, dirty cell where you continue to wait. At about 6.00 a.m. the inmates are all handcuffed and chained together and then returned to the holding cell to wait. The clean shirts and the crisp collars that wives had so carefully ironed are grubby after a few hours and the smart suit is starting to look crumpled, however carefully you sit. The steel bracelets around the wrists and ankles chafe and hurt; the steel chains around the waist are uncomfortable and pull the suit out of shape. It is important to try and keep the mind clear and prepare for the ordeal ahead in court. This means ignoring the endless, cynical obscenities and grumbles of the other inmates. Chained together, huddled on the unswept concrete floor around a well-used toilet, you hear: 'Where's the fucking paper? The motherfuckers ain't got no fucking paper!' Finally on our way to court in the prison bus, we look out at the world from which we've been removed.

The ride from MCC was particularly moving for me, as we passed through Coral Gables and I saw all the old familiar places from behind the bars. I passed the children's schools and saw their friends arriving for the start of a new day. Nothing, no words can convey the shame and horror of such a moment; frightened to see your own children; frightened they will see you. It was so strange to see proof that life indeed did carry on.

Most of the other people sharing the road with us were on their way to work, or to school. Car pools of young kids, freshly scrubbed, clean and wholesome in contrast to us on our Bus from Hell. Pretty young secretaries heading to the office, fixing their makeup in the mirror as the traffic inched slowly forward. If we were lucky, from our vantage-point high in the bus, we could see down their dresses or look where their skirts rode up the thighs. There was great competition to get a window seat.

In prison sex is inextricably entwined with violence, obscenity and misogyny, and the sight of the female public, so close, so varied, so tantalizingly out of reach, inflamed all those passions. Faces pressed against the windows, wild glittering eyes devoured and undressed the women, mouths and tongues gestured obscenely and hurled imprecations that negated, in one foul torrent, whole millennia of human progress.

252

Most riders in the early morning commute remained in air-conditioned ignorance, unaware of the closeness of the tumbril. But those who looked up and saw the faces and heard the cries were changed. They knew that the solid boundaries of their world had shifted momentarily. Swiftly they averted their eyes and returned to the security of their cocoon. Thus abandoned, we knew we had removed ourselves from normal human pity, and in such a frame of mind we approached the Court and the judgement of our fellow citizens.

I know you want to hear about the trial. Please bear with me. Before we finally leave that Bus from Hell I do have a request to make to you; a plea to anyone who drives on America's highways. Next time you are in traffic and you see an unmarked and scruffy bus or van with bars on the windows and barely-human faces snarling out at the world, please do not shudder and turn away in disgust. Please give a sympathetic smile and wave before you drive on. Somewhere in that alien horde beats an English heart; an embarrassed accountant grins sheepishly.

For the duration of the five-week trial (except for weekends) Peter Combs and I lived at Fort Lauderdale City Jail. It is not part of the federal system. By arrangement, two large cells are set aside for federal prisoners, and the city police are paid so much per body per night. Unlike the bank robbers, racketeers, drug lords and international arms dealers of the federal system, the clientèle at Fort Lauderdale were pimps and hookers, muggers, rapists and crack monsters. The reality of the city jail became an important part of our world and our impressions of the trial. Our perception of everything that happened during the five-week period was overshadowed by what happened in that God-forsaken place.

Federal and non-federal prisoners, by law, must be kept separate, and so rather than put us in the tank with the normal prisoners, Peter and I would be put with the female prisoners. There being no special place for the female prisoners in the reception area, their bodies would be cuffed or chained to any convenient but solid object: a metal table leg, steel bars, a door or even a heavy steel filing cabinet. So, wearing our smart bankers' suits after a day in court, we would spend an hour or so, after our return, sitting on the dirty floor of a corridor, chained to a filing cabinet as busy police officers went about their duty and stepped over our bodies.

The female prisoners were almost always there for soliciting. Their poor emaciated little bodies, ruined with drugs and 'good times', made a pathetic mockery of sex. Most of them were just kids. Chained in the strange intimacy of our shared misery and humiliation they would whisper obscene promises and flash me their soiled goods, their sad bodies. As my mind tried to analyse the events of the day I would realize that my companion on the floor was not wearing underwear and that, like her, I was just another piece of flotsam,

253

a reject, beyond hope and worth nothing. Most often, my lack of response to their charms would cause loud cackles about faggots. The desk sergeant would often explain that I was English and, as everybody knows, all Englishmen are faggots. But occasionally a glance would be exchanged, a smile, and some poor girl in her terrible shame and humiliation would know that she was still recognizably human in that awful place.

The Palm Beach marshals would collect us from Fort Lauderdale at about 6.30 a.m. and deliver us to the courthouse at West Palm Beach by about 7.30 a.m. We would be ushered into the courtroom usually just after 9.00 a.m., at the very last moment, just before the jury was admitted. The fiction was that the jury was not supposed to know that Peter and I were in custody. When the court was not in session, when everyone else went for coffee or a cigarette or a pee or lunch, Peter and I would be taken back through the door which led into the marshals' office, where we would be put in a bare steel cage with a hard metal bench and a clogged, seatless toilet open to the office.

Bridie, my youngest daughter, drew an extremely detailed picture of the courtroom. She showed the white-haired judge looking down from his dais. She showed O'Neill gesticulating and arguing to the jury, Lovato sullen in the witness box, the defence attorneys busily sorting through their masses of papers and, at the back of the room, behind the judge and below the American flag, she had marked 'the Bad Door', where Peter and I were taken.

Behind 'the Bad Door' was a whole other world: the world of the marshals. During the five weeks that Peter and I lived in that office, we became part of their lives. Peter and I were soon on Christian name terms, and friendly with them all. We watched budding romances and professional rivalries as they developed over the weeks. We listened to phone conversations and policy discussions. We knew who was having trouble with his wife, who was unhappy with this month's pay-cheque, who had a drinking problem.

Going into court was very much like appearing on stage. The marshals would check their guns and put on their jackets. They would adjust their ties and come to unlock our cage, one opening the door with his key while the other stood back to cover him in the approved manner. Peter and I would adjust each other's tie and jacket, each acting as the other's mirror. Whatever despair or fear we felt would be suppressed with a deep breath. The door would open and with a positive spring to our step, a virile bracing of the shoulders and a modest but self-confident smile, we would stride into the courtroom, for another brief moment free men in control of our destiny.

The sense of freedom in court was disorientating. We were human beings again. We were dressed like other people and were treated like other people. We joined in group laughter and shared jokes, we participated in conversations

254

which never once contained the words motherfucker or cocksucker. We expressed opinions and were listened to. Even after we were taken back through 'the Bad Door' to our cage, we were still among friends – Dave and Jerry and Bob, the marshals. We still shared jokes and agreed that it had been a long day. But gradually the charade would fade away and the demands of the real world intruded. The cuffs and chains would be put back on, the wrists and ankles still raw and sore from the morning. Within ninety minutes of shaking hands with my attorney, man to man in civilized surroundings, I would one again be lying in a corridor, chained to a door frame and next to a girl with bare breasts and broken teeth: 'Got any smoke, honey?'

The issue of the admissibility of the tapes dominated the first two days of the trial. The legal debate that took place was crucial, not only to these proceedings, the dress rehearsal, but also the main event that would follow – if and when Marks was extradited. If Judge Paine ruled that the tapes could not be used against Lane *et al.*, then Marks, in all probability, was free.

In advance of the trial, the defence lawyers had submitted voluminous written arguments to Judge Paine, savaging the government and its methods, and O'Neill had made a spirited reply. But Paine gave the impression that he'd been too busy to consider them. He said he would take verbal arguments – but quickly, please; he wanted to get on with it. 'Well, excuuuuuuuuse me, Judge Paine,' said Combs to Lane, back behind 'the Bad Door' during recess, 'but that's my fucking life you're trying to hurry through.'

Then Paine announced his decision. Lane, for one, could not believe it.

I don't care how sympathetic you are to Lovato. I don't care what a good cop he is, how hard he worked, what impossible odds he overcame, what brilliant detective work he accomplished and how sheer dogged determination, luck and cheek finally won the day. Those tapes were illegal, and should never have been admitted. The tapes were made casually to help in the preparation of the case and Lovato, quite reasonably, assumed that by the end of the day he would have tons of dope, bundles of money and a big cartel in fragrante delicto. In fact, he ended up with just the tapes, and had to base his case on those despite the fact that they violated every aspect of the Fourth Amendment. No other country would permit those tapes and probably no other judicial district would permit them other than Florida.

But the time was right and the place was right and after a couple of days' discussion in court, Judge Paine ruled that the tapes would be

255

admitted in evidence. It was a blow from which the defence team never properly recovered.

But for O'Neill, getting the tapes admitted was only half the battle. They ran for well over twenty hours in their totality, and once the voyeuristic novelty of listening to other people's conversations had evaporated, they were boring. To the uninitiated, they were also largely incomprehensible: a mind-numbing succession of different voices, many of them hard to understand, speaking in code. What did 'Bugs Bunny' mean, except as a cartoon character? 'Dog and bone'; 'Your dog is sick'; 'Champagne in Mozambique'; 'It's very south, around the bend, halfway up the squiggly bit' – it was all meaningless. The conversations might as well have been in Greek. No jury could be expected to make sense of them without more than a little guidance.

It was therefore essential, argued O'Neill, that Craig Lovato, with his long experience of drug traffickers and their devious dissimulations, be allowed to interpret the tapes for the jury, explaining who was talking and what they were really saying.

No, said Judge Paine. The jury could listen to the tapes and draw their own conclusions.

There was a great deal of gloom in the Comfort Suites Hotel that night. Lovato, for one, thought the judge's decision was a near-fatal blow. It was almost better not to play the tapes at all than to have the jury listen to hours and hours of conversations in which the words 'hashish', 'marijuana', 'cannabis' or 'drugs' were not mentioned once. Yet without the tapes, the RICO charges – the ones that counted – were almost impossible to prove. Lovato told O'Neill bluntly: 'Bobby, you've got to come up with something.'

Sure, Craig. Like what? O'Neill headed for the law library of the US Attorney's office in West Palm Beach, but it was locked for the night. So, too, were Judge Paine's chambers, where he might have found the law books he was looking for. Back at the hotel he hit the phone, calling lawyers he knew at their homes, slowly coming up with case law that seemed to support his position that Lovato should be allowed to interpret the tapes.

What clinched it for him, however, was a computer printout he'd been carrying around in his briefcase. It was a report of a drug case too recent to have made it into the law books, or even the supplements. It came out of the 3rd Circuit in Philadelphia, where the federal appeals court had ruled, a couple of months before, that an FBI agent should have been allowed to interpret tapes that were crucial to the government's case in *United States* vs. *Theodoropolous*. In *Theodoropolous* the conversations were literally in Greek. Nevertheless, it seemed to establish the point that in some circumstances case agents could testify as 'expert witnesses', allowing them to say not only what they had heard but also what they thought it meant.

The next morning, O'Neill came out fighting, quoting the case law that he said allowed Lovato to testify as an expert witness, saving *Theodoropolous* until last. The defence team included some highly experienced attorneys – three of them big-hitting lawyers out of Los Angeles – but they were not prepared to argue the merits of a case too recent to be in the law books.

Judge Paine reversed himself. He said Lovato could interpret the tapes.

One immediate consequence was that John Francis, the Mob-connected money launderer, did a deal with the government, pleading guilty to one charge of tax evasion. (Lovato strongly objected to the deal with Francis, scornfully dismissing his vague promise to 'co-operate' in return for leniency. Still, as he conceded, it was 'Bobby's call'. O'Neill thought the case against Francis was too weak.)

For Patrick Lane, Peter Combs and his wife, Patti, the consequences were slow in coming – but, from that point on, probably inevitable.

It was the tapes that linked us all together, and it was the sound of the tapes which filled the courtroom almost every day. Except for a couple of conversations, Howard's voice was on every tape. His unmistakable lilt, his laughter, the smoker's sharp intake of breath while he thought; his invisible presence filled the courtroom. By the end of the trial, Howard's voice and his mannerisms were as familiar to the members of the jury as they were to us who thought we knew him well.

For both Peter and myself it was an especially sobering experience as we learned that what we had individually thought of as a special relationship was no more than standard operating procedure for Howard on the phone. Like two men who had loved foolishly, we were forced to watch as our courtesan undressed and performed her intimate tricks for a succession of paying customers. Having both prided ourselves for so many years on our friendship with Howard, we both started to refer to him as 'your friend Howard'.

Poor Peter. I know how awful it was to listen to my voice on tape filling the courtroom with its sound. But it was so much worse for him. It was cruel. His conversations with Howard were terrible. The swearing, the racist

257

jokes: 'That cocksucking judge. I'd like to rip his fucking head off his fucking neck . . .' And for Peter the worst of all was the one where he described drinking champagne direct from the bottle and comparing it to how a girl must feel giving head.

Despite the foul language, Peter is sexually very conservative and very prudish. He is also very shy where women are concerned, and was extremely aware that there were nine women on the jury and at least two of them were young and attractive. He tortured himself imagining the tapes being played in front of them. 'What can I do? Where can I look?' He suffered terribly. It wasn't because the tapes were incriminating and would lead to a guilty verdict that worried him. It was the idea of having to sit in court, facing those women, that caused him to suffer. He told me on several occasions, only half-joking: 'I'll plead guilty if only they promise not to play the tapes.'

His shame and his suffering during that period were extreme and I shall never forget how brave he was, how he forced himself to keep going, to keep joking and not to give in to despair. Conditions at the jail were appalling. The air-conditioning was freezing, often we had no blanket or mattress and slept on hard, cold, filthy concrete floors. Several competing TVs all blasted at full volume. The other inmates howled, screamed and fought all night long. Often no razors in the morning, nor toothbrushes. We never ate all the time we were there – the food was literally like vomit which someone had thrown up on a plate. But Peter always had jokes, and however down I felt he always had me laughing again by the time we reached the courthouse. 'Maybe it will be your tapes today,' he would grin hopefully. 'Perhaps it will be you in the hot seat. Anyway, why don't you fucking Brits ever cuss on the phone? You all faggots, or what?'

In the witness box Lovato sat. Dark, brooding and bored. We all quickly realized that Lovato was a worthy foe. He was good at interpreting the tapes. Damned good. Too bloody damned good. Years of experience became depressingly apparent the moment the first questions were put to him. This was no man who was going to be pushed around or tricked or brow-beaten by any chicken-shit attorneys. Unruffled, serious, scornful, professional – we all realized that he was dangerous.

We had all been looking forward to getting Lovato in the witness box. We were all going to have fun with him. We had read all his affidavits, his reports and his grand jury statements. We knew all the mistakes and all the contradictions and inconsistencies. We rubbed our hands in glee. After nine months of being kicked around, the boot was on the other foot and we were going to have fun with this big, stupid, ugly cop. Within minutes all the attorneys were scrambling for cover, tails between their legs, and all the plans for cross-examination were changed. 'He's too dangerous,' they said, 'we don't know what he might say.' So because Lovato was good, but also because the attorneys – all of them – were cowardly, he got off easily and was able to sell his damaged goods to the jury.

Lord Moynihan was a strangely disappointing figure when he arrived. He seemed to have shrunk from the large man that I remembered. Both Jude and Peggy made the same comment. But he was not a man to underestimate. As with Lovato, we quickly realized that we had a formidable opponent. But where Lovato was constrained by law and his own sense of the rules of the game, Moynihan recognized no laws. He lied about the missing $1,250 without a flicker. Despite Judge Paine's repeated instructions, Moynihan continued to do things exactly the way he wanted to. He sat at his ease and conveyed to the bewildered jury that it was all a jolly jape. He read from his notes and he digressed and answered questions in whatever manner he chose. All through his testimony Jude and Peggy riveted him with a Medusa stare so fixed and laser-like that I feared the wall behind him would shatter if he moved his head. Peggy is endlessly fascinated by Moynihan, the first (and I hope only) truly bad person that she has ever known.

Gil Charette also looked smaller. Certainly less terrifying. He was so obviously a cop, and I wondered how I could ever have thought otherwise. I wondered if I'd known that all the time.

Dominating the whole room, with his boyish charm and winsome manners, was little Bobby O'Neill. You could see all the women on the jury wanting to take him home and feed him – or whatever. His 'Aw, shucks' manner, his shy smile, his moral outrage were guaranteed to win sympathy from the jury. Alone, he stood there against all the hired guns from out of town with their fancy Los Angeles ways. Judge Paine obviously liked him, and he respectfully treated Paine like a wise father. (Peter was extremely funny, and lying chained in the corridor or huddled together in our cell trying to keep warm, he would keep my spirits raised with his endless imitations. He did a very good one of O'Neill asking Paine for something outrageous to be admitted and Paine eventually waking up and granting the motion, at which point O'Neill says: 'Oh, gee! Thanks, Dad.')

The effect of all these law-enforcement officers from around the world should not be overlooked. Day after day they trooped into court; their strange titles and names, their accents – all contributing an exotic excitement to the proceedings. They were all law enforcement, from different countries, helping our government. They had flown around the world just to be here. They would not have done that if this was not terribly important. It sent two messages, both to us and to the jury. It showed how important this case must be, and how much time and effort and international co-operation had been invested – a not-guilty verdict would mean that this immense effort would all have been a waste. It also emphasized the power and resources of the federal government.

It reminded us that these were the people who had put men on the moon. They were moving men around the world to appear in court, they were speaking with the authority not just of Uncle Sam, but of Scotland Yard and the Mounties. Bobby O'Neill did not stand alone, he had Maigret and Sherlock Holmes standing beside him.

I know that O'Neill was flying by the seat of his pants, and that he and Lovato were getting no support or help. So you tell me. But from where I sat, it was a machine and it was grinding me to nothing. Even though there are last-minute hitches and panics and improvisations behind the scenes, the audience should still share Hamlet's indecision, still swoon at the love scenes, and still be moved by the sound and the fury. What is presented on stage is what counts: 'The play's the thing.' It does not matter that it was all improvisation and illusion. I was terrified. And the bars and the chains were real. The marshals' guns were real, Jude's pain was real, and seeing my children from a distance, growing old without me – all that was real.

We were made aware of the real power of the government every time we wanted to pee or kiss our wife. They had our bodies. They made us strip naked while they humiliated us with their body searches at least twice a day. They physically hurt us every day with their chains. To us, in jail, they were part of a big team that included the prison guards and the drivers of the vans and the marshals with their guns. These are not abstract concepts. These are the physical realities of the government. These are the actual flesh and blood, steel and concrete manifestations of the power of the machine that we were fighting. It might not have been well-oiled, but it was big, it was powerful and it worked. We were at all times aware that they controlled the vast Behemoth which held us in its maw.

The jury very quickly associated me with money, and money very quickly became the easily-understood metaphor for an otherwise confusing saga. From day one, the jury clearly understood, and were made to understand, that I was the money man. My role was easy to comprehend and to remember.

I doubt whether, at any point in the trial, the jury could have said: 'This specific amount of drugs was smuggled from this place to that place on this date by those people playing the following roles.' However, they were quite certain that over a period of years a whole bunch of us had been smuggling a whole bunch of drugs around the world and making a whole bunch of money at it. They did not really understand why Howard Marks was not in court. The one single thing which was clearly understood is that a heck of a lot of money had been made, and that I was the man who handled it. Every time the subject of money was mentioned I would watch the jurors' eyes all turn in my direction, or Judes's. And there I sat in my pinstripe suit, like a tall

City gent. Just what a money man is supposed to look like. Amid the welter of confusion the jurors took comfort in the clarity of my role. My wife and I were probably nice people, I was not involved in any violence or unsavoury activities, I spoke nicely on the phone, I did not use 'language' – and I was obviously guilty as hell. Each time more money was mentioned my guilt was clearly established. Each new dollar was another nail in my coffin. The fact that I was living in France and growing my own food when most of these events were taking place was not known by the jury. All they knew was that money was being made, and I was the money man.

I think the strongest image from the whole trial, the metaphor which sticks in our memories and sums up the whole case, was the million bucks in the cake tin. Some time in the early seventies, one of Peter's workers had $1 million in cash which he hid in a large box at his house. In court he testified that the cash remained sitting there for weeks because Peter was 'too busy' to come and collect it. The jury sat through that story with their mouths hanging open. That was the moment when they first understood what the case was all about and why we were there and where their duty lay. $1 million! And he is 'too busy' to come and get it! They looked at me and wondered why Peter did not send me to collect it. I was obviously too busy counting other money somewhere else. It was early in the trial that the jury were told about the $1 million in the box and from that moment on, for the rest of the trial, none of them would look me in the eyes again.

Judge Paine was exactly what a southern gentleman judge was supposed to look like. Large and physically imposing, thick silver-white hair, and kindly eyes which surveyed an increasingly distasteful world from over the top of his reading glasses.

There is no question that the government got everything ruled in their favour. I believe that the only defence motions which Paine granted were permission to have our wives deliver a change of clothing to the marshals' office, and that we should be allowed back to MCC at the weekends. Everything else was denied. Peter does a very good imitation of Judge Paine which can always raise a laugh among those who know: 'Denied. Denied. Denied.'

I think Paine's basic philosophy is to 'tip everything out on to the table and see what we've got. Let's rummage around and use our common sense to see what's been going on.' It is an approach which appeals to me and probably appeals to most laymen – certainly to most juries. Forget all the nit-picking and hair-splitting: let's see if it waddles and quacks. If it does, it's a duck. Unfortunately, in these days of RICO statutes and the New Guidelines, such an old-fashioned and common-sense approach is no longer appropriate. In selecting the precise charges on the original indictment, the prosecutor is also deciding what sentence will be given. Judges such as Paine are becoming an anachronism. There is no place for him in the 'brave new world' of the Sentencing Reform Act.

I will not even attempt to describe the horror of sitting in the holding cell, waiting for the jury to return with a verdict.

But they did eventually return and I, being the major name with the most counts, stood first and faced the jury. The verdicts were read out, one after the other, all the same – 'Guilty' – and I concentrated on standing upright and not showing any emotion on my face. I then sat down, feeling numb and unreal, and watched as Peter and poor Patti went through the same ordeal. Rick Brown stood with a smirk on his face. When he was acquitted he left the courtroom with a cheery wave.

Teresita Caballero also left the courtroom declared innocent and free. As Lane described it, only slightly tongue-in-cheek:

'If I remember correctly, there were 3,478 witnesses brought from seventeen different nations around the world. On 3,478 occasions, after O'Neill and the other defence attorneys had finished their questions, her attorney would leap to his feet with a bright smile and 3,478 times, as though it were the first time, he would say "Good afternoon. My name is Kevin Emus and I represent Ms Terri Caballero."

'He would turn and point to Terri.

'"She is the young lady sitting at the end of the table."

'The witness would obligingly look at Terri and she, expressionless, would return the stare.

'"Have you ever seen Ms Caballero before, sir? At any time, ever, anywhere?"

'Puzzled, the witness would shake his head. "No."

'"Have you ever heard Ms Caballero's name mentioned by anyone at any time?"

'"No."

'"Thank you. No more questions."

'Kevin drove us all crazy with his routine, and we could all mimic it – and often did – but it worked.' In her case, Judge Paine would not even allow the charges to go to the jury.

So of the six defendants, two won and four lost. In addition, three of those indicted by the grand jury had pleaded guilty and testified for the prosecution at the Lane trial: Wyvonna Meyer, Gerry Wills's former wife; Geoffrey Kenion, 'the Sewage Engineer', who'd abandoned his fight against extradition from Spain after nine months in jail; James Newton, Lord Moynihan's old school chum,

who'd gone voluntarily from England to Miami. (In return for their testimony, and a guilty plea to one token charge, all three were allowed to go free.) Not bad, thought O'Neill. Seven out of nine, thirteen to go.

Though it might have been premature, the hard core of the Eclectic team toasted their victory at a party held in a German restaurant near West Palm Beach. They capped the evening by presenting a plaque to George Pasenelli. It was inscribed: 'Presented To The Man Who Caught D.H. Marks From Your Around The World Colleagues.' Mounted on it were Pasenelli's by now widely-celebrated silver handcuffs.

Certainly, that two-month period between 5 May and 7 July was the blackest and most despairing experience in any of my family's lives. The Palm Beach edition of the Miami Herald *suggested that I would get eighty years, and the photograph of me which they published fully justified such a sentence. They added that I was a money launderer for the Bufalino family, and the photo suggested that I strangled small children in my spare time away from the laundry.*

Peter Combs and I remained in Fort Lauderdale for a couple more weeks after the trial because they forgot about us. Following our convictions, it didn't matter where they tossed us or where we lay. Lauderdale provided a suitable reflection of our mood, a chilling glimpse of our future.

I felt as though I was dead. I wanted to be dead. I didn't want to have died, to have been before and passed on, mourned and missed. I wanted never to have been. I needed Jude desperately, and she needed me. Peter and I alternately drove each other crazy and tried to comfort each other. My attorney told me that I would probably get thirty years but that we'd get copies of the trial transcript for free.

Jude and I had never seriously considered the possibility of my being convicted as a racketeer. We were prepared for me to be found guilty on some of the counts and had accepted that I might spend a couple of years in jail if things went badly. But never the RICO; we had never faced the reality of twenty plus years. We had to adjust to the new reality.

I quickly decided that there was no way that Jude could be expected to also serve that time. She could not lead a shadowy half-life in endless sorrow just because of my stupidity, and so I concentrated on how I could best organize the split. The children needed a man about the house even though I would remain their father. As far as I was concerned, my life was finished. In order to survive those sorts of sentences, a man has to cut all links with the outside world. He has to change, he has no choice but to conform to the reality of life within the walls, and the values of the prison population. Jude would have to

263

create a new life. She was still young and attractive and alive, and I could not allow her to throw it all away and to wither up, wasted. And then one day I received a letter from her. Even though I had kept my thoughts to myself, she had known what I was thinking and she told me 'No'. She would not leave me. She did not want to live without me. Don't even think about it.

So we decided to fight. We'd lost the battle but not necessarily the war. What remained to be decided was my sentence and we asked all our friends to write to the court, saying what they knew about me. The response was incredible, humbling. Jude made sure that the originals were sent to the judge over the three-month period, and copies were gathered and sent to the probation officer [who would make a recommendation as to how long Lane should get]. *Instead of seeing the probation officer with my attorney, which is the usual way, I went and met him by myself. Instead of arguing over what information he had a right to examine, I prepared a detailed history of my life with a list showing where he could get supporting evidence. Jude took the same approach, and we bombarded him with background.*

The wise guys at MCC gleefully forecast fifty years. My attorney, correctly, thought the government would be insisting on thirty. The probation officer warned me that I would be lucky to get twenty. He told Jude to prepare herself for twenty to thirty, but comforted her that I would probably get out after ten. He himself recommended fifteen, which was as low as his boss would allow him to go – and he had to fight O'Neill over that. The people who wrote my pre-sentence report wanted to ask for ten years, but I pushed and pleaded to drop it to six. We compromised by asking Judge Paine for eight years.

I was pleased not to have Peter with me when I set off for sentencing. I needed to be alone with my own dark thoughts. I spent another evening with the hookers, and a night on the floor in Fort Lauderdale. The holding cell at West Palm Beach was full. There was no big trial in progress and so we were just a bunch of numbers – for sentencing, parole violations and such like. In and out, wham, bam, thank you, ma'am! All the old intimacy with the marshals was gone. It was: 'Go in, collect your thirty years and get out again.' Whoosh! What was that? That was your life, mate!

In fact the whole thing took more than an hour. Jude sat in the front row. Neither of us had the spare resources to smile at each other. At school I was a star debater, captain of the school debating team; polished, glib, fast on my feet. Standing before Judge Paine, fighting for my life when I should have been at my best, I was a shambling mess. My heart was literally in my throat, and I could hardly speak for choking.

O'Neill responded with a speech about growing up in the Bronx, not having had all the benefits which I had had, and seeing sixteen-year-old unmarried mothers selling their bodies for crack while smooth-talking representatives from

264

the Medellín cartel in their smart English suits ran off with the money. He also reminded the judge, in case he hadn't seen that morning's paper, that the Medellín cartel were busy killing judges and bombing courtrooms.

Judge Paine told me to stand and receive my sentence. He started with the six conspiracy counts and gave me three years on each one, to run concurrently. This was good but no big surprise, as the maximum was only five years on each count. We were all far more interested in the RICO counts, and that is where everyone's attention lay. Paine saved the best for last. After shocking the room with 'Five years' there was a pause before he added – probation.

To say that we were all, in our own ways and for our various reasons, speechless would be an understatement. I stole a glance at Jude as I was hustled back through 'the Bad Door'. Her face was white: 'What did he say?' she mouthed, unable to comprehend or accept.

The rest of the day was a blur. I floated back to MCC. Prisoners are a superstitious lot: luck and hope are all we have got to believe in. Examples of good luck are so rare that great attention is paid to them. Everyone wanted to know how I did it, and who my attorney was. They wanted to touch me, as though some of the good fortune would rub off. They wanted my benediction. I was oblivious to everything. I can still remember sitting there with an insane grin on my face, unable to speak, unable to feel.

Peter was ecstatic. Tears were openly running down his face, and he hugged me. 'We are all going to be all right,' he said. 'It's going to be OK.'

Combs was wrong. When it came to his turn to stand up in court, Judge Paine looked over the top of his reading glasses and said 'Forty years.' Combs didn't flinch. Then Judge Paine looked at Patti and said 'Eight years.' Combs lost it then, lunging towards the table where O'Neill and Lovato were sitting. Each of them thought he was coming for them, and each of them squared off to meet him. The marshals dragged Combs away. Judge Paine did not appear to notice.

Both Lovato and O'Neill sympathized with Combs. Patti's sentence made no sense to them when compared to the leniency shown to Patrick Lane. ('You might want to record the fact that I'm surprised,' said Lovato after Lane received his three years. 'Surprised, baffled, cynical – and extremely angry.') Nobody who had been in court could doubt Patti's devotion to Combs. O'Neill said she didn't have a bad bone in her body. She simply did what Combs told her to do. If he'd been a doctor, she would have studied medicine. If he'd been an oilman, she would have

265

sold oil. But he was a dope dealer – and now she was going to do eight years.

'Patrick, three years. Patti, eight years. Make sense to you?' said Lovato.

Madrid, July through October 1989

Judy Marks had been visited by her children in prison in Madrid twice. The girls, Amber and Francesca, were coping better than she could have hoped, wise beyond their years. Baby Patrick, however, was a mess. The first time he saw his mother in jail he attacked her, scratching her face, pulling her hair – furious, apparently, at what he thought was her desertion of him. The second time he was fine until she took him for a walk to the prison commissary and he saw the armed guards in their watchtowers. He became hysterical. It was more than she could stand.

Marks, who had read the transcript of the Lane trial with intense curiosity, hired an American lawyer for Judy: Donald Re, a Los Angeles attorney who had represented Rick Brown at the Lane trial and won his acquittal. In late July 1989, just over a year after Judy and Howard were arrested, Re flew to Madrid and saw both of them. They all agreed that Judy would give up her fight against extradition and go voluntarily to Miami, in the hope of cutting a deal that would allow her to plead guilty to a token charge and return to her children. She arrived in Miami in handcuffs on 11 August, frightened, made cold by the unfamiliar air-conditioning, resentful and hostile. Within the DEA she soon became known as 'the Ice Maiden'.

Marks remained in Spain, determinedly so. The outcome of the Lane trial and the news of Combs's forty-year sentence depressed him enormously. He said: 'I mean, the difference between forty years and life is probably not too much, unless marijuana really is the sort of elixir I hope it is.' He was terrified by the thought of American jails and vowed to keep the fight going in Spain for months; years, if necessary. Gustavo Muñoz, his Madrid lawyer, still had many more creative tricks up his sleeve.

But the tide was inexorably turning against him. The Spanish authorities, irritated by his manipulation of the media, banned any further interviews with Marks. The Spanish courts, closely monitored by the American embassy in Madrid, methodically blocked every twist and turn, denying every motion Muñoz made and every appeal.

On 13 October 1989 the Spanish Council of Ministers, the final deciding authority, approved Marks's extradition. 'Got him,' said Lovato – and then quickly changed his mind. Howard was not done yet, he discovered.

It had all the hallmarks of a classic Marks ploy. Roger Reaves, also moved from Palma to the same jail near Madrid, had fought equally hard to avoid extradition to either the United States or West Germany, though his tactics were, if anything, bolder. He first tried to bribe his way out of prison, promising a guard hundreds of thousands of pesetas which, he said, he had stashed in Palma. When that failed, Reaves wrote to the American vice-consul in Madrid, offering to give the DEA 'invaluable first-hand information' about Jorge Ochoa, one of the founders and leaders of the Medellín cartel. Reaves said that all he wanted in return was 'freedom from prison and a new identity for my family and myself'. He had not yet received a reply from the DEA when West Germany's request for his extradition prevailed and he was quietly shipped to Lübeck, north of Hamburg. Lovato and O'Neill were caught unawares by that development. They thought they had a deal with the *Bundeskriminalamt* (BKA) that they would 'get the body'. But that 'misunderstanding' became utterly insignificant when they learned, in late October, that the BKA was now planning to go after Marks.

On arrival at Lübeck, Reaves had dropped his protests of innocence and agreed to plead guilty to the West German charges, in return for a sentence of seven years. He had also made a statement, thoroughly incriminating Marks in the plot to ship hashish to England. When Lovato first learned what had happened, the Lübeck prosecutor was preparing a Provisional Warrant of Arrest for Marks, along with a request for his extradition from Spain.

'They've cooked it up together,' Lovato told O'Neill, convinced that Marks and Reaves were attempting to throw a giant wrench in the works. If the Spanish received the West German extradition request the worst that could happen – from Marks's point of view – was that everything would be delayed for months while the competing claims for his body were weighed. Marks would happily admit his guilt to the West German charges and, with luck, the West Germans would win. Given the choice between Lübeck and Miami, Marks would choose Lübeck every time. 'He'd pay for his own ticket,' said Lovato.

But the BKA had a Drug Liaison Officer assigned full-time to the DEA in Miami, and he and Lovato got on well together. 'Horst, do me a favour,' said Lovato.

In Lübeck the prosecutor was told by the BKA that Lovato and O'Neill were on their way for urgent discussion. He agreed to do nothing about Marks until he'd talked to them.

They flew to West Germany on the weekend, ready for a meeting with the prosecutor on Monday 23 October, though he said he was busy and might have to put them off until the Tuesday. Fine, they said.

On Sunday, by coincidence or not, Marks was taken from the prison without warning to police headquarters in Madrid. The next morning – well before the Lübeck meeting could take place – he was put on a TWA flight to New York, en route to Miami, accompanied by two US marshals. He was totally surprised and extremely unhappy. 'There's a lot of sly tricks being played,' he said, not knowing the half of it.

Miami, Winter 1989

It was every bit as awful as he'd feared. Marks entered the United States at John F. Kennedy airport in New York in handcuffs, with a steel chain around his waist. The Immigration and Naturalization Service (INS) refused to let him in because he didn't have a passport. He sat in the arrivals hall for an hour, the object of curious stares, while the mess was sorted out. Then another delay, while the marshals replaced the tickets to Miami which they'd lost somewhere down the line. It was 1.00 a.m. the next morning before Marks was locked up in the holding cell at MCC. Two hours later he was woken up and told he was going to court. He then received his first taste of the routine that had become part of Patrick Lane's life: the humiliating prologue to the ride in the Bus from Hell. Arriving in court he felt totally forgotten: there were no reporters, no Craig Lovato – indeed, nobody from the DEA – and no Bobby O'Neill. He was distinctly peeved. He thought the least Lovato could have done was show up.

But Marks is nothing if not resilient. Within a few days he'd discovered that, as prisons go, MCC is not that bad, though overcrowded. It is laid out rather like an American university campus, set around a lake. It has extensive sports facilities, which did not interest Marks, and an excellent law library, which did.

He was greatly cheered to find he was among friends. Patrick Lane and Peter Combs were still there, awaiting transfer to the prisons where they would serve their sentences. So, too, were Jim Hobbs and William Robb, who had lost their respective battles to avoid extradition from Amsterdam, and Saleem Malik who – to everybody's surprise – had been extradited from Pakistan. (Malik, the first-ever Pakistani extradited from his own country to the US on drugs charges, was enormously aggrieved. He felt, with some justification, that he was a victim of Prime Minister Benazir Bhutto's resolve to improve relations with America. He felt, also with some justification, that it would have never happened in General Zia's day.) Marks and his chums sat by the lake, drinking Coca-Cola, reminiscing about old times.

His spirits thus restored, Marks began the serious business of concocting his defence. The only thing that alarmed him about MCC was the defeatism of most of his fellow inmates: they didn't consider the possibility of acquittal. By Marks's estimate, 80 per cent of them had become 'snitches' for the government, attempting to win themselves leniency by betraying others. Marks had no intention of becoming a snitch and he had no intention of being convicted. He had a couple of nasty surprises in store for Craig Lovato.

There are no facilities for women prisoners at MCC and there is no federal women's prison in Miami. Judy Marks therefore found herself parked in Dade County Jail, kept in a cage with eighteen other women, all of them black or Hispanic. There was no lake, no law library, no sports facilities. Breakfast was served at 4.30 a.m., dinner at 4.30 p.m., and the food was virtually uneatable. She slept on a metal bunk with a mattress just half an inch thick. There were male guards who leered at the women prisoners. She felt ill, but was afraid to see the doctor because other inmates told her she would then be transferred to somewhere called 'the Annexe' – which was much, much worse, they said.

Her Los Angeles lawyer was tied up in a trial in California and never came to see her. Bobby O'Neill was talking about doing a deal, but he was also talking about raising the ante – bringing a new charge that would raise her exposure from a maximum of five years in jail to a mandatory minimum of ten. She oscillated wildly between saying, 'To hell with them, let's go to trial,' and agreeing to anything if only they would let her go home. When she talked to her children on the phone, she promised she would be home in time for their birthdays in November, but she wasn't. When they asked her if she'd be home in time for Christmas, she didn't know what to say.

Then, thank God, she was moved to the North Dade Detention Center, where the federal government pays the state to house some of its prisoners. Howard was moved there, too – not out of compassion but because the DEA wanted him separated from his fellow defendants. Away from Marks's influence, Lovato thought correctly, most of them would do a deal. So Judy and Howard were able to see each other a couple of times, and they could talk on the phone. They agreed two things.

First, Judy would do a deal with the government, pleading guilty to a token count in return for a sentence of 'time served'. There was a savage additional penalty in that, as a result of her conviction, she would not be allowed to return to the United States. She would, in other words, never see Howard again so long as he remained in an American jail. Marks told her he didn't plan on being in jail for very long. Anyway, because of the children, there was no choice. At least she would be home in time for Christmas. (She was. Having pleaded guilty, she was deported from the United States on 18 December.)

Second, they agreed that Marks would hire the best attorney he could find. He had threatened to go it alone, and represent himself; or plead poverty and take whatever public defender the court assigned. But Judy convinced him to be sensible, and Marks interviewed a number of Miami's defence attorneys who had experience of drug trials and who were summoned to the North Dade Detention Center one by one.

He eventually settled on Stephen Bronis because Bronis, unlike many of the others, listened to what Marks had to say. Marks was never willing to place himself entirely in the hands of an attorney. His defence, he made clear, was going to be a collaborative effort. Marks would take advice but, in the final analysis, he was going to call the shots. Bronis could live with that.

Judy very much approved of the choice. She'd been told by a fellow inmate that while Bronis was not yet at the top of the Miami league, he was utterly dedicated, serious, and had a reputation as a workaholic.

When Bronis heard about that endorsement, he wrote Marks a wry note: 'Yes, I am serious. And though I'm not one of the top-ranking attorneys, I am a workaholic.'

Marks, now in fine form and growing more confident, wrote

back: 'I'm neither an attorney, nor very serious, nor a workaholic. But I *am* top rank!'

Miami, 1990

Howard Marks had a secret: He wasn't 'Mr Dennis'. He wasn't the mysterious Englishman who had delivered the crates of unusual dimension to Forbes, Forbes, Campbell and Company in Karachi – and he could prove it.

He was in England when the delivery took place, staying with Judy and the children at one of his favourite hotels, the Imperial in Torquay. He had the airline ticket, showing he left Karachi two days before the crates were delivered. He had a credit card slip, showing that he'd bought a ring for Judy at Athens airport en route to England, and he had the bill from the Imperial. This was no accident. Being somewhere else when anything risky was happening was one of the perks of his new role as a middleman.

But they couldn't prove that. The only evidence they had of his involvement in the Alameda load was their assertion that he was Mr Dennis. Their whole case had been predicated on mistaken identity. He couldn't wait to see the look on Craig Lovato's face.

They were wrong about Vancouver, too – though even Marks hadn't known that at first. The load the Mounties seized in September 1987 had nothing to do with Marks. It had nothing to do with Sparrowhawk, Wills and Allen or Denbigh either, for that matter. *That* Vancouver load belonged to somebody else. *Their* Vancouver load had never been seized. It was just an extraordinary coincidence, and bad luck. The Mounties had stumbled on two different organizations operating in the same city at the same time, and naturally assumed they were one – as had Marks when he'd first heard the news. Then later he'd found out: it was their money the Mounties had seized, but it was not their dope.

Of course, he couldn't very well say that in front of the jury, but he didn't have to. Luckily for Marks, the real owner of the seized Vancouver load had been arrested in Seattle, Washington, and in making his deal with the government, he'd confessed. Lovato knew about the confession but he continued to believe that the two organizations were one and the same. Well, he was wrong. He'd put two and two together and made five: coppers' mathematics. Howard was going to have fun with the Vancouver load in court. He thought that Bronis would be able to tie Lovato in knots.

But how to explain what he'd said to Moynihan about Vancouver

271

on the tapes? Easy: 'I was lying,' he would say, if he went on to the witness stand. (Marks and Bronis were still arguing about that. Bronis was very much opposed to Marks testifying, but he was coming round to Howard's point of view.) 'I was trying to impress him,' he would say of Moynihan. 'He wanted to believe I was still in the dope business and I wanted to accommodate him.'

Marks was going to use much the same approach to deal with all of Moynihan's evidence. Did he tell Moynihan he'd been in the dope business for twenty years, bringing in two or three loads a year? 'Yes, absolutely, I was bragging,' he would say. Did he discuss with Moynihan growing marijuana in the Philippines on an industrial scale? 'Yes, but it was his idea. I thought it was nonsense. I just went along with it for a bit of fun.' But didn't he pay $50,000 into the Hong Kong account of Moynihan's wife? 'Yes, but it was his money, not mine. He asked me to smuggle it out of the Philippines for him.'

And so on. Marks wasn't worried about the prosecution's star witness. There would be a couple of nasty moments, but all in all he thought he could negate Moynihan's evidence.

Which left the 1986 Los Angeles load. Marks knew he was in serious trouble on that charge because of the testimony of Geoffrey Kenion and Wyvonna Meyer, both saying they'd carried large sums of money for him from the United States. Worse, he knew that Brad Whites of the IRS had finally obtained the records of his Hong Kong bank account, showing large sums of money coming in from Patrick Lane and John Francis, and large sums of money going out – over $3 million in all – to Saleem Malik. Then there were the tapes they would play in court day after day, with all his hard-to-explain conversations with Combs and Wills. With Lovato giving his interpretations, the jury was likely to believe it was listening to a drug deal going down.

But, thought Marks, what the jury wouldn't know, and what Lovato couldn't tell them, was *where* the deal went down. Lovato would certainly say it was Los Angeles but that was just educated guesswork. He didn't have a sliver of proof. It was on the slender foundation of that piece of luck that Marks built the most ingenious part of his defence.

In jail in Spain, he'd spent months studying the transcripts of the tapes as though it was his life's work. He knew every mistake the transcribers had made – and there were literally hundreds of them – and every passage they couldn't understand. In jail in Miami, he'd pored over the thousand of documents the DEA had been required to produce under the 'discovery' rules, carefully calculating where they supported Lovato's interpretations and where they did not. He made copious notes on yellow legal pads, and drew elaborate charts in multi-coloured inks. Finally, he was sure he had a story that fitted almost all of the provable facts.

Yes, he admitted to Bronis, he was a drug trafficker, and yes, he worked with people like Peter Combs who operated from the West Coast. But no, they did not smuggle drugs into the United States, hadn't done so since the 1970s, because the penalties were too tough. They smuggled drugs to Australia, Canada, England, Spain – anywhere *except the United States*. Marks said he had broken the law of just about any country Lovato cared to name – *except America*. He said he knew that by admitting all this he was asking for trouble from the British, the Canadians, the Australians and God knew who else, but he would worry about the future when it arrived.

Marks wasn't sure he would totally get away with it. He thought the jury might find him guilty on a couple of counts. But he *knew* he could beat the RICO charges, and that is what mattered. If he had to serve five years on the rest of the charges, well, so be it.

By spring 1990, with his trial set for early August, Marks was feeling very confident, not least because the government seemed to be running out of steam.

The DEA hadn't found Wills or Allen or Bradley Weller, and it hadn't found George Lane either, though by then he was living openly in England. Phillip Sparrowhawk remained stubbornly in jail in Bangkok, defying all attempts to extradite him, aided, it was rumoured, by the payment of a large bribe to someone in authority. In Canada the case against John Denbigh seemed to be collapsing for lack of evidence and it looked increasingly likely that he would not be extradited. And though Saleem Malik had done a deal with the government, pleading guilty to one count of conspiracy in return for a sentence of four years, and though he'd promised to 'co-operate' with the DEA, he had sent a message to Marks saying the opposite: that he would never testify against 'my good friend, Howard'.

Best of all – and this was the most unexpected piece of luck – Marks's two main antagonists had left Miami.

Craig Lovato had been promoted to Group Supervisor and transferred (together with his wife, Wendy) to Phoenix, Arizona. He'd return to Miami for the trial, of course, but he was no longer the case agent. That job had been assigned to Ed Wezain,

Lovato's partner, who was simultaneously assigned to the DEA's investigation of Manuel Noriega, the former strongman of Panama. How Wezain was supposed to keep on top of both cases at the same time, nobody knew. 'I'm very pleased for Craig,' said Marks when told of his promotion, doing his best to keep a straight face. 'Delighted, in fact.'

And Bobby O'Neill had gone too, in his case quitting government service altogether to join a New York law firm that specialized in medical malpractice suits. O'Neill said he would return to Miami in August to prosecute Marks, but Bronis said that was just a pipe dream: Dexter Lehtninen, the US Attorney in Miami, would never allow a 'deserter from the ranks' to argue the government's case. That job would fall to another Assistant US attorney, William Pearson, who knew very little about the case and had no emotional stake in it. To him, Howard Marks was just another doper. There was no reason to believe that Pearson would make an exceptional effort to send Marks to jail for the majority of his remaining life.

In late May Marks was feeling as ebullient as any man can in jail, impatient for his day in court. Then the roof fell in.

Phoenix, Arizona, May 1990

It was happenstance that Craig Lovato and Peter Combs now lived in the same town: Lovato in a temporary apartment in downtown Phoenix, while looking for a house; Combs in the federal penitentiary at nearby Black Canyon, serving his forty years.

Lovato was grateful for the coincidence. It meant he didn't have far to travel when Combs's new lawyer called up and said his client wanted to make a deal.

The deal wasn't for himself, Combs said when Lovato went to see him in Black Canyon. He was appealing his conviction, on the grounds that he hadn't been caught fair and square. He still possessed the furious optimism of most prisoners beginning extremely long sentences: the self-protective denial of the stark reality. Convinced that in the end his conviction would be reversed, he was content to remain in jail, awaiting what he saw as his inevitable victory.

What he wanted was a deal for Patti. He couldn't abide the thought of her remaining in jail a day longer. She, too, was appealing her conviction, and in her letters to Combs she said she was fine: her jail in California wasn't that bad; she could take it. Combs, however, could not. He wanted her set free immediately.

So he told Lovato: 'I'll make a deal: I'll give you Howard, Patti walks out the door.'

Combs subsequently talked into Craig Lovato's tape recorder for more than three hours, while Wendy Lovato took notes, describing at least some of the secrets of his eighteen-year partnership with Howard Marks. He confirmed Marks's role in the 1973 Las Vegas load. He talked about more than twenty other loads he said they had brought into the United States during the 1970s. He described how Marks had become the middleman in the 1984 Alameda load, by getting Saleem Malik to supply the hash. Most crucial – and, for Lovato, most gratifying – of all, he verified the essential details of the 1986 Los Angeles load. Lovato's educated guesswork, it turned out, had been inspired.

'When you told Howard "Champagne in Mozambique", what were you talking about?' Lovato asked.

'The dope was in Mexico,' said Combs.

'And when you said it would be "in Connolly's place in about a week" what did you mean?'

'Los Angeles.'

'And when you told Howard, "I just got tickets to this play tonight"?'

'The dope was in Los Angeles,' said Combs, effectively slamming the cell door on Howard Marks. Lovato had no idea what Marks's defence was going to be – the *anywhere but America* defence – but it no longer mattered. Combs had just blown it out of the water.

There were things Combs would not talk about. He'd made it very clear to Lovato that he was unwilling to implicate other people. The deal was Howard for Patti, period. But yes, he said, he would testify at Howard's trial if necessary.

'You're doing the right thing,' said Lovato.

Combs had agonized for months before making the decision to talk. If it hadn't been for Patti, he said, he never would have done so. But the truth was, he was also angry at Marks – and, paradoxically, terrified for him.

Angry because he blamed Marks for being careless on the phone long after they knew it was being tapped by Lovato. ('If the commissary sold guns, I'd go and buy one now and blow your fucking head off,' Combs had told Marks when they were briefly reunited at MCC in Miami.)

Terrified for him because, nevertheless, he still loved Marks like a brother. Combs was certain that Howard's boundless egotism

275

would make him go to trial and attempt to repeat the miracle of his Old Bailey acquittal. But the South Florida of the 1990s was a much tougher forum, and Combs was sure that – with or without his testimony – Howard would lose, condemning himself to the rest of his life in jail. He thought Marks's only chance was to make a deal with the government.

Self-justification perhaps, but Combs was not alone in believing that the time had come for Marks, for his own sake and for the sake of other people, to pay his dues.

Oakdale, Louisiana, May 1990

Patrick Lane walked around the exercise track of the Federal Correctional Institution, surrounded by Louisiana swampland, in brooding silence, struggling to reconcile a host of complex emotions, almost all of them negative. He had become withdrawn and introverted, sometimes going for a week or more without speaking a single word. He survived the hostility of his fellow inmates by deliberately projecting an air of dangerous and barely suppressed violence. This acquired persona was hardening around him like a scab. He was totally alone with his thoughts too much; his grasp of reality slipping.

The sense of euphoria he'd felt at the unexpected lightness of his three-year sentence had sustained him for a long time. He'd expected to be released to a half-way house in not much more than a year. Meanwhile, he'd occupied the prison library at MCC, preparing his appeal against conviction. Like Combs, he was convinced he would prevail. He continued to believe that what he'd done for Howard was stupid and possibly illegal but that it did not amount to money laundering. He *knew* his conviction on RICO charges could not possibly be upheld. By the time the appeals court reversed it, it would be somewhat academic, since the nightmare would be over and he would be home with his family. Still, he looked forward to his eventual vindication. Then he'd felt the first chill winds of the government's wrath, rattling at the shutters of his naïve and comforting assumptions.

'I am the United States government,' Lovato was fond of saying. 'You're looking at it.' By which he meant that whether or not the government pursued a target and how far depended to a considerable extent on the determination of the case agent. Lovato could have shrugged his shoulders and walked away when Lane got off, in his view, virtually scot-free. In Lane's case, the thought never even occurred to Lovato. He was utterly determined that Lane would get what he deserved and Lovato's resolve, simply because it existed, meant that Lane still faced all of the awesome powers at the government's command.

First, in January 1990, O'Neill twice hauled Lane before the grand jury in Miami, under a grant of immunity that removed Lane's protection against self-incrimination.

'Mr Lane, how long have you been a money launderer?' O'Neill began the questioning.

'I am not a money launderer,' said Lane

'When did you stop being a money launderer?'

'I never was a money launderer.'

And so it continued, until Lane felt like asking O'Neill when he ceased beating his wife. But he was forced to admit that in the summer of 1986, on at least three occasions, he had gone to New York on Marks's behalf to receive suitcases full of cash, left outside the door of his hotel room, and that he'd arranged for that cash to be sent to Howard's Hong Kong account without meeting the requirements of the IRS to report any such transaction. Lane called it money moving, rather than money laundering, but that was not a distinction the government was inclined to recognize.

Meanwhile, the government countered Lane's appeal against conviction with an appeal of its own, against his sentence. The government argued that since some of the overt acts covered by the RICO charges had occurred after 1 November 1987, when the Sentencing Reform Act became law, Lane should have been sentenced under New Guidelines. If that argument was upheld, Judge Paine would have no choice: whatever his personal opinion of Lane's culpability, he would be obliged to sentence him to fifteen to twenty years in jail, with no parole.

Then – and this was no coincidence – the INS stepped in. Instead of being released to a half-way house as he had assumed, Lane was transferred to Oakdale, Louisiana, under an INS 'detainer' as somebody liable for deportation. He would remain there until the competing appeals were decided, even if that was long after his release date.

Even if Lane won in the appeals court, the government was still not done. Brad Whites of the IRS would bring a case against Lane for defrauding the United States, and the INS would prosecute him for illegally obtaining a green card.

In the interim, he would be called as a witness for the prosecution at Marks's trial, and forced to testify. If he did not repeat what he'd told the grand jury, he would be prosecuted for perjury. If he refused to answer, the government would press to have him jailed for criminal contempt. Then they would drag him back into court again. The process could go on indefinitely.

Only when they tired of it would he be deported, along with each and every member of his family. And – Lovato was assured by Terry Burke – when Lane was finally back in England, where there is no Statute of Limitations, Scotland Yard would take a very hard look at any offences he might have committed there over the previous eighteen years.

Lane could not believe it at first. He thought that after his appearances before the grand jury Bobby O'Neill had accepted that Lane's role in Howard Marks's affairs was limited – and he was right. O'Neill (though not necessarily Lovato) had come to believe that Lane was not the major player the government had once thought. Lane was guilty but not to the extent that he deserved to spend another fifteen or twenty years in jail. It would be a 'crying shame' if that happened, O'Neill said. But it *would* happen, O'Neill would make sure of it, unless Lane came to his senses and co-operated with the government. He was the only one who could save himself. So long as Lane remained on 'the wrong team', he was an opposing player and O'Neill's job was to knock him down as hard as he could. O'Neill would do it, without reluctance. Nothing personal, Patrick. It's the rules of the game.

Circling the exercise track, railing against the unfairness of it all, Lane thought he should contest the terrible power of this well-oiled machine, whatever the cost. But he knew he couldn't do it. His family had already paid an enormous price for his own conceit and his loyalty to Howard. They had no reserves left, and neither did he.

After agonizing for months, he essentially came to the same conclusion that Combs had reached: Howard wasn't worth it.

Miami, June 1990

Some nine weeks before his trial was due to begin, Marks received a letter from his brother-in-law:

> Dear Howard:
> I have just spent the past eight hours with agents Lovato and Wezain here at Oakdale and I have agreed to tell them

everything that I know about you and about this case. Consequently, I will be testifying against you at your trial in August.

I am informing you of this partly to ease my conscience by forewarning you, but also in an attempt to persuade you to plead guilty now and to make a deal with the government before it is too late.

After serving my time for the past two years in stoic silence, you can well imagine how painful and difficult a decision this has been. I am all too aware that little Amber who has always treated me with such reverence as her 'favourite uncle' will now only think of me as the man who betrayed her Daddy and sent him to jail for life. But I have had to weigh my love and duty towards Jude, Peggy and Bridie. I am facing the very real probability of a new 15/20 year jail sentence and I have no right to impose that on my family when I am offered a way out. In return for the government's agreement not to pursue the extra jail time, I have become a cooperating witness.

Cooperation is a bit like pregnancy; there are no half-way measures. Having agreed to tell the truth, I will have to tell the whole truth; from when I first met you till when I last saw you – and everything in between. They started asking me questions today, slowly and methodically, and they will be back again tomorrow, and the next day, and the day after that, until they are satisfied that they know everything that I know. As I answered their questions, part of me felt detached, listening to my voice as though it belonged to somebody else, speaking in the courtroom. As I listened to that voice, speaking slowly, telling only the truth, I finally realized that you do not stand a chance. If you go to trial you will be destroyed and I will be one of the instruments of destruction.

I am all too familiar with the way evidence is presented in an American courtroom. I know what it sounds like and how it affects the jury. I am horribly aware of the meagre amount of evidence needed to convict me on the exact same charges that you are now facing. But the evidence that they have collected since then is so much more considerable, and so many people have agreed to testify against you. I have not heard from Peter for a long time, but Patti is still in jail and I know that his love for her is far greater than any loyalty that you can reasonably expect to claim. Lovato tells me he has six or seven new witnesses willing to testify. O'Neill told me of a ton of new financial records. I suspect that all the gaps in the first trial have now been plugged.

But even if it is all government bluster, my evidence alone will sink you. We have been good friends too long, you and I, and I know too much about you.

This is not England, and it is no longer 1980, let alone the 60s. South Florida in 1990 is a whole different world, and the judicial system expresses a darker public mood. I do not care how imaginative or resourceful you are, and I have never underestimated your abilities; this time you will not pull it off. Miracles are against the law, and witches are burned at the stake. If you go to trial before twelve American citizens, you will be convicted. If you are convicted in the Southern District of Florida, especially with all the public notoriety, you will quite possibly go to jail for life. For you to spend the rest of your life behind bars will not only be a shameful waste of all your gifts but will be a terrible tragedy for all the people who love you and need you and whom you will leave behind.

In talking with Lovato and Wezain I did not sense any personal animosity towards you. I suspect they have even grown to like you after all this time, and certainly they feel that it would be a senseless waste for you to spend the rest of your days in jail. If you concede defeat, I do not think they will be vindictive. But for as long as you remain unbowed, they will be merciless and implacable in the exercise of their awesome power.

So, as a lapsed Catholic to a Welsh Baptist, I am recommending submission to a greater power. *Extra ecclesiam nulla salas* – no salvation outside the church. I'm afraid it involves a humiliating loss of face and a painful swallowing of pride, but if you wish to rejoin your children while they are still little children, I see no alternative to a complete and utter surrender. You are surrounded, outgunned and outnumbered – there is no dishonour in such a defeat. But as a father, as a husband, as a son and as a brother – you have no right to throw away your life in a futile gesture of bravado.

The world media will, of course, be very upset if there is no big trial for them to showcase, and Miami's legal community will regret the loss of so many rich possibilities. The chaps in the cell blocks will jeer and grumble, and your public will be generally disappointed to be denied so promising a drama. Around the world there will be many who worry that what I am doing to you today, you will be doing to them tomorrow. There is no question but that your image is going to be destroyed if you plead out now. But for those people who do not care about your image and care only about you, for yourself; if pleading out will bring you home sooner, then the sooner you do it the better.

I am not going to plead with you on behalf of your children, or my sister or your parents. I am pleading on my own behalf. I want to remain Amber and Golly's favourite uncle. I want little Patrick to be proud of my name. I do not want to have to stand in a Florida courtroom and point my finger at you and reveal to the cold scrutiny of strangers all the secrets of twenty years of friendship. Please don't make me do that.

Whatever you decide, all my prayers are with you.

Patrick

They gave Marks twenty-one days to make up his mind. They said that because of the testimony of Patrick Lane and Peter Combs, and other new evidence, the case against him was now overwhelming. They said that if he agreed to plead guilty, to avoid the expense and trouble of a trial, they would ask for a maximum sentence of forty years but under Old Guidelines – meaning that he would be eligible for parole after serving one-third. If, on the other hand, he went to trial and lost, the government would demand a sentence of more than 100 years, under New Guidelines – meaning he would die in prison. They said that if the government had its way, that prison would be Marion, Illinois, the toughest there is, where there are cells underground reserved for the most recalcitrant prisoners. They said that this was the last and only deal the government would offer: 'Your choice, Howard.'

West Palm Beach, 13 July 1990

There was only a handful of people, and no pack of reporters, in Judge Paine's court to witness the surrender of Howard Marks. Few British newspapers, and only one in America, recorded the fact that he pleaded guilty to one count of RICO and one count of conspiracy. He was yesterday's news, no longer important.

He looked much older than when he was arrested, and when his picture had dominated the front pages and the television news, just two years before. His hair was long and unkempt and his teeth were rotting. He did not look like the King of Cannabis, the biggest dope dealer in the world. He looked very much alone.

When it was over – after the judge had accepted his pleas and set a sentencing date three months hence – Craig Lovato asked the marshals to let him talk to Marks. They brought him back into the courtroom through 'the Bad Door'. Lovato went over and shook his hand, and they sat down together.

He said he knew how Marks must be feeling but the worst was over now. Now that he'd accepted the inevitable, things would get better. The government wasn't going to be vindictive, Lovato said. If, later on, Howard wanted to co-operate with the government, tell them what he knew, all things were possible. Lovato said he would make sure that Marks served the first year of his sentence in Phoenix so they could talk, if Howard wanted to. He could be home, back with his family, in just a few years.

You've made the right decision, Howard, Lovato said. Finally, you've done the right thing.

EPILOGUE

In the visiting room of the North Dade Detention Center, Howard Marks and his best friend were debating the theory of chaos.

Put at its simplest, the theory says that in both science and human affairs, chaotic events – the deviations dismissed as pure chance and random error – are not random at all but part of a pattern. In other words, chaos is not chaotic, as we define the word. Since the theory challenges some of the fundamental assumptions of Newtonian physics, it appeals greatly to Marks, who likes the idea that things are not always what they seem. His friend said the theory of chaos was 'a bunch of bullshit'.

'Well, take the two of us,' said Marks.

Two young men from similar, modest backgrounds. Both are clever enough to win scholarships to Balliol. Both of them become thoroughly captivated by the mores of the Swinging Sixties, from which Balliol was not immune.

One of them, Howard's friend, puts all that behind him and goes on to become a doctor and one of the leading epidemiologists in the world. The other, Marks, becomes the most persistent, prolific and audacious dope dealer that Balliol, or perhaps any other university, has produced.

The disparity between their lives is extraordinary. From similar starting points, they ended up poles apart; one at the peak of his profession, the other, at the age of forty-five, facing up to forty years in an American jail. Was that a random accident, pure chance, or

283

something that would fit the theory of chaos? If there had been ten clever young men at Balliol from similar backgrounds, would only Marks have turned out bad, or would there have been a pattern? Was it random or chaos? 'Random,' said Howard's friend.

They argued for a while, but it was difficult to concentrate in the windowless claustrophobia of the visiting room, against the background chorus of slamming cell doors, the occasional explosions of angry voices and the blaring television set. After half an hour, Marks got bored with the debate and conceded. 'OK, it was random,' he said.

But he didn't really believe it. He is not happy with randomness; too 'mechanistic' to accept that things happen by pure chance. He is sure that things are determined by pre-conditioning; something in our background, or make-up, or character, that determines what we become. He thinks the theory of chaos may have a lot to say about human affairs and, perhaps, his own life. If he could study the lives of hundreds of bright young men of similar backgrounds, a pattern might appear: for every so many epidemiologists, a potential dope dealer would emerge.

He says it is a task he might undertake, now he has the time for it.

It was impossible to visit Marks in jail in Miami and not be fascinated, charmed – and manipulated – by him. As Patrick Lane says, Marks works his magic best one-to-one: 'Howard has the ability to listen very intently and to make people feel that they are the centre of his attention. He has a very mobile and expressive face and he provides a mirror to show people themselves the way they want to be seen. He makes serious people feel profound and intelligent. He makes most people feel sharp and witty, and those with a problem feel less alone. Each of his many and intensely personal relationships are mini-conspiracies. To be friends with Howard is to be "Thee and me" against the world. The rest of the world are all those people who are not intelligent enough to understand these great truths which you and I share, too insensitive to share this secret sorrow, too dumb and plodding to enjoy this sparkling wit and too bourgeois to see that it is all a joke and none of it is real. Thus, with no obvious effort on his own part, without ever being loud or domineering, without seeming to assert himself in any way, Howard is always able to make himself the centre of attention. I have seen the magic work with spaced-out hippies in the sixties, with the beautiful people at the smartest parties in

London and New York, and with the cream of the criminal crop in an American prison.'

In jail he would submit to interviews for hours on end, day after day, answering questions with disarming – his lawyer might say reckless – candour. Even when he obviously lied, which was rarely, he would tell you he was doing so with an enormous grin that the tape recorder couldn't capture. Whatever his public position, in the interviews he made no pretence about it: he was as guilty as hell of at least some of the charges. He was a doper. It was what he did, what he'd almost always done. He did it to make money – though not 'unfortunately' the great sums Craig Lovato believed he had stashed away in some numbered account – and because for most of his career – though not towards the end – he enjoyed it. It was, he said, against the law but not wrong. It was the laws against cannabis that were wrong, mindless and stupid. He said he wondered what would happen if every American who used marijuana (6 million people by official estimates) simultaneously turned themselves in to the police. He recognized that most people, certainly most people in America, thought that selling dope *was* wrong but he blamed that on the 'hysterical' coverage of the war on drugs on American television, 'which does to the brain what plaque does to the teeth'. The strategy of the war, which differentiated hardly at all between cannabis and cocaine, bewildered him.

For a while during the darkest period – before his surrender but after he knew that Peter Combs and Patrick Lane would testify against him – he said he would go to trial, and risk spending the rest of his life in Marion, Illinois. He thought that if he lost and went to Marion, America might 'come to its senses' and he, and all the other dopers in jail, would receive amnesty. Persuaded that his martyrdom would almost certainly go unnoticed, he changed his mind, but he continued to question what will happen in a country that, under the New Guidelines, allows its judges no discretion and fills its jails to bursting point with dopers and crack kingpins alike, offering them no possibility of parole and, therefore, no incentive to rehabilitate themselves.

He held no animosity towards Craig Lovato – whom he always calls Craig just as Lovato always calls him Howard. ('Well, you see, we think we know each other,' said Marks.) He said it was Craig's job to catch him, and his job not to get caught, 'and he did his job better than I did mine'. Nevertheless, he said he could not understand why Craig, and what seemed like half the world's policemen, pursued him so relentlessly when the cocaine cowboys of the Medellín cartel were running rampant, practically unchecked, poisoning America with their wares, producing outright war in the ghettoes and a generation of crack babies. He said that if Craig Lovato, and a few others like him, went to work with the same resolve against the Kings of Cocaine, instead of Cannabis, America might not be in such a mess.

The question underlying it all, of course, was 'Why *me?*'

After playing a game of tennis – which he also does with un-relenting determination – Craig Lovato sipped a glass of Chivas Regal, discussing the toxic substances with which people poison their bodies.

He said he did not differentiate between them, whatever the medical consequences of their use. If Craig Lovato made the rules, all of them would be legally available to adults (though selling all and any of them to children would be a capital offence). He said he believed it was not the government's job to dictate which drugs people could, and could not, ingest into their bodies. He believed that partly because, as a veteran 'narc', he knew the futility of enforcing laws that, by their existence, created and encouraged an obscenely profitable illegal black market. It was also part of his ethos: he is a product of the western United States, where people generally believe that matters of personal responsibility – what we do to ourselves – are none of the government's goddamned business.

It may seem paradoxical that, holding those views, Lovato should have devoted most of his adult life to putting drug traf-fickers in jail. Not so, he said. He was first and foremost a cop. He believed in the rule of law – not speed limits and pettifogging regu-lations – but the fundamental laws without which society could not operate. He understood, he said, that governments might impose unjust laws that should be broken: anti-semitic and race laws, for example. He also understood that people sometimes broke laws in the passion of the moment, or out of desperate need, and he could sympathize with them to some degree. What he could not understand or tolerate was professional criminals who cynically broke laws out of greed; who made their profits out of other people's misery. That was particularly true if they had a choice: if, unlike the desperado in Douglas with whom he'd traded bullets, the circumstances of their birth and upbringing did not condemn them to a life of crime.

He became a cop – or, rather, he remained a cop – because he wanted to do what he could to put such people out of business. He despised them, he said. He refused to read books that glamourized, or even made human, the 'bad guys'. (*High Time* was the exception, but then he had a special incentive to read that.) He became a narc because drug trafficking, of all organized crime, attracted through its enormous revenues the worst of the bad guys. Like Howard Marks.

It did not matter which illegal drug Howard profited from, he said. It didn't really matter how many tens or hundreds of tons he had smuggled (though Lovato continued to believe that Marks had been far more industrious than he ever admitted). It didn't matter that Marks genuinely believed that cannabis should be legalized; his trafficking had nothing to do with ideology.

What mattered – what had made Howard the subject of the longest and most intensive investigation of Lovato's career – was this: for almost all his adult life, Howard had used his intelligence, his charm, and his talent for manipulation deliberately to break the law. His motive was greed. He had never shown remorse. On the contrary, he'd boasted of his success: as Lord Moynihan said, 'He made it sound such fun.' He was, in those terms, Lovato said, as bad as any cocaine kingpin.

Why pursue him, though, as opposed to any other utterly incorrigible trafficker? Because he was there, said Lovato, like a mountain waiting to be climbed.

As he continued to sip the Chivas Regal, Lovato was asked how far he would take the paradox of enforcing laws he thought unreasonable in order to pursue the bad guys. What if, for example, prohibition had been reintroduced a week before, and here we were, drinking bootleg Scotch, determined to continue doing so even if we had to become bootleggers ourselves to ensure our supplies?

'I'd arrest us all,' he said.

Is Howard Marks rich? Is there hidden away in some Swiss bank, or in Dubai, an enormous stash of drug profits? Not according to Marks, or judging by the straitened circumstances of his wife and children. Craig Lovato believes there is a hidden haul – and that Marks is sufficiently selfish to leave his family in poverty, if necessary, in order to make his denial more credible.

Patrick Lane believes there is no fortune awaiting Howard on his eventual release. Lane may not be an unbiased source – he remains incurably fond of his brother-in-law – but he knows more than most about Marks's finances.

287

'He's never been interested in saving or hoarding money,' said Lane. 'Howard has always been against the idea of interest, and I think he genuinely regards money in the bank as "dead" money. Howard liked his money to be moving, he liked to spend it. Not to acquire "things": he always bought the latest toys, gadgets and gizmos but he never became attached to them because he was always prepared to flee at a moment's notice. Howard liked money solely in order to spend it. Not to spend it quietly and carefully, but to be seen to spend it as lavishly as possible.

'Howard has a theory that the more you spend, the more you get. To keep the rivers of money flowing you must encourage it to pour and splash freely, and as soon as you try to divert some of it or control the flow, the stream will dry up and the flow will go elsewhere. This is easy to do when the river is in full flood, but it takes an act of faith in the dry season to continue to hold the sluice gates open and not to try and conserve a little. Howard always had to live up to his image of fabulous and careless wealth, even when he was broke. Money is drawn to money, and as long as people think he is rich they will be attracted to him. And I think it was that tension that he most enjoyed, spending those last few dollars – taking the giant risk – and, just at the last moment, generating a new flow. Certainly, when he did have money he couldn't seem to get rid of it fast enough.

'So I don't believe he has hidden millions, at least not on the scale that Craig Lovato thinks. Nor do I think that Howard saved money for his children. He genuinely believes that inherited wealth is bad for the recipient. He also believes that the accumulation of wealth blunts "the hunger" and he fought always to maintain the vitality and alertness that is a part of hunger. He believes that rich children grow up spoiled and ill-equipped for the "battle" of life. He believed that his business partners, if they became rich and successful, would become soft and careless, and I suspect that he himself was frightened of becoming bored once the need to survive was no longer so keen.

'Apart from anything else, I doubt whether Howard could have kept a hidden fortune secret. Howard loved to tell his secrets. It was part of the one-to-one relationships; another ingredient in the Marks Magic.'

The length of sentence Marks should serve became a matter of intense debate. The principal recommendation to Judge Paine was made by Michael Berg, the probation officer responsible

288

for preparing the pre-sentence report. Berg was accustomed to receiving conflicting information – it comes with the territory – but in this case the discrepancies were exceptional.

The government continued to insist that Marks was, by any standard, a 'major violator': not, perhaps, the head of an international organization, as the DEA had originally claimed, but a first among equals – at least on a par with Peter Combs, and therefore deserving of similar punishment. Based partly on what Combs had told them, they claimed that Marks was responsible for seventy-seven loads imported into the United States. The government said justice demanded that he get the full forty years.

On the other hand, Howard's friends – and they are legion – and his acquaintances and, of course, his family pleaded for mercy. The Howard Marks they portrayed in their letters, sent by the sackful, many directly to the judge, was no international gangster; rather, a misguided hippy doper left over from the sixties, when marijuana was not regarded as a great social evil even by the law. Times had changed, he had not. He was not a criminal so much as an anachronism.

And in stark opposition to the government's harsh assessment stood this letter from Marks's twelve-year-old daughter, Amber:

Dear Judge Paine,

First of all, I would like to tell you about all the things my father has done for me. Whenever I had a problem with schoolwork, he was there. He could explain it to me like no-one else. He helped me to really enjoy my work, and to be ambitious in life. He taught me to be patient and to forgive people. He told me how everyone has their own ways of living and I should respect them, however different they are to my own. He taught me that the most important things in life were not money but family and friends.

Please, I need him home to teach me more, to be a father to me. I miss him so much. I haven't seen him for over a year, and at the moment we can't afford to fly over. I miss him at Parents' Night and at prize giving. I'm so proud of how gentle, clever and kind he is. I want to introduce my father to my new friends, but I can't. When I need help at school, I write to him so he can explain it to me. He often writes pages of biology or maths to me, whatever I need help in. But it does not reach me in time. I hate having to look at those same old photo albums of him. I don't want him to miss out on the rest of my childhood.

In two months' time I will be thirteen. If he comes home in only ten years I will be twenty-three, my younger sister twenty, and my younger brother, who has hardly ever seen him but knows and loves him, will be fourteen.

If you were to let him out soon, I know he would never smuggle again, I wouldn't let him. I never want to lose him again. I don't think he would want to, anyway.

I want to be a lawyer when I'm older and Daddy, if he gets out soon, wants to be one, too. He said we could have a business together.

Please, sir, don't give him long. I will wait for him forever, but please don't make me.

Amber
XXX

Judge Paine took the middle course, sentencing Marks to twenty five years: far less than the government wanted; far more than Amber feared. Howard Marks will be eligible for parole before the end of the century.

WHAT

HAPPENED TO

Craig and **Wendy Lovato** live in Phoenix, Arizona, where both continue to work for the DEA, still chasing bad guys. There is no shortage of bad guys in Phoenix. For the Lovatos, caught up in the press of new business, the Marks case has become nothing more than a memory.

Judy Marks lives with her children in Palma, though she hopes to return to England to live. She remains convinced that she and Howard were the victims of vindictive zeal on the part of the DEA.

Terry Burke is now assigned to the National Drugs Intelligence Unit at Scotland Yard, where he continues to specialize in international cases of great complexity. **Tony Lundy** divides his time between homes in England and Spain, where he has been working on his own account of the events that caused his downfall. **Peter Nelson** of Her Majesty's Customs has been transferred from London to Bristol, his home town.

Harlan Bowe returned from Karachi after six years and works for the DEA in Fresno, California. **Art Scalzo** finished his tour of duty in Manila and is a DEA group supervisor in San Diego, California. **Brad Whites** continues to work for the IRS in Washington DC. **Randall Waddell** is now SAC for the Naval Investigative Service in New Orleans.

Julie Desm finally got her wish to quit Los Angeles and lives with her husband, their son, three dogs and a cat in El Paso, Texas, where she is assigned to the EPIC intelligence centre. **Neil Van Horn** also left Los Angeles – and the DEA. He is now back in Portland, Oregon, which he much prefers, working for US Customs.

Lawrence Ladage suffered a heart attack in New Orleans. He recovered and is now the regional SAC for US Customs in Seattle, Washington. He no longer uses **Reiner Jacobi** and **Thomas Sunde** as informants because of 'all the grief'. He is, however, not yet convinced they did anything wrong. Sunde and Jacobi have kept distinctly low profiles since Marks's arrest, supposedly spending most of their time in Hong Kong and Japan. Lovato has left messages with their families in America, saying he wishes to talk to them. At the time of writing, Jacobi and Sunde had not responded.

George Pasenelli works for the DEA in Houston, Texas, where his wife continues her high-flying career with the FBI. The plaque on which his silver handcuffs are mounted has pride of place in his den.

Bobby O'Neill works for the Manhattan law firm of Kramer, Dillof, Tessel, Duffy, Moore. He lives with his wife and son not much more than field goal range from his beloved Edgewater.

Jim Hobbs and **William Robb** were both released from prison after pleading guilty to token counts in return for 'time served', and returned to Europe.

Saleem Malik is serving his sentence in America, hoping he will soon be allowed to return to Pakistan. He continues to blame 'political chicanery' for his extradition to the United States, and rejoiced in the downfall of Prime Minister Benazir Bhutto, his nemesis. Saleem was joined in jail in Miami by his nephew, **Aftab Malik**, who flew to Miami from Karachi voluntarily, hoping to do a deal with the DEA. He offered to provide further evidence against his uncle, Howard Marks and high-ranking Pakistani officials in return for money, a 'safe house' in America, and permission to carry a gun. Instead he was arrested on a Belgian warrant, accusing him of heroin trafficking.

John Denbigh went free – at least for a while. After a two-year legal battle in Vancouver, the American request for his extradition was denied for lack of evidence. Canadian charges against Denbigh, accusing him of importing the Vancouver load, were thrown out by the courts. The DEA was annoyed but sanguine, because Denbigh could be re-arrested in any other country that had an extradition treaty with the United States. **Ed Wezain**, who remains the case agent for the DEA in Miami, said: 'It's like hunting big game; sooner or later he's going to walk into our sights.' Denbigh did waltz into their sights in Amsterdam, in November 1990, and the battle to extradite him began all over again.

Phillip Sparrowhawk remains in jail in Bangkok, still resisting extradition. Wezain is content to let him sit there for now. Like Denbigh, Sparrowhawk will always remain a DEA target.

Gerald Wills, Ronald Allen and **Bradley Weller** remain fugitives, last heard of by the DEA in Thailand, negotiating yet another deal. Meanwhile, **Roger Reaves** became a fugitive – again. In September 1990, he escaped from his German prison in Lübeck.

George Lane also remains a fugitive, though in his case there is no obvious hue and cry. Living now in England, he seems to have become the forgotten man of the saga.

His elder brother, **Patrick Lane**, was released from prison in Oakdale, Louisiana, after Marks pleaded guilty – though only after agreeing, much against his will, to drop his appeal against conviction. He lives in Miami with his wife and daughters, rebuilding to revive his desktop publishing business.

Patti Hayes was also released from jail after Marks pleaded guilty. Her husband, **Peter Combs**, is serving his forty-year sentence in Phoenix while his lawyers pursue various lines of appeal. He remains convinced that his conviction and sentence will eventually be overturned.

Lord Moynihan returned to the Philippines. After receiving medical help in California, his wife, **Editha**, gave birth to a son and heir. Tragically the child died of pneumonia when he was not much more than one year old.

Howard Marks can substantially reduce his sentence by agreeing to co-operate with the DEA, telling them what he knows. If he refuses to do that – and he insists he cannot betray other people, 'exchange my pleasure for their pain' – he will nevertheless survive. As John Nicholson, one of his old friends from Balliol, says: 'Howard has the gift of enjoying himself pretty well everywhere. I can see him in prison walking around greeting everybody, cock of the roost. Everybody will love him. Howard will survive in any society.' He hopes with Lovato's agreement, he will spend most of his time in prison in Butner, North Carolina, where inmates can study for degrees awarded by Duke University. Marks's thesis might well be on the theory of chaos.

AUTHORS' NOTE

Though we hope it doesn't read like it, this book is based on: thousands of documents produced as evidence by the US government under the pre-trial discovery process; tape recordings and transcripts of the 433 telephone conversations recorded in Palma by Craig Lovato; the transcript and exhibits of the West Palm Beach trial of Patrick Lane *et al.*; documents supplied to us by Howard Marks; our own interviews and conversations, and other interviews we had to access to, with, among others: Mark Bastan, Harlan Bowe, Terry Burke, Tom Cash, Peter Combs, Phil Corbett, Julie Desm, James Hobbs, Geoffrey Kenion, Lawrence Ladage, George Lane, Natasha Lane, Patrick and Jude Lane, Craig and Wendy Lovato, Tony Lundy, Howard and Judy Marks, Tony Moynihan, Peter Nelson, Bob O'Neill, George Pasenelli, Art Scalzo, Neil Van Horn, Randall Waddell, Ed Wezain, Brad Whites.

Pat Barry, our researcher, organized and analysed that mass of material and, from it, produced a detailed chronology several times the length of this book. It became our bible. Without 'the chron', and Pat, we could not possibly have told the story of *Hunting Marco Polo*.

We have other debts to pay.

James McFadden and Nigel Bowden came up with the original idea for this book and generously allowed us to take it over.

Peter Gillman conducted interviews for us in London, dug deep into the newspaper archives, allowed us to 'borrow' invaluable

295

information from *The Duty Men*, his definitive account of Her Majesty's Customs, and vetted the manuscript for errors. (Any that remain are our responsibility, of course.)

Christopher Olgiati of BBC Television (with whom we collaborated in the making of a documentary on the Marks case) gave us access to his interviews and often shared the research load. Shirley Whitton, his assistant, was extraordinarily helpful.

Andrew Neil, editor of the *Sunday Times*, supported the project with encouragement and money from the outset.

Frank Shults and Con Dougherty of the DEA in Washington, and Tom Cash and John Fernandes of the DEA in Miami, trusted us sufficiently to approve almost unlimited access to Drug Enforcement agents. Mike Fleming of the US Customs Service in Los Angeles was equally helpful in arranging interviews with Customs agents.

Jim Simmons of the US Marshal's Service in Miami was forbearing in permitting us frequent access to Marks while he was being held at the North Dade Detention Center. The staff of the prison were also exceptionally helpful in making the long interview sessions as comfortable as possible.

Bill Murphy and Felice Myles of Uptown Travel in Washington DC efficiently organized, usually at the last moment, our journeys to England, Spain, Thailand, the Philippines and New York, New Orleans, Oakdale, Los Angeles, San Diego, El Paso, Houston, Phoenix and, more often than we care to remember, Miami.

Irv Goodman and Mark Barty-King, our editors at Little, Brown & Company and Bantam Press respectively, inspired us and were endlessly tolerant of the difficulties inherent in covering a moving story.

Robert Ducas, more our partner than our agent, was, as always, indispensable. Neither he, nor we, could manage without his assistant, Jeanie Curtiss.

For moral support, love and generous hospitality we owe gratitude to: Dallett Norris and Bill Wesbrooks; Betty and Bill Kutzke; Betsy and Ira Silverman; June Hawkins and Al Singleton; Jodi Cobb; Alicia Maris; Sarah Burke; Louise Chinn; Linda Melvern and Phil Green; Joan Vernon.

Of all those who submitted to interviews, and our disingenuous appeals for the answer to 'just one more question', four are due special mention.

Ed Wezain, having taken over as the DEA case agent, also

inherited our voracious demands for information. He never once balked, though he undoubtedly had better things to do.

Patrick Lane answered our questions with perspicuous, insightful and sometimes brutally honest letters than ran to a total of more than 120,000 words. Only a fraction of his output is represented here. Somebody should get him to write his own book.

Finally, and most of all, we wish to thank Craig Lovato and Howard Marks. In talking to us, each of the two main protagonists knew that we were simultaneously talking to the 'other side'. Since the contest between them was still going on, it took great leaps of faith on their part nevertheless to trust us with their confidences. Neither of them asked us to betray the other's trust. Both of them accepted that we would reach our own judgements. Every writer should be blessed with such stimulating and articulate subjects.

Paul Eddy and Sara Walden
London, December 1990

INDEX

301